The Story of
NELSON'S PORTSMOUTH

JANE SMITH

HALSGROVE

This book is dedicated to

Ellie, born in 2000,

and Ruby, born in 2002:

our new millennium generation.

First published in Great Britain in 2005

British Library Cataloguing-in-Publication Data
A CIP record for this title is available from the British Library

ISBN 1 84114 476 2

Halsgrove House
Lower Moor Way
Tiverton, Devon EX16 6SS
Tel: 01884 243242
Fax: 01884 243325
E-mail: sales@halsgrove.com
Website: www.halsgrove.com

Printed and bound by CPI, Bath

FOREWORD

By the First Sea Lord and Chief of the Naval Staff
Admiral Sir Alan West GCB DSC ADC

In this very special year for our maritime heritage, I am delighted to have been invited to write this foreword to *The Story of Nelson's Portsmouth*. 2005 will see a concerted campaign by many maritime organisations to draw attention to our nation's dependency upon the sea and to all of those who serve at sea. Few places more than Portsmouth capture the essence of that relationship between our island and the sea, and no man more than Admiral Lord Nelson signifies the character and spirit of our seafaring nation.

Nelson was and remains a hero, inspirational by his endeavours and through his character. Decisive and unfaltering in battle he nevertheless possessed many of the frailties and weaknesses which we all share. Despite uncommon vanity and an unusual opinion of his own place in the world, he cared deeply for his people and would countenance nothing but humanity towards the enemy in victory. It is this humanity which draws us to the man, while his dedication, courage and selfless loyalty to his country provide the benchmark for those of us following in his footsteps within the modern Royal Navy.

Perhaps his enduring legacy is in drawing our attention from time to time to the spirit of the seafarer, spirit as manifest today as it was two centuries ago when opposing forces at the Battle of Trafalgar engaged. That spirit is more often than not captured in writing, in the musings and thoughts of every sailor who, far from home, commits his thoughts to paper and sends them on to loved ones far away. From the painstaking despatches of 1805 to the immediacy of the modern e-mail, the messages have changed little; they tell an unvarying story of the pain of separation, the joy of homecoming and, in between, the things which matter most to a sailor abroad – the next promotion, the next operational engagement and above all, when the chance presented, the next run ashore.

The City of Portsmouth has changed much since 1805 but it remains a thriving naval city with clues at every turn of the men and women who lived there and who built, maintained and served in a navy that was to rule unchallenged in its superiority for over a hundred years. With HMS *VICTORY* as the proud centrepiece to that history, and still used as a Flagship, the naval dockyard, with its hustle and noise, its people and its determined industry is in many ways unchanged in its character since Admiral Nelson's day. In 2005, the city will be the focus of our nation's celebrations of his famous victory at Trafalgar and will also provide the backdrop for the commemorations of the life of a great British seafarer and commander. This book tells the story of a city that delivered and continues to deliver one of the world's greatest navies, and the people of a nation whose lifeblood is the sea. To those interested in our maritime heritage, this book has been eagerly awaited.

Admiral Sir Alan West GCB DSC ADC
First Sea Lord and Chief of the Naval Staff

An engraving by W. I. Mosses entitled, 'The Anniversary of Trafalgar on Board the Old Victory at Portsmouth' published as an extra supplement to the *Illustrated London News* on 22 October 1881. The setting of this picture is essentially a *tableau vivant* symbolising that family group which links youth and old age beloved of the late Victorians, the three generations. We see the charming young girl waiting to lay her posy and the fatherly sailors arranging the laurel wreath. The oldest generation is represented by the grandfatherly captain who brings authority and maturity to the scene.

Our eye is drawn upwards and we see that Lord Nelson himself is present in the form of his famous signal on the wheel with his own Latin motto, *Palmam qui meruit ferat* (Let him bear the palm who has deserved it). He took this motto on receiving the Knighthood of the Bath and it was also the motto of the battleship HMS *Nelson*. It comes from Jortin's *Lusus Poetici*, written in 1748, *Ad Ventos*, stanza iv:

Et nobis faciles parcite et hostibus,
Concurrant pariter cum ratibus rates:
Spectent numina ponti, et
Palmam qui meruit ferat.

Just above the wheel we see the crown of the British Sovereign, at this date Edward VII. Looking down again we see the two kneeling sailors paying the homage of the Royal Navy to his memory. In the background sailors prepare for Trafalgar Day, one climbs the rigging with another laurel wreath and a further two prepare to hoist the signal 'England Expects Every Man Will Do His Duty'.

As for HMS *Victory* herself, the motto and crown do not exist today although they could still be seen in a photograph entitled, 'Old Sailors' Visit to HMS *Victory*', reproduced in Agnes Weston's autobiography *My Life Among the Blue Jackets* which was first published in 1909. The skylight behind the figures also appeared in the photograph but is not there now. There are, however, examples elsewhere on the ship. The plaque marking the spot where Nelson fell is still there although of a slightly different design. Otherwise, the spot is remarkably unchanged today. (COURTESY *THE ILLUSTRATED LONDON NEWS*)

CONTENTS

Acknowledgements   6

Introduction   9

Chapter I   1623–1714: A Grandchild of the Stuarts   11

Chapter II   1726–1778: An Influential Uncle   33

Chapter III   1782–1783: 'I want much to get off this d....d voyage'   75

Chapter IV   1784–1787: 'I am fonder of the sea than ever'   81

Chapter V   1793: 'there is no certainty in wind and waves'   95

Chapter VI   1798: 'the times are big with events'   102

Chapter VII   1803: 'that horrid place Portsmouth'   106

Chapter VIII   August 1805: 'this is the first time in quarantine'   110

Chapter IX   September 1805: 'but my fate is fixed and I am gone'   113

Chapter X   2005: The Immortal Memory   133

Bibliography   157

ACKNOWLEDGEMENTS

The recreation of Nelson's Portsmouth has been a wonderful project to work on, especially in this year of the 200th anniversary of the Battle of Trafalgar. I have received tremendous help and support from many local people in 'Nelson's Portsmouth', in particular the Bowker family. Jean provided the initial impetus and encouragement two years ago when she suggested that, 'I write something for 2005'. This is the result!

Also her husband, Dr Carey Bowker, has very patiently put up with, for him, interminable discussions on Nelson's malaria and agues. Last but not least, I would not want to leave out that other very important "member of the family" whose acquaintance I made while working on the book, the catamaran *Life Begins*.

I am most grateful to David and Jackie Baynes of the Friends of Old Portsmouth Association for heroically reading the book proofs through for me.

Other people in Old Portsmouth who have helped me are Commander Paul Bolas of the Royal Naval Club & Royal Albert Yacht Club. He very kindly arranged for me to take photographs in the club on the Trafalgar Dinner Night and allowed me to reproduce an image from a book in the club's library. Bob Knox of the Portsmouth Sailing Club talked me through the state of the tides on 14 September 1805. Colin Harris let me look at his specialist collection of postcards; John Henry Pounds helped me with Nelson's last walk; Trevor Gale, the Secretary of the Friends of the Royal Garrison Church, gave me useful information about the interior; St Thomas's Cathedral gave me permission to reproduce photographs taken inside, and the Vicar at St George's Church, Portsea, the Revd Karina Green, also gave me permission to take photographs inside.

I have also been helped by a great variety of other people and have enjoyed working with them all: my Uncle Peter Nex came up with some excellent references; Bob Irwin of J.A. Hewes (Photographers), The Studio, 91 Lawrence Road, Southsea, made his technical expertise and local knowledge available to me as usual; Mrs Anna Tribe very kindly gave me permission to photograph her on Trafalgar Night; John Montagu, the eleventh Earl of Sandwich introduced me to his illustrious forebear, the fourth Earl of Sandwich; David White, the Somerset Herald at the College of Arms, gave advice on the heraldic symbols in Portsmouth and Anthony Triggs, local historian and author very generously lent me photographs from his collection.

Russell Fox very kindly gave up his morning to 'walk the walls' with me and lent me copies of his work on the fortifications.

During the last four years the two local groups I have worked with have been a great source of help and inspiration. Firstly, the Thomas Ellis Owen Festival Research Group of Sue and John Pike, Jackie Baynes, Trish Lovell, Lucy Johnson, John Tims, Margaret and Rod Ward and Trevor Clark.

Secondly, the Diggers in the Storehouse, Wendy Smith, Norman Gordon, Peter Ardern, Richard Brooks and Dr Val Fontana. A special thank you goes to Charlotte Frost for her ability to proffer a much-needed helping hand at crucial moments.

Outside Portsmouth, this book would not have been complete without the help and advice from Judith Goodman of the Merton Historical Society. She very generously shared her research findings on Nelson's last journey with me and enabled me to link up Merton and Portsmouth in more detail. I am grateful too, to the landlord of the Royal Anchor, Liphook, for permission to reproduced a photograph taken inside.

Over the water in Gosport, I am grateful to Linda Hedley of Gosport Museum for finding an image of Haslar Hospital and Oonagh Palmer for permission to reproduce it; at Haslar Hospital, Surgeon Captain J. K. Campbell, the commandant, gave me permission to reproduce a photograph taken on the hospital site and Eric Birbeck took me on his most fascinating guided tour. I am also grateful to Richard Martin, the authority on Martin Snape.

As always, I am most grateful for the assistance I have received from the public archives in Portsmouth and permission to reproduce images from their collections. Alan King, the Historical Collections Librarian at the Norrish Central Library, Portsmouth, has been a source of help all through the project, and the library staff have done wonders in tracking down obscure books via the inter-library loan scheme.

At the City Museum, the local history officers, John Stedman and Katy Ball, have been of great assistance in finding and reproducing images and my thanks go to Diana Gregg and the staff in the search room for all their help.

Other museum sites I visited in the course of my research are the Square Tower – Portsmouth City Museum very kindly allowed me access to the top to take photographs and Paul Hitchcock, museum attendant, waited patiently while I took them; at Southsea Castle I had a very useful discussion with Stanley Kitchener, museum attendant, and at Eastney Beam Engine House, Tim Gower, the site manager, let me photograph him with a very large spanner.

At the City Council, I am grateful to Val van der Hoven, the city manager, for permission to photograph the keys of the city and to David Collins, the Lord Mayor's butler who has since retired, for showing them to me.

My thanks must of course, go to the Royal Navy whose year this is, in particular to the First Sea Lord and Chief of the naval staff, Admiral Sir Alan West, for taking time out of a very busy schedule to write a foreword for this book; to Lt-Cmdr Ford, the base security officer at HM Naval Base, for permission to take photographs of the Landport Gate and in the dockyard, and to MGS CO3 Tony Martin for taking me round. The verger at St Ann's, Neil Rowe, very kindly allowed me to take photographs.

On HMS *Victory*, I was pleased to find that the tour of the ship, on this occasion led by ex-Navy guide Trevor Fawcett, was as exciting and enthralling today as it was when I first did the tour as a child back in the 1950s.

I am also very grateful to Lt-Cmdr Mark Barton, the secretary of the Royal Naval Fencing Association, who very generously lent me archive materials from his collection. My thanks go too, to Matthew Sheldon, curator of manuscripts at the Royal Naval Museum, for his assistance with the sea charts.

I very much enjoyed my contact with the Defence Diving School and the chance to visit Horsea Island. I am most grateful to Lt-Col. Alan Taylor for permission to reproduce photographs of the Ceremony of the Keys; Lt Lanigan for showing me around the school and to Mike Galbraith, storeman, for the walk out to the bungalow.

At the Camber, my thanks go to Paul Fryer, senior pilot and assistant harbour master for giving up his time to tell me all about the pilot's work and for permission to reproduce his photograph.

Another good day out was to Eastney Pumping Station which was organised by Penny Hodge, the press and PR officer of Southern Water. I am very grateful to her for all her efforts plus permission to reproduce a Southern Water photograph. Also to Mark Gregory, the section leader; Lee Wilkinson, the shift controller, and in particular, to Ron Shipp, process operator, for his fascinating and gripping tour of the works.

As for the national archives, I have had a lot of involvement with the National Maritime Museum over the last 18 months and am most grateful to David Taylor and Lucy Waitt, picture librarians, for their help and for permission to reproduce museum images; Brian Lavery, curator of ship technology; Brian Thynne, map librarian; Roger Quarm, curator of pictures, and Peter Finch and Bernard Bryant, store managers.

In particular, I am grateful to John Graves for sharing his research findings on the model dockyards with me, and Polly Larner of the Friends for tracking down an article about them. My especial thanks go to Tina Chambers, the deputy head of photography at the museum, for her wonderful close-up shots of the interior of the model dockyard.

At the Science Museum, I am grateful to Kate Pink, the picture researcher, for digging out a photograph of the model dockyard and to the Science and Society Picture Library for permission to reproduce it.

I am also grateful to the staff of the Reproduction Unit of the British Library for the images of the 1698 survey and for permission to reproduce them all.

The staff at English Heritage have always been helpfulness itself, both at their regional office in Guildford and their head office in London. At Fort Cumberland, Tracey Wahdan, the regional director of visitor operations, very kindly gave permission for me to visit the fort and Cynara Davies, outreach officer, organised it. My thanks go to David Webb, the facilities manager there, and David Fellows, archaeologist, for showing me round when I got there. David I am especially grateful to, as he gave up his time to take me round the site in the teeth of a freezing cold wind.

I would also like to take this opportunity to pay tribute to two groups of local people who beaver away year in year out on the history of Portsmouth with not a lot of recognition. They are firstly, all the local historians who work away just for the love of it and whose research can be consulted in the Central Library and the search room at the City Museum: I owe them all a great debt – we all owe them a great debt.

Secondly, the stalwart guides of the Portsmouth Tourist Guides Association who lecture in the City Museum and trudge around Portsmouth in all weathers regardless of the number of people in their group – it can be 20 or 1! The only way to learn about a place is to go and see it on foot.

The guides do a great service in keeping the history of Portsmouth alive especially in this year of the 200th anniversary of Trafalgar. Two events stand out from all my research over the last 18 months, Madeleine Selby's lecture on the life of Nelson and her walk 'In Nelson's footsteps'. Hopefully, she will continue with them after 2005.

Lastly, my thanks go to Steven Pugsley, the chairman at Halsgrove for publishing not only another book on Nelson, but yet another one on Portsmouth! I am much appreciative of all the hard work and support from everyone there.

Jane Smith
Southsea,
April 2005

INTRODUCTION

The Letters – What Was In them?

Horatio Nelson wrote almost 60 letters from Portsmouth itself and on board ship from the anchorages of Spithead and St Helen's. Ranging over a period of 23 years, 1782–1805, they cover vast changes in his career. His first letters are those of a young captain in the process of building a naval career. His last, those of a senior naval officer and national hero.

However, whether written by a famous admiral or the lowliest seaman, the letters share all the characteristics of the letter home written by servicemen and women, particularly those on active service. Firstly, they are one-sided, it is very rare that both sides of the correspondence are united. Secondly, they often refer to people and events that are unfamiliar to the reader, and thirdly, can seem excessively concerned with details such as the food, the pay and promotion or lack of it. Trivial, perhaps, to those not in the services, but extremely important to those who are.

In reading Nelson's letters we are linked directly and immediately with him and his life. The fact that he was on active service and had to face death all the time, as do many servicemen and women, gives him an authentic voice which is not found in many other types of correspondence.

In any case, Nelson wrote a good letter. The eighteenth century was the golden age of letter writing and diary keeping and Nelson was no exception to this rule. Gossipy, warm and pithy, his letters are timeless.

He wrote to let his family and friends know where he had been the day before, where he was then and where he was going the next day. He asks about the latest family news, relates his adventures to them, describes the ins and outs of rows with senior officers and repeats chitchat about colleagues. So often the letter home is about stark contrasts, on one hand, the minutiae of routine daily doings and on the other, the immediacy of momentous national events.

As for his connection with Portsmouth, although Nelson does refer to it as a 'horrid place', this was right at the end of his career in 1803 when the circumstances were different from earlier times in that he was having to leave Lady Hamilton. In any case, to the serviceman, one place looks very much like another and anywhere else is bound to be better than the place he is in at the moment.

For the purposes of this book, the letters have been taken from the seven volumes of correspondence compiled by Sir Nicholas Harris Nicolas (1799–1848), plus a few from outside sources. Nicolas served in the Navy from 1808–1816, then following the end of the Napoleonic Wars in 1815, he studied law and was called to the Bar in 1825. He spent the rest of his life compiling and editing scholarly books.

The collection of the dispatches and letters of Lord Nelson is his main work which was published between 1844 and 1846. The letters commence when Nelson was 18 in 1777 and end in 1805. All collections of letters are a creation of the editor and this is a compilation very much of its own time. Nicolas was writing for the early Victorians and edited the letters in his personal style, for example, damned is shown as 'd....d'.

Further, he was a contemporary of Nelson's daughter Horatia. She was never able to acknowledge Lady Hamilton as her mother and Nicolas, who was friendly with her, felt unable to include any of Nelson's letters to her. Nevertheless, his was not only the first collection of Nelson's letters but a collection which was accompanied by very detailed notes. It remains an essential work of reference today.

The Island – What did It Look Like?

'The Account of Hampshire' published in 1750 in the *Universal Magazine* sums up eighteenth century Portsmouth, its dockyard, the town, harbour and Portsea in a nutshell. Firstly, it describes the island of Portsea as, '...about 14 miles in compass surrounded at high tides by sea water, of which they make salt...and is joined to the continent by a bridge'. The description continues as follows:

The town of Portsmouth is said to be the only regular fortification in Britain and the key (quay) of England. After the revolution (1688) this port flourished mightily: and the fortifications are as regular as those in any port in Europe.

Here is a good counterscarp, and double mote, with ravelins in the ditch and double palisadoes and advanced works to cover the place from any approach where it may be practicable.

The town is also strongest on the land side by the fortifications raised of late years about the docks and yards. Within these few years the Government has brought more ground for additional works and no doubt it may be made impregnable since a shallow water may be brought quite round it.

It is amazing to see here the immense quantity of all sorts of military and naval stores. The rope-house is almost a quarter of a mile long and some of the cables made here require 100 men to work at them; and their labour is so hard, that they can work but four hours in a day.

The least number of men continually employed in the yard is said to be a thousand and they but barely sufficient. In short, the docks and yards resemble a distinct town and form a kind of marine corporation within themselves.

The situation of the place, being low, and full of sea-water and ditches, makes it aguish and in want of fresh water.

Here are many good modern buildings; the town is large and so full of people that the streets seem always in a hurry, by the continual resort of seaman, soldiers, and their dependants to it.... the inns and taverns are crowded continually and this concourse makes both provisions, fuel and lodging very dear.

Here is a garrison but its number is occasional... It is observed to the great credit both of the civil and military government of this place that the one does neither corrupt not interrupt the other.

The Church is large and handsome and the Deputy governor has a very good house and a neat chapel.

A 1000 sail of ships may ride safe in this harbour. The mouth is secured on the Gosport side by 4 forts and a platform of above 20 great guns level with the water; and on the east side by Southsea Castle built by Henry VIII. Gosport is itself a large town of great trade, mostly inhabited by the sailors' wives and well provided with lodgings for travellers, but though it is a different parish with Portsmouth, it is generally called by the same name.

As this town of Portsmouth cannot admit of any enlargement in building and the inhabitants have increased so prodigiously of late years not only Gosport has received considerable additions, but a sort of suburb has been built on the heath or common adjoining to Portsmouth which is in a fair way to outstrip the town itself for numbers of inhabitants and beauty of houses and the rather as it is independent on the laws of the garrison and unencumbered with duties and services of the corporation.

Trafalgar 200 – 21 October 2005

The approach to the 200th anniversary of the Battle of Trafalgar gives us an unusual opportunity to take a closer look at the letters that Nelson wrote from Portsmouth against the backdrop of Portsea Island as a whole.

In addition to the letters, the purpose of this book is also to catch a glimpse of all the places he was familiar with through the eyes of the chart makers, the artists, the sculptors, the builders and model makers and even the reporters from the local press who were contemporary with the town he knew. In the process, we can follow the story of Portsmouth as it unfolded.

But first, to set the scene before his arrival, we need to go back in time.

Chapter I

1623–1714:
A GRANDCHILD OF THE STUARTS

The year 1698, the ninth year in the reign of William III, was a turning point both in Nelson's family history and in the history of Portsmouth. For Nelson it was the year in which Mary Nelson, his paternal grandmother was born, so linking him closely with the seventeenth century.

As for his maternal grandmother, Ann Suckling, she had been born seven years earlier in 1691. This was in the second year of the joint reign of William and Mary, both grandchildren of King Charles I and just thirty-one years after the Restoration of the Monarchy (1660).

Nelson was born less than a century later, in 1758. Both grandmothers are shadowy figures to us now, but help us to remember that Nelson's world was one which was dominated by the Stuarts and Hanoverians. The Industrial Revolution was still to come, the age of the horse had not yet been overtaken by the railway, and the era of sail had not been supplanted by the steam engine.

As for Portsmouth, the year 1698 saw the completion of a very comprehensive survey of the buildings in the dockyard. This was intended to estimate their monetary value and to set out the improvements carried out during the reign of William III, who had expanded the size of the dockyard by reclaiming land and building a new dry dock and two wet docks.

Its significance for us today, though, lies in the fact that the details of the buildings are illustrated in delicate colour. This enables us to catch a glimpse of how the old timber and brick dockyard must have looked just before it was gradually replaced by brick and stone in the coming century into the buildings we know today.

Also in 1698, Portsmouth Dockyard was on the itinerary of Emperor Peter the Great of Russia, when he spent three days there as part of his grand embassy to Europe. The survey enables us to see what he saw, at least in representational form. This visit was important too, because it established a connection with the Russian Navy which continues to this day.

Portsmouth was essentially a fortified medieval town and dockyard, whose development and expansion had been continued by the Stuarts, Charles II and his nephew William III. By the time that Nelson had joined the Navy in 1771, and been introduced to Portsmouth in 1776, the Hanoverians had been in power since 1714. However, the Stuarts had left a distinctive legacy which would have been familiar to Nelson. To see the Portsmouth that he saw, we must go back to the early 1660s.

A Garrison Town

Nowadays, Portsmouth is thought of primarily as a naval city but for seven hundred years it was a garrison town with a substantial military presence: this is how Nelson would have known it. The head of it, originally known as the governor, was a powerful personality within the town and his residence, an important and imposing building.

The history of the role of governor dates from the end of the thirteenth century when the Constable of Portchester Castle on the western side of Portsmouth Harbour had also become governor of Portsmouth. Up till this time, the governor had no specific residence and had simply lived in part of the existing fortifications known as the Square Tower.

The Royal Garrison Church

Near to the Square Tower stood the Domus Dei, another medieval building which had been founded in 1212 as a chapel and hospital for the pilgrims who landed at Portsmouth on their way to the shrines at Winchester and Canterbury. In 1540, the Domus Dei and its lands were surrendered to the Crown as part of the Dissolution of the Monasteries. This enabled the military to acquire a site in the centre of the town with a dominating position by the harbour entrance and easy access to the water.

The site was developed as a complex of buildings with a new residence for the governor constructed in 1580. The site remains in the possession of the Ministry of Defence to this day. In the 1860s, the church underwent a major rebuilding programme which changed its appearance and is now known as the Royal Garrison Church.

During the renovation Queen Victoria's son, Prince Alfred the Duke of Edinburgh, dedicated a seat in the chapel just inside the door on the left to the memory of Nelson; the inscription reads, 'Vice Admiral Horatio Viscount Nelson K.B., killed at Trafalgar Oct. 21 1805 aged 47. D.D. Captain HRH the Duke of Edinburgh KG'. This can still be seen today.

In 1970, the building was transferred into the care of the Ministry of Public Building and Works: this eventually became English Heritage, which retains responsibility for its maintenance and management today. The Royal Garrison Church is Grade II listed. As regards the interior and its artefacts, these are cared for by the Friends of the Royal Garrison Church who organise guided tours. The church is also used for military funerals and memorial services.

The area of green surrounding the church is known as Governor's Green. It is not only buildings which are Grade II listed – this area is bounded by wrought iron railings and gates dating from the early to mid-nineteenth century. They were Grade II listed in 1999, but at the time of writing though, they are badly in need of restoration. Adjacent to Governor's Green is Grand Parade, a name reflecting its original military function.

Government House

The governor's new residence became known as Government House and the ground surrounding it as Governor's Green. During the existence of the Portsmouth garrison, there were at least three different buildings by this name. There was the one next to the Domus Dei, which was demolished in 1826, then a house in the High Street and lastly, a building opposite what is now the City Museum which was built in 1882. None of the three survives today as the last two were destroyed during the Second World War.

This is the version of Government House dating from 1580 engraved by Armstrong and Tom in about 1717. It is shown from its western side with Domus Dei on the left, and on the right-hand side is an entrance through the fortifications. (© NATIONAL MARITIME MUSEUM, LONDON, REF. No.: PU 1073)

An Infanta Arrives

Returning to the 1660s, the proximity of Government House to the harbour was put to good use when the Portuguese Infanta Catherine of Braganza landed at the Sally Port on 14 May 1662. She was to be the bride of Charles II who had been on the throne for two years and was consolidating his position as monarch by marriage with a European royal family.

In London, Samuel Pepys (1633–1703) noted in his diary for 15–17 May 1662,

...At night all the bells in the towne rung, and bonfires made for the joy of the Queene's arrivall; who came and landed at Portsmouth last night. But I do not see much thorough joy, but only an indifferent one, in the hearts of people, who are much discontented at the pride and luxury of the Court, and running in debt. So to bed.

Back in Portsmouth, Catherine was obliged to await the King's arrival but they finally married in Government House a week later: this plaque in the Sally Port commemorates her arrival and wedding. The Sally Port was also the embarkation point for many naval heroes. (AUTHOR'S PHOTOGRAPH, 2003)

The Square Tower

Above left: The Square Tower was built in 1494 as a fortified residence, possibly for the governor of Portsmouth. A century later, however, its use changed when the governor moved into a residence next to Domus Dei. The Tower was then used for storing gunpowder. Nelson, though, would have known it as a meat store when the Admiralty converted it to that use in the late 1770s.

In the early nineteenth century the Tower was returned to its function as part of the fortifications and a shutter telegraph station was erected on Southsea Common. In 1822 this was replaced when a semaphore station was placed on the top of the tower. The Tower acquired a new lease of life for a while as this formed the first link in the chain of semaphore stations between Portsmouth and the Admiralty in London. Eventually, the station was made obsolete by the development of the electric telegraph and the semaphore tower was removed in 1848.

Portsmouth Museums and Records Service acquired the Square Tower in the 1960s and it was Grade I listed in 1969. The Tower was restored to its present condition between 1979 and 1986 and today is used for weddings and other functions. (AUTHOR'S PHOTOGRAPH, 2005)

Above right: The Tower has, of course, a commanding view of Portsmouth Harbour and the fortifications: its solid stone mass looms over the west end of the High Street. In addition, a niche high up in its east face contains a gilt bust of the martyr King, Charles I. From this vantage point it gazes down the High Street as a memorial to the King and to Portsmouth's Stuart heritage. (COURTESY ALLAN SMITH, 2005)

Charles I – A Portrait Bust

James I had been King since the death of Elizabeth I in 1603. His son the Prince of Wales, who was to become Charles I, set out on a expedition in 1623 with the Duke of Buckingham to Madrid as part of negotiations to marry the Spanish Infanta Maria, sister of Philip IV of Spain. However, the plans came to nothing and they returned home. Twelve years later when he had became monarch, Charles donated a bust of himself to the town in commemoration of his safe return. Donated during his lifetime, the bust, in effect was to become his own memorial.

The significance of the bust lies in the fact that the Stuarts were the first to introduce the artistic form of the portrait bust into Great Britain; it had been almost unknown here until then. It was designed by Hubrecht le Sueur (c.1585–1670), who was a French royal sculptor who had been brought to London in the retinue of Princess Henrietta Maria of France in 1625 when she married Charles I.

The purpose of the portrait bust was to establish a standardised version of the image of the monarch in the public mind. There is no record of Charles actually sitting for a bust – le Sueur was considered to be an image maker rather than a portraitist and his real skill lay in casting in bronze. His best known work is the equestrian figure of Charles I in Trafalgar Square, made in 1630–33; the same design of Charles's face was to be repeated many times in the future.

During the fourteen years that le Sueur was the sculptor to the English Crown he produced about fifty commissions for the King. These included busts and statues which were made for public and official places and placed in purpose-designed niches. Locations included Canterbury Quad at St John's College, Oxford (1634); the Whitehall Banqueting House and the Square Tower in 1635; the Market Cross at Chichester (1637); the churchyard of St Paul's Covent Garden and Inigo Jones's screen in Winchester Cathedral (1638); and Duke Humfrey's library in Oxford in 1641.

All these were produced in the period known as the King's Personal Rule when Charles I ruled without Parliament from 1629 until 1640. Although they were a personal initiative on his part, they did follow conventional design and were closely modelled on French busts of Henri IV, the father of Henrietta Maria. Le Sueur received his last royal payment in 1639 and in 1641, just before the Civil War, he returned to France.[1]

The busts were produced at public expense and the version in the Square Tower cost £50, a immense sum in those days. It was made of gilded bronze with the niche encircled by a stone wreath of laurel and oak. The royal coat of arms was placed on a protruding shelf below.

The original must have been in place barely a decade, and Nelson would have seen the copy as we do today. The bust is a fascinating and important part of Portsmouth's history and, were it not for the English Civil War, Portsmouth would have had an original Hubrecht le Sueur bronze as well. (Courtesy of Portsmouth Museum and Record Services)

There are two inscriptions, one on a small slab above the bust reads 'Charles the First'. The other originally read:

King Charles the First: after his travels through France and Spain, and having passed many dangers both by sea and land. He arrived here the 4th day of October, 1623: there was the greatest applause of joy for his safety throughout the kingdom that was ever known or heard of.

At some point in its history, the wording after the date was removed.

This photograph shows the bust in the museum which is thought to be a copy made in about 1660 and regilded in 1814. Its caption in the museum states that the original bust was destroyed during the Civil War. In 1982, a fibre glass copy was made and placed in the niche in the Square Tower so that the 1660 copy could be kept in the museum for conservation.

The Royal Coat of Arms

The royal arms had its origins in the twelfth century and has been interpreted in many different ways. The Stuarts, though, attached great importance to its design and understood its wide scope for interpretation in three dimensional form. This gave a simple yet very effective visual shorthand to symbolise the monarchy and Great Britain which is still in use today. The concept of the circular convex shield as a base is taken for granted now, but the Stuarts were the first to introduce it along with the supporters on either side. These consist mostly of animals and human figures either in realistic or allegorical and mythical form.

The Stuarts introduced the lion of England and the unicorn of Scotland as the supporters, and they remain in the royal arms today. In this photograph we can see that although the stone work is very worn by the sea air they are full of vitality.

Portsmouth does not have much in the way of decoration on its public buildings probably because the fortifications and dockyard were built with public money and were concerned primarily with function. There were no rich merchants or wealthy industrialists to build ostentatious mansions or lay out large estates all over Portsea Island.

The nearest equivalent to the country house could perhaps be the fine buildings constructed as officers' messes. Examples of these today are the building now used as the City Museum in Museum Road; the Wardroom of HMS *Nelson* in Queen Street; the building used as the Royal Marines Museum in Eastney, and Gatcombe House in Hilsea.

Yet none of them is associated with one individual. Not all the buildings display the royal coat of arms but, where it does appear, it quietly and subtly symbolises service to the monarch and country that has characterised Portsmouth throughout its history. (AUTHOR'S PHOTOGRAPH, 2004)

The Cathedral Church of St Thomas of Canterbury

This engraving from the *Illustrated London News* dated 8 April 1882 shows the church from the junction of St Thomas's Street and Lombard Street. It was one of the two medieval churches on Portsea Island, the other being St Mary's, Kingston. Founded in 1180, St Thomas's was to become the Parish Church in 1320 and the Cathedral Church of Portsmouth on 1 May 1927. For many years the church was hidden away behind other buildings, so pictures of it are very sparse. The open view of it from the High Street that we have today is a post-Second World War development. This view shows its north side which has not changed quite so much.

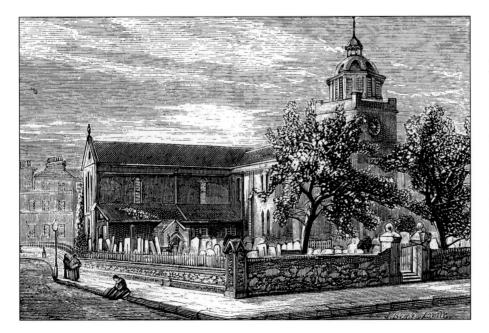

As to whether Nelson ever worshipped here, or anywhere else in Portsmouth, is not known. Today no one church is associated with him, although memorials to him exist in at least two: St Thomas's Cathedral and the Royal Garrison Church. That does not mean Nelson was not religious, indeed he did have a profound religious faith but it may well be that he was never in the town long enough to have worshipped regularly in one place. (COURTESY *ILLUSTRATED LONDON NEWS*)

'In this very town, fatal theatre of monstrous murder'

George Villiers, Duke of Buckingham and Lord High Admiral of the British fleet was a favourite of Charles I and has left a prominent legacy to the city in the form of a house and a pub named after him, and a striking memorial in the cathedral. He was stabbed to death by Lieutenant John Felton at No.11 High Street on 23 August 1628.

This engraving by Hamilton and Reeves published in 1803 is a late-Georgian interpretation of the scene. The artist has captured the moment in time as frozen in shock; the group see the assassin, the figure in the centre, raise his knife to strike the duke, the figure with the Cavalier-style hat, cloak, sash and rosette at his knee. Felton's hat falls in slow motion, the figure second to left clutches his heart involuntarily, while Buckingham holds his arms wide in acceptance of his fate. Felton was later executed and his body exhibited from a gibbet on Southsea Common.

Engravings of dramatic historical scenes such as this were extremely popular and very typical of the sort of thing that would have been on sale in the High Street in Nelson's time. Today, of course, its understated and subtle, naïve-style charm might be overlooked as we quibble that it is obvious the artist had never actually seen the High Street. It appears as though the building has apparently moved across the road and much nearer to the sea.

Moreover, according to the accounts of the murder, it took place in the hall of the house, not outside in the street. The design of the house owes more to fifteenth century Bologna than seventeenth century Portsmouth and the unusual rigging of the ship in the background suggests a continental influence on the artist. A knife which is reputed to be the one used to do the deed exists and was stolen from the house in January 2004. Luckily, it was recovered intact in April 2004.[2] (AUTHOR'S COLLECTION)

Buckingham House

The house where the murder took place still exists but at the time it was an inn, called Ye Spotted Dog. It is a timber-framed house dating from the sixteenth or early seventeenth century and is an important feature of the High Street. William Gates, however, described it as being much altered from its original design and it was refronted in the late seventeenth or early eighteenth century. This fine black and white photograph was one of a series taken just after the Second World War in 1949 when the house was unoccupied. It has been Grade II* listed since 1953.

Nelson was not the only famous historical character to walk the streets of Portsmouth of course. In 1661 Samuel Pepys visited the dockyard and town with a group of friends and stayed at the old Red Lion Inn, which at that time was situated on the corner of High Street and Church Lane. His diary entry for 2–4 May 1661 reads:

Then we and our wifes all to see the Mountagu, which is a fine ship. And so to the towne again by water; and then to see the room where the Duke of Buckingham was killed by Felton. So to our lodgings and to supper and to bed.

Left: It had been thirty-three years and a Civil War since 1628 but the assassination had not been forgotten. In the meantime, Buckingham House had become a tourist attraction. Pepys and his party must have been a sight worth seeing too, with them all trying to crowd into the small house: the gentlemen with their periwigs, large feathered hats, cloaks and swords and the ladies with their long dresses and elaborate hair styles, plus a retinue of servants and a few nosy passers-by. (COURTESY J. A. HEWES)

Above left: The spooky atmosphere of the empty house is brought out well by this black and white shot of the old wooden staircase. (COURTESY J. A. HEWES)

Above right: Another wooden staircase leading to a higher floor. The steep, winding staircase is very typical of houses in Old Portsmouth today. (COURTESY J. A. HEWES)

Above left: A close-up of the imposing front door and carved wooden ornamental portico. The plaque reads, 'In this house George Villiers Duke of Buckingham was assassinated by John Felton 23 August 1628.' (COURTESY J. A. HEWES)

Above right: The hall of the house where the murder is supposed to have taken place. Interior shots are particularly interesting as the house is not open to the public, although it has been used as offices in the past. It gives a good opportunity to see the timber work inside. (COURTESY J. A. HEWES)

Right: Lastly, a very unusual view, the rear of the house in autumn. (COURTESY J. A. HEWES)

The Buckingham Memorial

The Buckingham Memorial is Portsmouth's best example of an early Baroque monument. It is certainly the largest in Portsmouth cathedral and it is so large in fact that originally it stood against the far east end wall as a centrepiece in place of a reredos, as shown in this watercolour by R. H. C. Ubsdell dated about 1840. Ubsdell was a Victorian artist with a naïve style who painted many scenes in Portsmouth. However, by early Victorian times the Baroque style had fallen from fashion and it was moved to its present, much more cramped, location during reconstruction work in 1843.

It is interesting to note that this work was carried out by Thomas Ellis Owen, the architect and developer of Southsea, and to wonder if he had a hand in the resiting of the memorial. He was certainly no fan of the ornate Baroque style, preferring to introduce elements of the neoclassical, Gothic Revival and picturesque styles into the design of his houses.

A report in *The Builder* of 1843 describes the works:

St Thomas's Church – This church is closed for repair. The contemplated works are a restoration of the groined roof and east end of the chancel to its original condition, with the entire and thorough repair of the external roof of the chancel, and the restoration of the stone parapet instead of the present projecting eaves – the erection of several new pews at the west end, instead of the unsightly lobby which now occupies so large a space and forms only a loitering place for idle people.

The church will be cleaned throughout, and that most important point, a proper ventilation, in which the church is now so extremely defective, will be attained. The works will be done by Messrs. Hendy, of Portsmouth, under the superintendence of T. E. Owen, Esq., and of – Herbert, Esq., of London, the architect to Winchester College. Besides this the organ will be thoroughly repaired, and its different parts, which have been added at different times, will be completely harmonised.

(COURTESY OF PORTSMOUTH MUSEUMS AND RECORDS SERVICE)

✻ ✻ ✻

The memorial was designed by Nicholas Stone in black and white marble, and erected by Buckingham's sister, the Countess of Denbigh, to his memory in 1631. The duke's body, though, was buried in Westminster Abbey, but his bowels and those of the countess remained in the cathedral.

The design of the memorial has a lot to tell us concerning the religious symbolism of the time and the way in which the duke was represented. Firstly, the religious symbolism. The top half of the memorial resembles a one-dimensional mausoleum with its 'entrance' in the form of a tall recess containing an elongated funerary urn. Traditionally, the bowels are actually thought to be inside it.

The urn is surmounted by a phoenix rising from the ashes. According to Greek legend, the phoenix was a fabulous Egyptian bird and the only one its kind. It was said to live a certain number of years, at the end of which it makes a nest in Egypt or Arabia consisting of spices, sings a melodious dirge, flaps its wings to set fire to the pile, burns itself to ashes and comes forth with new life. The phoenix is also a symbol of the Resurrection.

The figure below the urn on the right holds a heart aloft and may indicate a connection with the Feast of the Immaculate Heart of Mary. This was a special form of devotion to the Virgin Mary which developed

from the seventeenth century and whose Feast Day was 22 August. The duke was murdered on 23 August.

A very typical and striking feature of Baroque monuments is the memento mori in the form of skeletons and single bones. Here, a skull rests at the base of the memorial symbolising the grave, in stark contrast to the cherubs balanced on the 'top of the mausoleum' who are nearest to heaven.

While the monument was dedicated to an individual, the opportunity was taken to remind the onlooker very powerfully of their own mortality too and to concentrate their minds on how to save their immortal soul from hell.

Secondly, Buckingham's worldly status is represented by the carvings on the panels either side of the recess. First the military: on the left at the top we see a shield, drum and trumpets, then a torso in Roman uniform, which associated the duke with the military ideals of ancient Rome, then a knight in armour holding a seventeenth century musket. The right hand panel shows us naval symbols: at the top another Roman torso, then a ship's sail, an anchor, compass and rope.

For his badge the duke used an anchor with the cable entwined. Henry Slight, a late Georgian historian, points out that the cable has disappeared from this monument, probably because of damage done to it during the Civil War. The anchor and cable were originally picked out in Or, the colour yellow used in heraldry. This may explain the significance of the painted gold elements of the monument today.

Surmounting the memorial we see his coronet and family coat of arms. The cherubs supporting the arms blow trumpets symbolising fame, as does the figure in classical garb below the urn on the left. (COURTESY OF PORTSMOUTH CATHEDRAL; AUTHOR'S PHOTOGRAPH, 2004)

***

Thirdly, a Latin inscription tells the duke's story. The Brothers Henry and Julian Slight, offer this elegant translation:

To George Villiers, Duke of Buckingham, who, from both parents, was most nobly descended: his father was Sir George Villiers, of Brooksby in the County of Leicester; and his mother, Maria Beaumont, Countess of Buckingham. He enjoyed every distinguished gift of nature and fortune, with the favour of two most prudent princes. His merits surpassed even the wishes of all who knew him: he was equal to bear the mass of the most weighty affairs, and only unequal to sustain the pressure of envy.

Whilst he was preparing, in this town, his army to encounter the enemy again, a merciless slaughter – that inundated the fatal shore with a new ocean of blood and tears, caused him to fall by the atrocious hand of an accursed assassin, A.D. 1628, August 23.

To this man, born to all that was great, and to his here buried remains, Susanna, his sister, Countess of Derby, with tears and perpetual mourning, erected this monument, A.D. 1631.

Thou passenger, if possessing any bowels of compassion and indignation, lament the undeserved fate of such a man.

And farewell.

All in all a most elegant and harmonious piece of sculpture with its spiritual, temporal, literary and artistic elements precisely balanced. The duke's sister is to be admired too for her devotion and taste. (COURTESY OF PORTSMOUTH CATHEDRAL; AUTHOR'S PHOTOGRAPH, 2004)

King James's Gate and Sir Bernard de Gomme (1620–1685)

For almost two hundred years, King James's Gate meant Portsmouth to anyone landing at Point. Situated in Broad Street, just before it turns left and becomes the High Street, it faced towards Point and was the first structure that they came across. It had been built in 1687 to commemorate the visit of James II to Portsmouth in that year. This photograph captures the gate at some point during the short period of time between the development of photography in the 1850s and the gate's removal in the 1860s. A group of workman pose to have their picture taken too.

The earliest and most flamboyant of the great gates of Portsmouth, the classical design was reminiscent of ancient Rome with Corinthian pilasters, a cupola and a broken pediment and ball.

The first and the last gates to be built were the only ones dedicated to individuals, King James II and King William IV whose gate was built much later in 1833/34.

King James's Gate, however, was the only one to carry an inscription, 'JACOBVS SECVNDVS REX A: REG: III: AN:DOM I. 1687.' Below, there is James's monogram also with the date 1687, and just below this at the top of the arch three cannon on a shield represent the ordnance arms. They are too indistinct to make out in this photograph though. (COURTESY OF PORTSMOUTH MUSEUMS AND RECORDS SERVICE)

❋ ❋ ❋

Charles II's greatest contribution to Portsmouth was to bring in a Dutch engineer by the name of Sir Bernard de Gomme in the 1680s to expand the fortifications and to redesign them in the latest European style. Andrew Saunders in a recent book describes him as the most notable military engineer in England, contemporary with de Vauban in France, Hoffmann in Denmark, Dahlberg in Sweden and Simon Stevin and Menno van Coehoern in the Dutch Netherlands.

The art of siege warfare has been consigned to history for so long that it is almost impossible to appreciate the significance of de Gomme's work, particularly as in Portsmouth it was never put to the test. By the seventeenth century, war itself was conceived in terms of the siege and its defence and the whole subject developed into a subject of philosophical study.

De Gomme, however, was not a man for intellectual debate, such as Sir Christopher Wren and other contemporaries, but was essentially a practical man of action with a huge capacity for hard work.

This enabled him to combine the duties of two prestigious posts: engineer in charge of all the King's castles, and assistant surveyor at the office of the Board of Ordnance. In 1682, he became the surveyor general and chief engineer.

However, as he got older his energy faded, his health declined and he spent more time in London occupied with administration. In Portsmouth, all that remains today of his work is the Spur Redoubt, the King's Bastion (originally Wimbleton's Bastion) and the long curtain wall and its moat.

He was the complete professional and his forte was that of administration, always an under-recognised skill. This made him inconspicuous in his own day and he has remained so in ours. He was Dutch at a time when the Dutch were unpopular, and his English was very limited. The lack of background material means that there has never been a detailed biography of him and he is completely unrecognised in the Netherlands. De Gomme died in 1685, the same year as Charles II, and their deaths represented the end of an era which had encompassed Civil War and the Restoration of the Monarchy.

King James's Gate though, is thought to be his work. It was intended to be part of the complex system of fortifications around Portsmouth and cut off the town from Broad Street and Point. It led to a moat and drawbridge and the area beyond it became known as Spice Island.

According to the historian of Portsmouth, Henry Slight, in about 1783 the marble ball fell from the summit of the tower of the gate during a tempest and split into fragments at the feet of two ladies who were passing at the time. In 1826, the gate was restored and the ball replaced.

Unfortunately, the gate is no longer there, having been relocated twice. First by the Victorians, when the fortifications were demolished in the 1860s, and then secondly in November 1948, when it was re-erected on the north-west side of Burnaby Road by the Ministry of Public Buildings and Works. It is Grade II listed. Luckily, it was not destroyed completely, but Portsmouth certainly lost a monument of major importance. No doubt it saw Nelson come and go a few times too.

Today, King James's Gate stands impotently at the edge of the United Services recreation-ground with the ball and pediment lost. Now, it is flanked by two identical side entrances. An interesting point though, originally the fine classical façade was precisely that, a façade built on to an existing smaller brick gateway. This photograph demonstrates how it must have looked, ornamental stonework on one side, plain brick on the reverse. (AUTHOR'S PHOTOGRAPH, 2004)

Above left: The interior brick arch shows up well. As for the ornamental iron gates, presumably there would have been some sort of interior smaller gate. However, no pictures exist of the gate with the interior gates closed. (AUTHOR'S PHOTOGRAPH, 2004)

Above right: A close-up of one of the side entrances. (AUTHOR'S PHOTOGRAPH, 2004)

A closer view of the Corinthian pilasters. (AUTHOR'S PHOTO-GRAPH, 2004)

Above left: This close-up of the date 1687 reveals the worn stone-work. (AUTHOR'S PHOTOGRAPH, 2004)

Above right: James II's monogram almost worn away. (AUTHOR'S PHOTOGRAPH, 2004)

Above: A last view through the decorative iron work to the modern buildings beyond which surround Guildhall Square. James II however, was never to visit Portsmouth again as he gave up the throne in 1688. He was replaced by two grandchildren of Charles I, the Dutch William of Orange and his wife Mary, who ruled jointly. (AUTHOR'S PHOTOGRAPH, 2004)

St Thomas's Church Tower

Left: St Thomas's Church began to take on the design that we see today when it was altered in the 1690s and a new church tower built in Portland stone by John Mitchell. (AUTHOR'S PHOTOGRAPH, 2004)

Above: This was also to function as a watchtower and the work was commemorated by a date outside on the north wall of 1691 plus the Portsmouth crescent and star. A very dramatic memento mori is placed in the classical pediment above and shows a skull wearing a laurel wreath symbolising the transitory rewards of fame, two crossed bones and an hour glass lying on its side – the sands of time have run out. (AUTHOR'S PHOTOGRAPH, 2004)

William of Orange and Mary Stuart Coat of Arms

A very decorative royal coat of arms was fixed to the pillar above the Portsmouth Corporation pew in the quire to commemorate the rebuilding of the church. The lion of England and the crown are highlighted in gold, and the wooden carving below displays the Portsmouth crescent and star. Cherubs were mythical figures which featured frequently in the coats of arms of this time and here, one links the lion and unicorn. The ribbon under the cherub is inscribed with the motto of the Dutch House of Orange, *Je Maintiendray* (I will uphold – the Law.)

The Order of the Garter with its ribbon and motto, *Honi Soit Qui Mal Y Pense* (Evil to him who evil thinks) surrounds the arms on which we can see a tiny shield in the centre. This was the arms of Nassau and represented William's status as Stadtholder of the Netherlands. The arms of Nassau are the Dutch royal arms today. All this is surmounted by the crown of Great Britain.[3]

The fine wood carving beneath shows the date 1695 and the Portsmouth crescent and star. (COURTESY OF PORTSMOUTH CATHEDRAL; AUTHOR'S PHOTOGRAPH, 2004)

The Survey of the Royal Dockyard

To move on now to 1698. By this time Queen Mary has died (in 1694) and William III rules alone until his death in 1702. The Stuart period is coming to an end but before it does so, Portsmouth Dockyard begins its change into the modern dockyard we know today.

The dockyard dates from 1194, when King Richard I granted Portsmouth its first charter and ordered a dock to be built at Portsmouth for the maintenance and preservation of the King's ships. The importance of the dockyard fluctuated in medieval times until Henry VII decided that Portsmouth, with its sheltered, protected and deepwater harbour should become the home of his Navy: his work was continued by Henry VIII.

During the wars with the Dutch in the seventeenth century, Chatham was the most prominent dockyard, but once the Protestant William of Orange had become King, the enemy changed from being the Dutch to the Catholic French. Portsmouth's fortunes were on the upturn due to its accessibility to the English Channel.

A major survey of the Royal Dockyards was undertaken in 1698 and the buildings illustrated in delicate colour. The large document produced was kept in the royal collection of George III which eventually formed the basis of today's British Library.

This highly decorative title page illustration of King Neptune in his chariot and the fleet symbolises the importance that was attached to Great Britain as a maritime nation in the eighteenth century.

In addition, King Neptune, the ruler of the sea, was closely associated with William III and considered to be his protector when William travelled across the sea from the Netherlands, not only to rule England but to return it to civilisation. Here, Neptune is shown bearing the royal standard of England. (COURTESY BRITISH LIBRARY REF. NO.: KING'S MS. 43, TITLE PAGE)

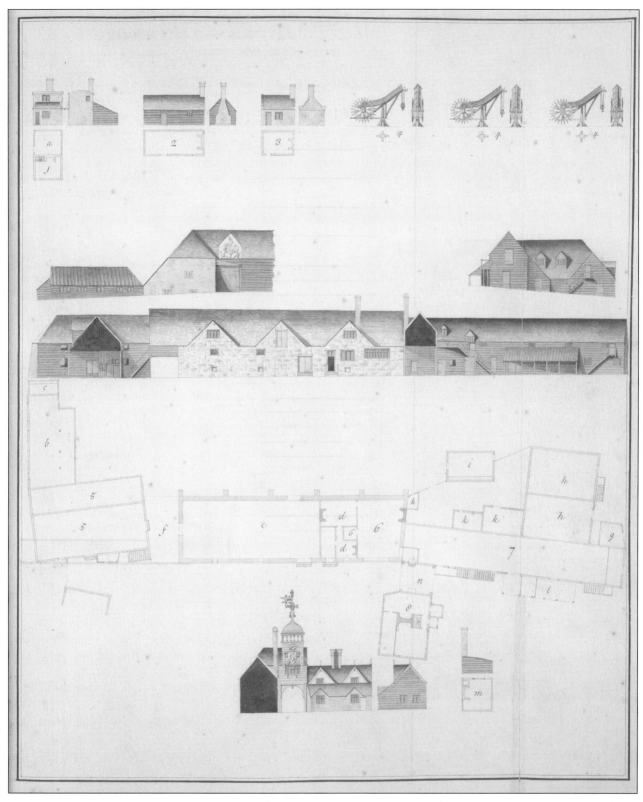

The page illustrates the porter's lodge made of brick, no.1; an old guard house, no.2; the pay office and cash room made of stone, no.6 and the porter's dwelling house made of timber, no.8. No.4 shows a front and side views of a crane. (Courtesy British Library Ref. No.: King's MS. 43, p.95)

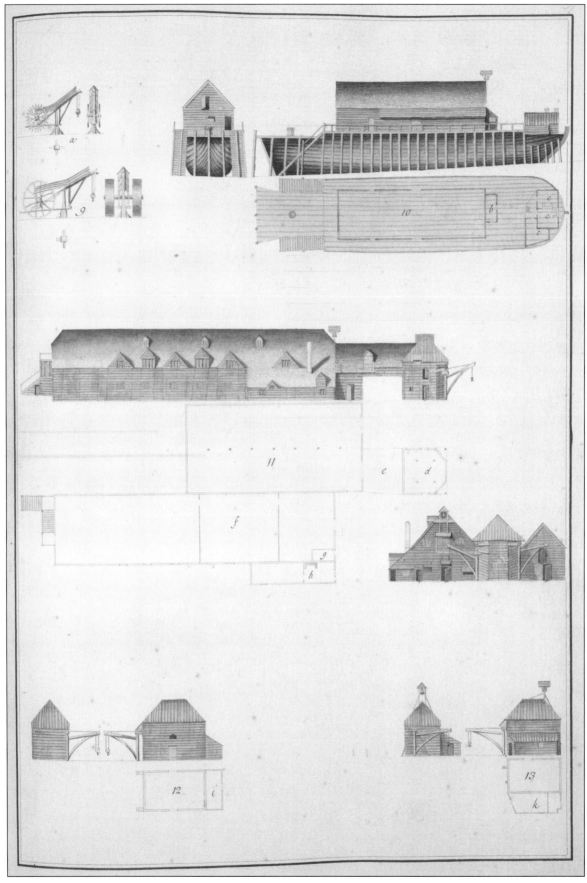

The large building in the centre is the timber storehouse, no.11. (COURTESY BRITISH LIBRARY REF. NO.: KING'S MS. 43, p.97)

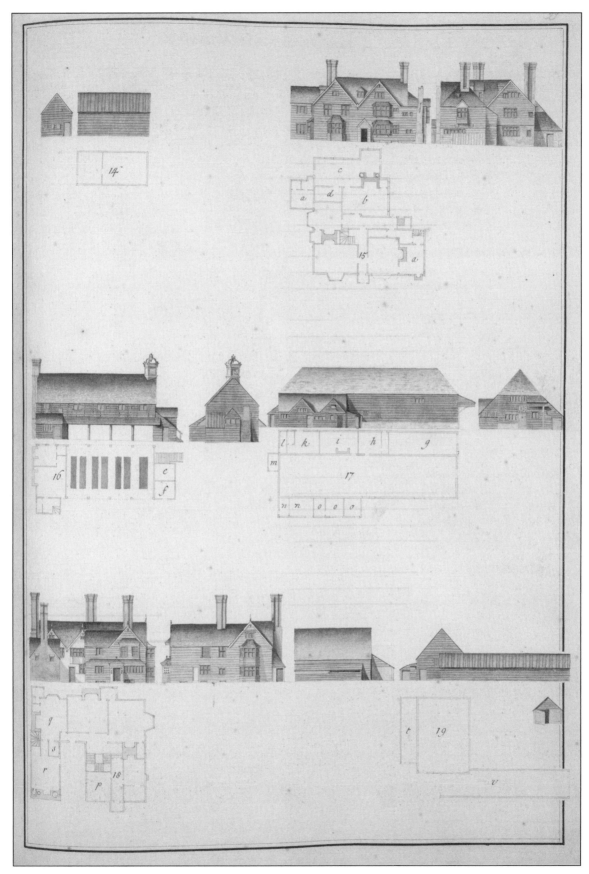

No.15 is the master shipwright's dwelling house made of timber and brick; no.16, the tap house, made of timber; no.17 is the great store house, also of timber; no.18 is the dwelling house of the clerk of the cheques, also of timber. (COURTESY BRITISH LIBRARY REF. NO.: KING'S MS.43, p.99)

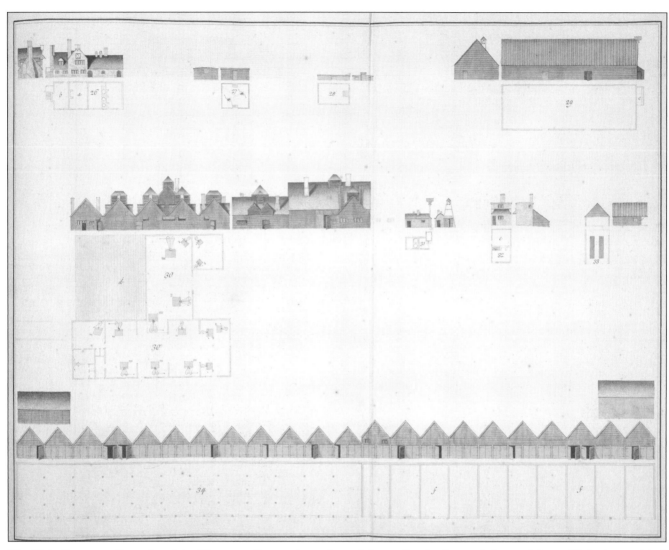

No.26 is the scavellmen's cabin (the scavellmen cleared mud from the docks and channels); no.30 is the smiths' shops and cabins, made of timber, and no.34 shows twelve timber boathouses, six with their doors ajar. (COURTESY BRITISH LIBRARY REF. NO.: KING'S MS. 43, p.108)

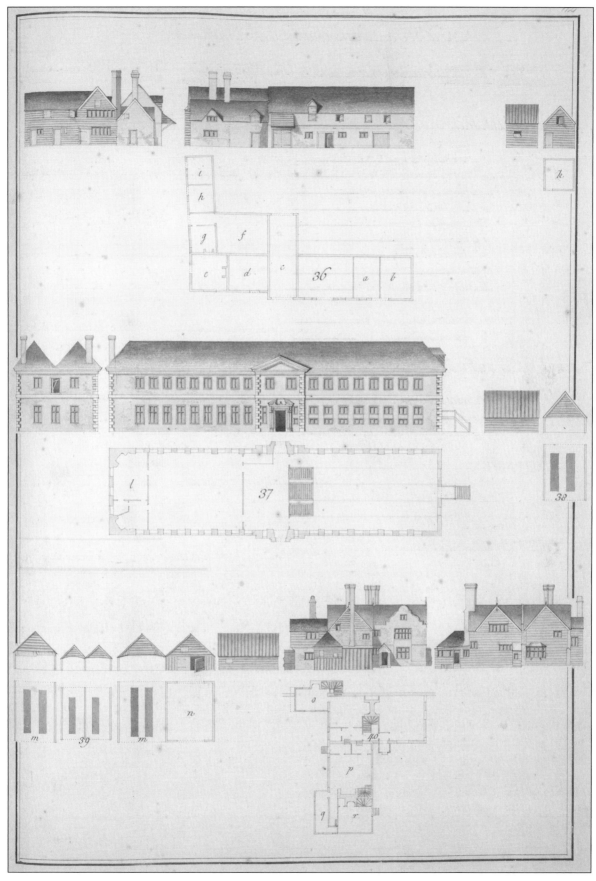

No.36 is the commissioner's stables made of brick; no.37, the new store house, made of brick and no.40, the storekeeper's dwelling house which is made of timber. (COURTESY BRITISH LIBRARY REF. NO.: KING'S MS. 43, p.112)

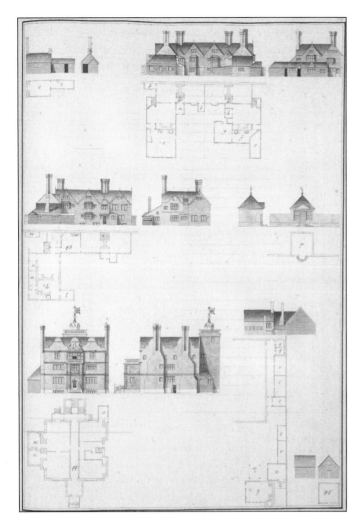

This page shows no.41, the master caulker's dwelling house, made of brick and timber; no.43, the master attendant's dwelling house, made of brick and timber; the very grand commissioner's house at no.44, obviously of brick; and at no.45, the pump house, of timber. (COURTESY BRITISH LIBRARY REF. NO.: KING'S MS. 43, p.114)

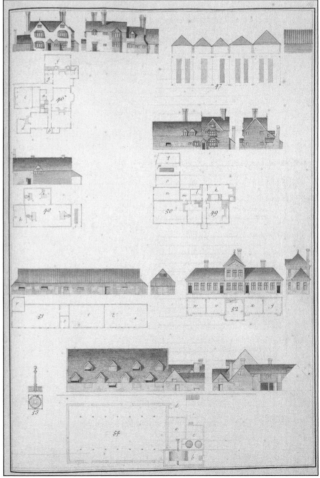

At no.52 we can see the new offices, all of brick and at no.53, an ornamental column in classical style described as made of Portland stone with dials about its capital and a spherical dial on a terrestrial globe aloft.

It does not need much imagination on our part to see that, with a little encouragement, the loving attention to detail in all these floor plans and elevations would enable them to jump off the page into the three dimensional model. However, this stage would have to wait until the next century. (COURTESY BRITISH LIBRARY REF. NO.: KING'S MS. 43, p.116)

Peter the Great of Russia Visits the Dockyard

A major event occurred in 1698 when Emperor Peter the Great visited the dockyard as part of his grand embassy to Europe, which lasted for eighteen months between 1697–1698. Peter was the first Russian ruler to visit the West but his mission was the acquisition of knowledge. Travelling incognito as 'Petr Mikhailov', his intention was to create a Russian Navy and to do this he needed to learn the art of navigation, the handling of ships and ship building. Peter and his entourage would visit Holland to learn the artistic techniques of building a ship and in England, the scientific technology to create a fleet.

William III encouraged Peter's interest and ordered Vice-Admiral David Mitchell who spoke Dutch, as did Peter the Great, to arrange a visit to Portsmouth, the home port of the Royal Navy. The visit lasted for three days, from 22–24 March 1698; on the first day the vice-admiral took the Russians on a tour of inspection of the fleet.

The following day, the mock engagement planned was delayed by calm weather so they all gathered on one ship and 'made rather merry'. This must have appealed to Peter whose appetite for drink was prodigious. On 24 March the weather changed and Peter watched the naval manoeuvres from the deck of Mitchell's ship, the *Humber*. The visit went off very successfully and then Peter returned to London to continue his trip.

Right: A plaque was placed near HMS *Victory* to commemorate the 300th anniversary of the visit in 1998, during the International Festival of the Sea, in the presence of many Russian sailors. (AUTHOR'S PHOTOGRAPH, 2004)

1711 – The Dockyard Wall

Between Peter the Great's visit and the death of Queen Anne in 1714, the landward boundaries of the dockyard were marked with a high brick wall which was constructed from 1704–1711. This wall replaced the modest defences which were already in existence and from that day on, the dockyard was set apart as a town within a town.

Left: A plaque on the main gate commemorates its completion in 1711 and around the corner in Admiralty Road, the date may also be seen picked out in different colour bricks. (AUTHOR'S PHOTOGRAPH, 2004)

Above: This photograph looking south towards Queen Street, Portsea gives some idea of the dimensions of the wall which is almost three-quarters of a mile long. Today, protecting as it does Portsmouth's inner garrison, it is the only part of the fortifications still to retain its original function. The entrance in the wall, now blocked up, gave people from Portsea access to the original St. Ann's Chapel. (AUTHOR'S PHOTOGRAPH, 2004)

1716 – The Camber Bastion

Left: Around this time a new Bastion was constructed at the Camber but disappeared long ago. One of King James's monograms was saved. This is what it looks like today after it was remounted following the development of Captain's Row.

There are two plaques. One reads 'A development by Sea Containers Waterside: King James Quay, Old Portsmouth 1995–1997'. The other reads 'King James's Gate monogram. There were two such monograms on this site, one on each face of the original Camber Bastion'. (AUTHOR'S PHOTOGRAPH, 2004).

Above: A close-up. (AUTHOR'S PHOTOGRAPH, 2004)

The Stuart Era Ends

The Stuart period was brought to an eventual close and in 1714 the resulting Hanoverian succession saw George I, the elector of Hanover, ascend the throne. The Georgian era had begun and brings us closer to the next generation in Nelson's family, his maternal uncle Maurice Suckling.

Right: This uncle is the link between the early and late periods of the Georgian age and our own modern world. He was to be a decisive influence in his nephew's life and to connect Nelson with Portsmouth for the first time. By chance, the dates on this tombstone outside Portsmouth cathedral straddle both centuries. (AUTHOR'S PHOTOGRAPH, 2004)

References
[1] *The King's Head: Charles I: King and Martyr*, pp.36–40.
[2] *The News*, 21 January 2004, p.19, and 2 April 2004, p.14

[3] *Friends of Portsmouth Cathedral Yearbook 2004*, pp.13–15.

Chapter II

1726–1778:
AN INFLUENTIAL UNCLE

Captain Maurice Suckling was born on 4 May 1726, just before the end of the reign of George I in 1727. He had made the Navy his career, becoming a lieutenant in 1745, a commander in 1754 and a post-captain ten years later in 1755. During these years though, he had no particular connections with Portsmouth and in fact, the houses he possessed were a long way away in East Anglia.

This is a portrait after Thomas Bardwell who painted him in 1764 at Woodton Hall near Norwich which was the ancestral home of the Suckling family. The captain's plain but elegant coat with the lace ruffles at the neck and wrists denotes a well-to-do, smart but modest naval man. His unadorned appearance for a picture is quite a contrast to the assortment of medals, ribbons and sashes that Nelson was to wear in his portraits in his later years.

(© NATIONAL MARITIME MUSEUM, LONDON, REF. NO.: BHC 3045)

A Western Prospect

So how was Portsmouth depicted during the twenty or so years before Captain Suckling became its MP in 1776? From considering the features of individual buildings we are now able to turn to pictures of the town itself. This engraving entitled, 'The West Prospect of Portsmouth in Hamp-Shire', is not just a pretty picture.

The prospect and its view was considered to be an art form in its own right in the eighteenth century and was very popular, this one for example, comes from the *Universal Magazine* which was published in the 1750s. Possibly today's equivalent of the *Reader's Digest*, engravings were an important part of its content and in particular, the engraving of the prospect.

How widely available was it? The magazine was printed monthly and cost sixpence. It is very difficult now to judge how cheap or expensive this was at the time, but certainly the eighteenth century saw a tremendous rise in the availability of all kinds of printed material. More people had access to education and could read and write. Street literature was a thriving industry and hawkers and pedlars earned their living by travelling the country selling ballads and halfpenny sheets of poems.

One of them, David Love, known as a flying stationer, noted in his autobiography that garrison towns were a good source of demand particularly in time of war. In 1791 he spent some time in Gosport and recorded that, '...the sailors gave sixpence or a shilling as freely for a book, as a half penny is given elsewhere when times are hard.'[1] It is reassuring to know that sailors did not spend all their money on alcohol and that a copy of the *Universal Magazine* was just that, something which could have been purchased universally by working people and not just the educated middle class.

To return to the prospect then, this could be defined as a scene viewed pictorially from a position of detachment. The resulting view could be categorised in many different ways, for example, as beautiful, genteel or enchanting. Prospects were intended to give pleasure and the view itself was to be viewed as a work of art rather than as simply a depiction of reality.

The subject matter and composition then was not just random, but considered very carefully for its effect on the viewer. Some views were better than others of course, and landscapes were considered to be the most superior. Next down the list was a combination of built landmarks and monuments with landscapes and gardens.

Seascapes and marine views were also very popular. Portsmouth's significance as a port and royal dockyard already made it a worthy subject for the prospect. Here, the artist has also noticed its potential as a scenic spot. There is something for everyone – a combination of the imposing buildings of the dockyard and town with a lively view of shipping and in the foreground a rustic vista, reminiscent of the views from Portsdown Hill.

Human interest has been added by the boatloads of sailors coming ashore, perhaps returning from war and greeting their waiting loved ones – a very familiar scene in Portsmouth. The location of the picture is emphasised by the crescent and star of Portsmouth at the top.

This prospect of Portsmouth is actually based on a similar version produced in 1749 by the British engravers Nathaniel and Samuel Buck who had produced earlier engravings of other seaside resorts. The 1749 version is less interesting though, as the buildings of Portsmouth are obscured by the shipping.

This version of 1750 was produced by the *Universal Magazine* and had been altered to show them much more clearly, although, apparently, from a great height. It would be difficult to imagine the same viewpoint today. Prospects were also an early form of guidebook, they supplemented written information about a place and were expected to be informative. As in this case, the buildings were numbered and a handy key printed underneath for reference:

1. *North Dock.*
2. *Boat-houses.*
3. *Officers' Houses.*
4. *Dock Clock.*
5. *Commissioner's House.*
6. *Sail and Mould Loft.*
7. *Rope House.*
8. *Royal Academy.*
9. *Landing Place at the Dock.*
10. *Rigging House.*
11. *The Common.*
12. *Officers' Lodging in the Gun-wharf.*
13. *Lamport [sic)]Gate.*
14. *Portsmouth Church.*
15. *The Point.*
16. *Flag on the [Saluting] Platform.*
17. *Round Tower.*
18. *Spit-Head.*

The 1749 version also extended further to the right and included a no.19, Blockhouse; no.20, St Hellen's Point; no.21, the Isle of Wight; and no.22, Part of Gosport.

Today, the prospect's attribute of the view from a great height has been completely superseded by aerial photography which may be more accurate, but does not have the same charm.[2] (AUTHOR'S COLLECTION)

Portsea Island – a Fort in the East and North

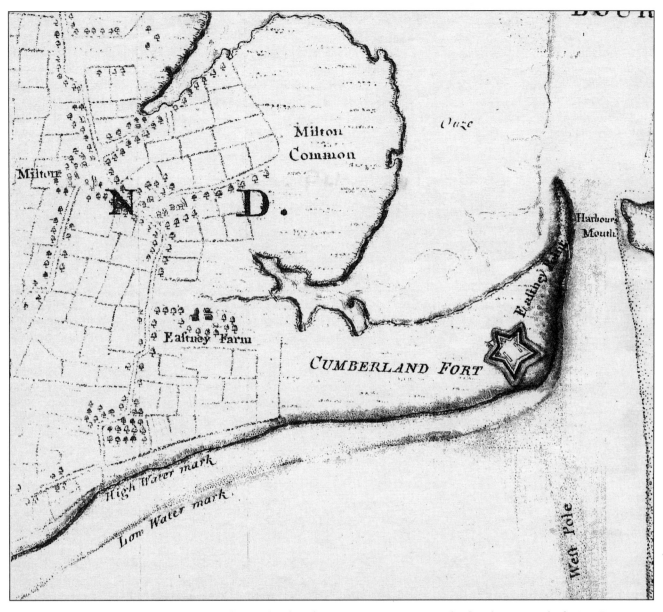

Portsea Island was seen as a whole as far as the fortifications were concerned. On the east side facing Langstone Harbour there had been an earthwork battery since 1716. However, following the Jacobite Rebellion in the mid-1740s, the Duke of Cumberland carried out a review of the nation's defences and concluded that the works were inadequate. Work was commenced on building Fort Cumberland in 1747.

This segment of a plan of Portsea Island dates from 1751 and shows the fort at Eastney Point. Its star shape was the latest thinking in fortification design in that any attackers could be seen from all sides. However, a contemporary report considered it to be useless from the start and its effectiveness in protecting the east side of Portsea Island from invasion was never tested. (COURTESY BRITISH LIBRARY REF. NO.: KING'S TOP. COLLECTION, vol.43–88, XIV–14)

After a very varied history, Fort Cumberland still stands today as Portsmouth's forgotten fort. Its enormous site is sunk mainly below ground level so it is almost invisible from the road and the sea. Eastney Point remains desolate and isolated from the rest of Portsmouth even though Eastney itself has been developed in recent years.

The fort is run by English Heritage as the Centre for Archaeology and maintains a very low profile as the public are only admitted on open days during the summer. Here, David Fellows the archaeologist, stands on the wall overlooking the sea to give some idea of the sheer size of the fort.

The tall chimney in the distance was the 'stinks' chimney constructed as part of Eastney Beam Engine House. (AUTHOR'S PHOTOGRAPH, 2004)

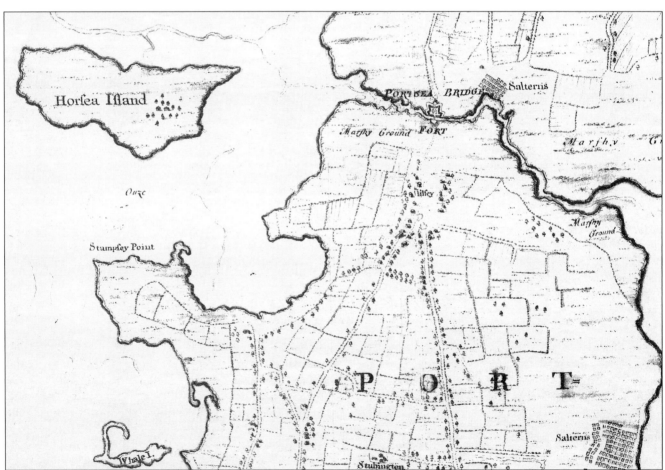

From the same plan of Portsea Island in 1751, this segment shows the north, in particular Hilsea and Portsea Bridge Fort. The northern and eastern sides of Portsea Island have more in common with each other than with Portsmouth itself. Both were desolate spots with few habitations and were only developed for military purposes to protect the dockyard. The fort at Portsbridge was the gateway to the island for many years but no trace of it remains now.
(COURTESY BRITISH LIBRARY REF. NO.: KING'S TOP. COLLECTION, vol.43–88, XIV–14)

St George's Chapel: The Shipwright's Church

To return to developments within the town, by the 1750s, the wars with France had resulted in a huge increase in shipbuilding and repair work in the dockyard. The area just outside the wall, known as Portsmouth Common, was being developed to cater for the corresponding increase in population and was to become known as Portsea in 1792.

Prior to this, Queen Anne had encouraged the expansion of the area in the face of opposition from Portsmouth itself and the main street was now named Queen Street in her honour with one running parallel named Prince George Street in honour of her husband, Prince George of Denmark. It is the development of Portsea which really began to separate the Georgian Portsmouth from the Stuart and would have been very familiar to Nelson.

However, apart from the dockyard chapel, the nearest church was St Mary's Kingston, so the local people petitioned the city fathers for permission to build their own church on a piece of waste land near the dockyard. The people not only raised sufficient money to build the church (which cost £2,209) but also to pay the stipend of a priest to conduct services; the foundation stone was laid in 1753.

St George's Chapel was built by 15 shipwrights from the dockyard. It is known as the 'shipwright's church' and was constructed out brick and timber from the dockyard known as 'dockyard splinters'. The building was completed in six months and dedicated to St George.

The overseer and probable architect was Nicolas Vass, a master shipwright or carpenter from the dockyard. Vass had a son, also Nicholas who was to follow in his father's footsteps. Eventually, in 1875 the church became a Parish Church serving its own area.

❊❊❊

As for the design, the builders made the most of the fact that they were not constricted by space and unlike so many Georgian churches, there were not houses or other buildings on either side. This meant that they could build outwards as opposed to upward.

The typical components of neoclassical architecture were adapted to fit the site, such as symmetrical windows, an imposing door-case and a rectagonal cupola. The pavilions on either side of the main door housing the staircases to the gallery are emphasised at the expense of the main entrance. A more expensively built church perhaps would have had the stairs inside, but the large pavilions do give the church a sense of balance and solidity. Vass resisted the temptation to put a large Venetian window in the west end having just one at the east end.

(AUTHOR'S PHOTOGRAPH, 2004)

Inside, the reredos dates from 1900 and consists of four plain wooden panels, their shape mirroring the design of the windows, to illustrate the word of the Lord. The three most important texts of the Anglican Church are set out here, the Ten Commandments, the Lord's Prayer and the Nicene Creed, taken, of course, from the Authorized Version of the Bible. The angels' heads around the windows are a touching addition.

This interior view also allows a glimpse of the wooden pews which disappeared at some point after the Second World War as in so many churches. Early undated photographs can be hard to date but the photographer has just caught a table with an inscription in the bottom foreground. It reads, 'In Memoriam Florence Cooper 1906–1911', which suggests that the photograph was taken before the First World War. (COURTESY PORTSMOUTH MUSEUMS AND RECORDS SERVICE)

This is a photograph of the church which was commissioned as part of a souvenir volume of the Conference of the National Union of Teachers held in Portsmouth in 1937. It was taken by W. J. Lawrence whose father, J. C. Lawrence, had established a photographic studio in Elmhurst Road, Gosport in the 1880s. The firm became very well-known, and Lawrence Square, off Gosport High Street outside the Town Hall was named after the Lawrence family.

Most unusually, it shows the east end with its attached building. The photographer has caught an atmospheric winter view which allows us to catch a glimpse of St George's Square as it was before the Second World War. The elegant Georgian houses on the left were all destroyed in the bombing. In the foreground, a sailor waits by a handcart for his comrade. (COURTESY OF J. C. LAWRENCE)

Far Right: Although the church survived the Second World War it was badly damaged. During the 1950s it was closed for a time and some restoration took place but the main refurbishment did not take place until the 1970s. This most unusual photograph dating from around that time shows the church from the air, so we can see the rudiments of its construction. (COURTESY THE VICAR OF ST GEORGE'S CHURCH)

Right: As for the appearance of the church today, this view shows the interior with the Venetian window, now plain glass, at the east end. (COURTESY THE VICAR OF ST GEORGE'S CHURCH) / AUTHOR'S PHOTOGRAPH.

Right: Here the Tuscan column shows up very clearly with the wooden galleries behind. Restoration work is being carried out on the west wall.

Overall, Nicholas Vass and his shipwrights not only did a good workmanlike job but created a most attractive church. As the first church of the Georgian period, St George's stands today as a focal point between the medieval St Mary's and St Thomas's, and the extensive Victorian church building programme in Portsmouth of the 1830s–50s: it celebrated its 250th anniversary in 2003.

While the squat shape and plain façade may seem unsophisticated compared to later Georgian churches, the architecture does have a certain energy and style which they lack. Today, the quiet authority of St George's and its square has quite a different atmosphere from Old Portsmouth.

The church would also have been instantly recognisable to Nelson. The same cannot be said of St Mary's, Kingston, however, which was completely rebuilt in the 1880s. At St Thomas's too, many alterations were made over the years culminating in the final completion of the nave in 1991.

Lastly, St George's connection with those shipwrights of the eighteenth century is maintained today by a display of shipwrights' tools in the entrance mounted by the Dockyard Historical Society. (COURTESY THE VICAR OF ST GEORGE'S CHURCH)
AUTHOR'S PHOTOGRAPH 2004)

'[See] a Stately Fabrick Rise': The Royal Hospital Haslar

The late seventeenth and eighteenth centuries were a golden age in the design and construction of hospitals in Britain and the American colonies. Between 1660 and 1815, the great veterans' hospitals at Chelsea and Greenwich were constructed, the ancient London foundations of Bethlem (Bedlam), St Thomas's and St Bartholomew's completely rebuilt and more than 50 other hospitals and asylums were purpose-built for the first time by charities or the Navy.

Naval hospitals, however, were distinctive in that they had to take all patients, irrespective of their condition and they only treated a single sex. Their main characteristic was that they had to maintain the security of a ship while avoiding the foul air, cramped conditions and even worse food which caused so much disease, especially scurvy, among sailors.

One of these hospitals was opened in Gosport on the western side of Portsmouth harbour to treat sick and wounded seamen. Up till now, they had been cared for in ships moored in the harbour which had become increasingly inadequate. In 1745, after much deliberation, the Admiralty commenced planning for the hospital which was built on open farmland on the peninsula overlooking Portsmouth harbour and between the fortifications of Gosport. Fort Monckton stood at its south-western end and Fort Blockhouse at the north-east.

The architect was Theodore Jacobsen, who had recently designed the Foundling Hospital in London, the foundation stone being laid in 1742. The original building was demolished but the charitable foundation remains in existence as the Thomas Coram Foundation. His designs in Gosport were implemented by James Horne and John Turner, a master carpenter.

The bricks were made on the site and the stone imported from the Isle of Wight. The site even had its own water supply which was obtained from artesian wells. The Royal Hospital Haslar was opened in 1753 although not finally completed until 1762. It celebrated its 250th anniversary in 2003.

The significance of the design was that it was influenced by that of the Royal Hospital at Greenwich which had been built for the Navy in 1694. Theodore Jacobsen however, was no Sir Christopher Wren and the ornate Baroque style of architecture had fallen from fashion but he was able to utilise the new classically-based Georgian architecture to give the design an elegant utilitarianism.

The hospital consisted of great courts lined with galleries and built on a series of arches to protect the building from flooding at high tide. There were three storeys of wards doubling back on each other, set end to end and alternating with lower storage blocks. The galleries between them were originally designed to open on both sides: the combination of courts and galleries was intended to reconcile security with salubrity.

However, this design was not quite as healthy as had been thought initially, and by 1799 the architecture was being blamed for high mortality rates, the doubled wards apparently impeding the free passage of air.

This aquatint by John Wells, based on a sketch by Revd J. Hall, the chaplain to the hospital in 1799, illustrates the sheer size of the place and its desolate site with no habitations and sparse vegetation. Revd Hall has tried to minimise its bleakness by reducing the size of the buildings and showing them from a viewpoint across the creek from the Gosport fortifications. (Courtesy Gosport Museum)

Water as the Prison Wall

Not only was it the largest hospital in England, on a site covering 32 acres, but the largest brick building. In 1758 Dr James Lind, one of the first physicians there, described it as, 'An immense pile of a building and when complete it will certainly be the biggest hospital in Europe!' It was probably also the most difficult hospital to get to, as originally there was no bridge across the creek and access via the land was round the Gosport peninsula. The sea was only a few yards away from the main gate and served the double purpose of providing easy access from the ships at Spithead and keeping the patients in once they got there.

The architecture reflects Haslar's additional function of a prison. Many of its patients had, of course, been press-ganged into the Navy and saw a stay in hospital as the ideal opportunity to escape. No one was to be in any doubt that the needs of the individual were always to be subordinate to those of the state. If they were unsure, they would soon be reminded by the austere architecture, with its forbidding walls towering over them and the high wall all around the site, not to mention the Marines at the gate.

No money was to be spent on decoration either apart from a splendid frieze on the pediment crowning the administration block in the centre of the north side. This carving was made by Thomas Pearce in 1752 and has at its centre a magnificent carving of the royal arms of George II. Two female figures sit either side of the arms representing the dual pillars of the British Empire which was dependent on the Royal Navy and the Merchant Navy: navigation and commerce.

Henry Slight described it much more romantically in a poem all about Portsmouth published in 1820:

...While on the rising ground is seen THE HOSPITAL.
Let India boast her caravanseras,
Of hoar antiquity – rich princely works
For wandering Pilgrim, fainting traveller;
Boast Greece and Italy their classic fanes,
Their marble columns, and their towers fair:
But where shines ought, more noble or more grand
In genuine kindness, angel charity,
Than Haslar's sumptuous pile...

On the rich pediment behold
The arms of England's monarchy,
The various sculptures which unfold
The pomp of naval dignity.
First, Navigation, boldly shining,
Her arms on blazoned Prow reclining,
While bending low with gesture sweet -
A wounded sailor at her feet -
She bathes his wounds in charity,
With care Samaritan attends
His every want, each woe befriends.

High in mid-air the Northern star,
Sure guide to ancient mariner;
On the fore-ground the compass wheel,
The mystic polar-pointing steel;
And at the angle, low reclined,
The Guardian of the Western wind;
While stern of ship – rich pearly ore -
And shells complete th' entablature.
*   Next Commerce, with unsparing hand,*
Sheds plenty oe'r the smiling land;
And fruits and never failing flowers
From golden Cornu-copia showers -
On Bales of Merchandize her seat.
The world's vast treasure at her feet.
Near this a ship-wrecked Sailor stands,
in mute despair on barren sands;
To whose distress and prospects drear
A friendly Bird doth minister;
While Boreas bids the tempest roar,
And shells and coral crown the shore...

More prosaically, hospital design was seen as part of the ideas of the Enlightenment which was to develop more fully in the second half of the eighteenth century. The concepts of order, harmony and balance were thought to be the means whereby the works of man could be reconciled with those of God.

The composition of this frieze would have been seen at the time not only as an attractive carving, but also, and more importantly, as a symbolic summing-up of the works of man as part of those of God. (Author's photograph, 2004)

A Place of Fashionable Resort

As for Nelson's connection with Haslar, or rather the lack of it, this does throw an interesting light on medical care in the eighteenth century. There is no record of his visiting the hospital as a patient and in view of all Nelson's health problems, it might be assumed that he would have been treated there. However, in his day, it was taken for granted that officers would consult and pay for their own personal physicians. His eye surgeon though, Thomas Trotter did serve at Haslar.[3]

While smart society might not consider visiting Haslar as a place for treatment, by the end of the eighteenth century it had become a tourist attraction and a place of fashionable public resort. People would visit the hospital to admire the architecture and the views just as they would the fortifications at Portsmouth.

In London, Nelson did just this with the Foundling Hospital in London. An account of its history records that:

> *In 1801, the hero of the Nile and some of his friends honoured the establishment with a visit and stood sponsors to several of the children. The names given on this occasion were Baltic Nelson, William and Emma Hamilton, Hyde Parker etc.*[4]

The Navy was seen as a good way of life for its boys but one does wonder though what became of the children with names like that. It also adds a most poignant note to Nelson's story bearing in mind that he had had no children with his wife and Horatia, his daughter by Emma Hamilton, was to be born that year on 1 February. She was almost a foundling herself, born illegitimately in great secrecy in London with neither parent able to acknowledge her publicly and looked after by foster mothers in her early years.

The Sister Building Over the Water

Portsmouth Dockyard and the Royal Hospital Haslar have much in common with their main characteristic being their enormous size. The dockyard of course, had a four-hundred-year start on the hospital but they both were to develop in similar ways, one as the largest brick building in Europe and the other as the largest industrial complex in Western Europe. Both have similar architecture, the dockyard acquiring its own austere, forbidding buildings when it was rebuilt in the 1770 and 80s in the neoclassical style of elegant utilitarianism.

In addition, both sites had a major economic and cultural impact on the surrounding communities. The dockyard and hospital each became a town within a town. While the equivalent of Portsea did not develop around Haslar as it did not have the thousands of workers that the dockyard employed, it could nevertheless accommodate about two thousand patients plus medical staff.

Both enterprises were the main employers in the area and the Haslar staff also purchased food and supplies from local farmers and sold off surplus stock to local people. The hospital also played an important role in the development of naval medicine with the work of physicians such as James Lind, known as the Father of Naval Medicine, contributing much to the health of the ordinary seaman.

Both Haslar and the dockyard were products of the theoretical ideas and political and military policies of the eighteenth century. The Royal Navy was at the height of its powers particularly between 1750 and 1805 when, if not actually at war, was preparing for it with the hospital and dockyard providing essential support.

So, what of the hospital today? Ideas and policies have changed considerably but the description of 'Stately Fabrick' by a Mr Maxwell in the 1750s still applies.[5] The site has been greatly extended and enlarged since it was first built and now, the hospital combines military and naval medicine with the NHS. Unfortunately, the future it faces is uncertain. Its modern crest at the main gate symbolises its naval history. (AUTHOR'S PHOTOGRAPH, 2004)

1766: The Sea Coast in the Neighbourhood of Portsmouth Surveyed and Navigated by M. Mackenzie

The development of the accurate and reliable sea chart was of vital importance to Nelson's Portsmouth as it was an indispensable tool for safe navigation. By this time, Britain was beginning to play a leading role in chart making, particularly by Murdoch Mackenzie senr (1712-1797), who was an important surveyor and chart maker. He was employed by the Admiralty to carry out hydrographic surveys but his contribution extended far beyond the official confines of the job.

His significance to British chart making lay in the fact that for the first time, he adopted the use of a rigid triangulation framework and measured base line from continental cartographers. In addition, he made standard use of a system of conventional signs and detailed abbreviations to indicate the nature and consistency of rocks and shoreline. This system is still in use by the Admiralty on their charts today.

This chart shows Spithead and Portsmouth Harbour with the figures indicating the depth in fathoms. On land on the right-hand side, he indicates Fort Cumberland, Southsea Castle and two brackets which represent military encampments on Southsea Common. In the top right hand corner he shows Horsea Island with one habitation. On the left-hand side, the Royal Hospital Haslar is marked very clearly. Portsmouth itself is shown as a fortified town although in 1766, Portsea has not been developed or fortified.

The sea chart also indicates very clearly the channel of deep water which ran alongside Southsea Common and up into Portsmouth Harbour. Portsmouth owes its entire development to two factors. Firstly, the situation of a large harbour opposite the English Channel with its proximity to the Continent. Secondly, a deep water channel which allowed access to large ships but could easily be defended. (COURTESY ROYAL NAVAL MUSEUM)

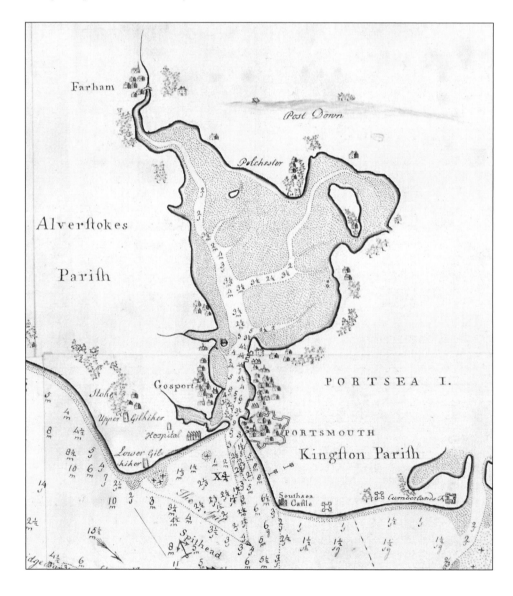

This photograph sums it all up perfectly – the combination of the shallow draught of the car ferry and the depth of the water allowing it to sail so close to the Square Tower and the fortifications. The car about to turn right into High Street appears to be just yards away. A fascinating and very familiar sight to local residents. (AUTHOR'S PHOTOGRAPH, 2005)

Catherine the Great's Captain

By the time Haslar Hospital was complete in 1762, George III had reigned for two years, having ascended the throne on the death of his grandfather in 1760. His fellow monarch, the Empress Catherine the Great, now came to the throne of Russia. In Portsmouth cathedral a tombstone is set in the floor, just below the monument to the Duke of Buckingham, with the following inscription:

Here lies the body of Captn. Ivan Karsakoff of her Serene Highness the Empress of Russia's ship... who departed this life Janry. 9th (O. S.) 1770.[6]

The cost of cutting this inscription on a new stone was paid by Russian friends bearing the name KORSAKOFF in the year 1915. (COURTESY OF PORTSMOUTH CATHEDRAL; AUTHOR'S PHOTOGRAPH, 2004)

So who was Ivan Karsakoff, what was he doing in Portsmouth and what was his story? In Portsmouth cathedral on the 8 August 1998, in the year of the 300th anniversary of Peter the Great's visit to Portsmouth, the Russian Orthodox Community of St Peter and St Paul of Portsmouth celebrated a Panikhida, which is the Requiem service for the departed, for the soul of Captain Karsakoff in the presence of the provost and precentor. A member of the community, Gervase Bradley, researched the captain's history using a variety of contemporary sources and has generously given his permission for an edited extract to be reproduced here:

Catherine and her Navy

The captain's full name was Ivan Alexievich Karsakov and he was captain first class of the Russian warship *Europa*. The Empress of Russia was of course, Catherine the Second, 'The Great', who had been sole ruler of Russia for eight years since the overthrow and murder of her husband Tsar Peter III in 1762.

One of her ambitions was a restoration of the Byzantine Empire under Russian influence, which would be ruled by her second grandson, the Grand Duke Konstantin

Pavlovich, but to attain this ambition she needed a fleet and Russia had had no fleet to speak of since the time of Peter I (the Great). So Catherine set about creating one and called in Sir Samuel Grieg and other British advisers nearly all of them Scots like Sir Samuel.

The first Russian fleet was modest consisting of a battleship of 66 guns and several frigates of 32 guns. At this time, Catherine was advised by the Orlovs, her lover Grigorii and his brother Alexis, who many authorities believe was instrumental in the despatch of Catherine's unlamented husband Peter III. Alexis's idea was to stir up the Orthodox Greeks against the Ottoman Turks by dangling before them the concept of an independent Christian Greece and then to support them with the fleet that Catherine had just created.

Alexis Orlov was commander in chief in spite of the fact that his knowledge of naval affairs was minimal. The two admirals under him were Spiridov and John Elphinstone. Elphinstone was another Scot of the Balmerino clan who had served with Greig under Commodore Keppel in Havana after coming into the Royal Navy from the merchant service. He was a man of dogmatic views and owed his Russian appointment to his outspokenness at a dinner party in London, 'The Dardanelles impossible? I will do it as easily as I drink this glass of wine!'

Spiridov left Kronstadt, the port of St Petersburg, first taking with him the three most efficient 66 gun ships and most of the available stores. He crossed the North Sea in bad weather making first for Hull, where temporary repairs were made to his squadron. He was uncertain if he should go round the northern tip of Scotland or risk the passage of the Downs, as the French at that tine were not friendly to Russia and were alarmed at her new power and aggressive naval policy. He eventually chose the latter route, calling at Portsmouth on the way and arrived at Gibraltar in the third week of November 1769.

Elphinstone was to follow Spiridov, but there was the usual Russian delay with stores and his officers could not cope. To make matter worse, the crews were of many nationalities and had to try to communicate with each other by speaking Dutch!

Soon after leaving Kronstadt, one of the 66 gun ships disobeyed every signal from the flagship and finally returned to port while one of the frigates sank. The remainder of the squadron straggled through the Baltic in an unseamanlike manner that must have broken Elphinstone's heart. As soon as they entered the North Sea they encountered bad weather which forced them to put into Copenhagen.

Once safely in harbour, all discipline vanished and the Russians, officers and men, at once abandoned themselves to the delights of Copenhagen, forgetting all about the purpose of their voyage. When reminded of their duty they grumbled and expressed dislike of an expedition into which they had been forced against their inclinations.

With the help of His Excellency M. Philosoph, the Russian minister at Copenhagen, Elphinstone managed to get the squadron to sea on the 12 December 1769, two days before the harbour froze for the winter. This was, no doubt, the reason why the disgruntled officers had employed their delaying tactics. Their worst fears were soon realised as a severe storm struck the fleet and scattered the ships like sheep. The dispersed squadron was forced to seek shelter in various English ports.

Elphinstone began to gather his scattered squadron together in Portsmouth at the beginning of January 1770. An examination of the ships had proved them to be a sorry state and Elphinstone asked the Russian ambassador to the court of St James to ask for full Admiralty assistance to facilitate repairs. An order was dispatched to the officers of the dockyard , 'To be on the most friendly terms and render every service in their power'. The Russian squadron stayed in Portsmouth until April 13th.

While the ships were being repaired, the crews were taught, 'the marine exercises and manoeuvres of small arms, hand grenades etc. aloft and in the tops', under the critical gaze of the Royal Navy.

A Death and Funeral in Portsmouth

Many of the seamen and soldiers were ill, four hundred were being nursed at Hilsea and many more at the Royal Hospital Haslar. One thousand were also encamped on Southsea Common. With Elphinstone in Portsmouth was Karsakov's *Europa*. She was in fact, attached to Spiridov's squadron but had stayed behind for repairs.

While leaving port she had gone aground near Southsea Castle, damaging her rudder, loosening her bolts and starting her timbers. The cost of repairs was £1000 and she finally got away by the 22 February. However, her captain, Ivan Alexievich, had been ill for two months and eventually died aboard the Russian hospital ship *The Northern Eagle* on or before the 22 January 1770.

Karsakov was buried on 23 January at four in the afternoon in his uniform. Presumably, in accordance with Russian and Orthodox custom, the coffin remained open to show the deceased lying probably with an icon on his breast, until the commencement of the actual funeral.

At eleven in the morning, 150 grenadiers were landed from the squadron to attend the corpse to the grave. They were described as 'very fine fellows' in their uniforms of green and gold lace. They were said to be expert in their exercises or drill. Apparently, Russian custom dictated that a man of Karsakov's rank, captain first class, should have had a thousand armed men to attend his funeral.

The Russians' applications for this number to land, however, was turned down by the authorities, as it was deemed imprudent to allow so many armed and disciplined men to land in one of the country's principal garrison towns, as Portsmouth was in those days. At length, it was decided to let them have another hundred men, presumably on top of the 150 grenadiers already landed. They disembarked from the ship's boats and marched up Grand Parade where they were marshalled with their arms grounded to await the funeral.

At about 3p.m. they commenced the march to the house where the corpse lay with drums and fifes playing and trumpets sounding. About 4p.m., when it must have been getting dark, the procession commenced when a company of about 20 men wheeled round from the ranks and came to attention at the door of the house where the captain's body lay.

First out came two Russian Orthodox priests in their black robes over which they wore what were described as, 'waist length cloaks of blue and pink satin respectively ornamented with hieroglyphics'. These were probably the Orthodox phelonion or chasuble which would have been worn with an epitrachelion or stole. Behind the priests came the corpse in a 'genteel' black coffin carried by six naval lieutenants with six other officers supporting the pall. On the coffin lay an unsheathed sword.

The deceased was followed by two young men in mourning clothes said to be Karsakov's nephews. Finally, came Admiral Elphinstone and another Russian admiral. This may have been Count Muschin Puschin, the Russian ambassador to the court of St James in his official uniform. Then came all the sea officers in white uniforms trimmed with green with black hat bands and scarves. The total company of troops brought up the rear marching to the beat of a drum and the tolling of the bell.

The cortege arrived in the chancel of St Thomas's Church where the curate read the Anglican burial service after which the body was interred. At the moment of interment, the troops outside discharged three general volleys and then returned to the house were Karsakov's body had lain with drums beating and trumpets sounding amid a large concourse of people who had gathered to see the unusual spectacle.

The captain had lain in state in his uniform of green and white with his hair elegantly dressed, 'and in every respect as if he were to attend a ball'. While he lay, he was attended by six priests with long beards wearing black robes and cowls over their heads, who had sung a panikhida and read the whole psalter over the body of the deceased as is the Orthodox custom.

The Departure of the Russians

When the last Russian squadron left Portsmouth on 13 April 1770, it proceeded to the Mediterranean to join its fellows under Samuel Greig and Spiridov. They were joined at Livorno by Count Orlov who gave Grieg the sad news that his prematurely born child was dead.

The Grand Duke of Tuscany, in whose territory Livorno lay, had a friendly relationship with the Russian Empress, who at that time was trying to obtain the use of the great harbour of Valetta in Malta from the Grand Master of the Knights of St John. This however, came to nothing. Early in May, the Russian fleet left Livorno and sailed east. It consisted of Orlov's squadron with two battleships and a bomb ketch; Spiridov's squadron with four battleships and one frigate; Elphinstone's squadron with three battleships and two frigates. In addition, there were three sloops and a small transport.

When the fleet reached the coast of Greece an attempt was made to rouse the Orthodox population against the Turks with the aid of agitators, proclamations and arms but there were not enough of the latter to be effective and plans for a landing were muddled. However, Orlov did manage to blow up a Turkish fort at Navarino, which would be the scene of a famous sea battle in the next century.

He then won a battle at Chios on 5 July 1770 and two days later on 7 July, he defeated and burned the Turkish fleet at the battle of Chesme Bay. The Turks lost fifteen ships of the line, nine frigates and over eight thousand men.

Orlov should then have advanced into the Sea of Marmora with the intention of taking Constantinople, but a French officer, Baron Tott, helped the Turks to put the Dardanelles into a state of defence. The Russians occupied about twenty islands in the Aegean but were never to achieve the main object of the exercise.

A Final Interment

Captain Karsakov was to lie undisturbed in the cathedral until the twentieth century. It is interesting to note that his tomb lay in St Thomas's Chapel, the most ancient part of the building which was constructed in pre-Reformation times. The Russian Orthodox Church bypassed the years of the Reformation and Counter-Reformation in sixteenth century Europe because of the Great Schism between East and West in 1054; the Orthodox Divine Liturgy remains unaltered, except for translation into other languages, since AD6.

In the period 1903–4, the church was closed and extensive repairs undertaken. There had been too many burials in the church in the preceding centuries and the condition of the foundations was foul. All the burials in the church were taken up and replaced in one large vault including the captain who could be identified by the richness of his gold lace and numerous buttons.

Unfortunately, the original tombstone was broken in the process and its whereabouts is not known but a replacement was provided in 1915 by the Korsakoff family. The Empress's captain who died so far away from home continues the link between Portsmouth and the Russian Navy and is not forgotten today.

A Marine Prospect of the Ordinary

Maritime engravings continued to be very popular and the 1770s saw the Royal Dockyards portrayed by John Cleveley the Younger (1747–1786) and published by the Bowles family who were a popular firm of printmakers in London.

In the eighteenth century, Portsmouth Dockyard was considered as two parts, the land side, known as the Extra-Ordinary where ships were built and refitted, and the water, known as the Ordinary, where ships not on voyages were moored and repaired.

The hustle and bustle of the activities in the Ordinary come over very well. The viewpoint is set almost at eye-level so we are much more closely involved in the everyday comings and goings than in the more remote and aloof prospects.

The harbour is seen as a place of work, not as an attractive setting for leisure pursuits. For example, the emphasis of the composition is placed on the masting hulk in the left foreground, which is about to lower a new mainmast in place on the vessel next to it. The dockyard itself forms the backdrop to the scene where we can see ships under construction in the dry docks of the Extra-Ordinary.

The Dockyard in Transition

In 1771, elements in the story of Nelson's Portsmouth gradually come together. By this time Nelson, who had been born in 1758, was twelve years old and thanks to the good offices of his uncle had joined the Navy. Maurice Suckling, a captain now for 15 years, in his turn had received promotion from his patron. On 26 June 1771, he had been given additional responsibilities which involved superintending naval affairs in the Medway and the Nore plus a considerable range of other duties.

This patron was John Montagu, fourth Earl of Sandwich (1718–1792) who was to have a profound effect on the careers of Captain Suckling and through him, Nelson. Prior to this though, he had made his reputation as a traveller, scholar and orientalist by undertaking his version of the grand tour throughout the Turkish empire when most aristocratic young men were content to settle for Italy and France.

Lord Sandwich's subsequent career had been devoted to the Royal Navy. From 1744 to 1747 he had served as admiralty commissioner and then three terms as first lord of the admiralty. The first term from 1748-1751 lasted three years and the second just six months in 1763.

His longest and most important term was the third and this lasted from January 1771 to March 1782. Lord Sandwich was to make his greatest contribution to the Navy during these eleven years which also coincided with Nelson's first eleven years in the Navy.

Most significantly for Portsmouth, as first lord of the admiralty he was to oversee the transformation of Portsmouth Dockyard from the timber and brick buildings of the Stuarts to the Georgian stone buildings we know today.

On the 12 January 1771 he became first lord of the admiralty after an absence of almost twenty years, and commenced his period of office with a major reorganisation and rebuilding of the six Royal Dockyards: Deptford and Woolwich on the Thames, Chatham and Sheerness on the Medway, and Portsmouth and Plymouth on the south coast. Lord Sandwich was to oversee this intense period of work and brought an immense capacity for hard work to the task.

So what led to this transitional stage? It had been prompted in 1770 by a series of fires which had damaged many dockyard buildings. These had to be replaced in any case and there was also a programme of new works to be completed. The Admiralty then took the opportunity to initiate a programme of annual inspections of all the dockyards.

Lord Sandwich – a man who believed in seeing for himself, a most unusual attribute in those days – commenced a rigorous series of investigations. He was an indefatigable visitor with plenty of stamina who saw everything there was to see, including the Royal Hospital Haslar and the Naval Academy in the dockyard. In June 1772 for instance, in Portsmouth, he visited 34 ships in one day!

The earl was also a man who had grasped the importance of background research. He understood the significance of the 'Survey of the Dockyards' carried out in 1698 and the fact that it could be used to study their development over the last 70 years and compare present improvements with the past. He borrowed it from King George for this purpose and crucially, realising the importance of retaining documents of this nature, returned it to the King's library, where over two hundred years later it can still be consulted.

It may seem incredible today that the first lord should be doing administrative tasks like this, but the Admiralty of the eighteenth century could not be compared with the vast bureaucracies of our modern word. Government departments were tiny with no distinction made between overall policy and routine business.

A first lord could be formulating foreign policy one minute and dealing with requests for leave from junior officers the next. With the concept of delegation yet to be developed, ministers were expected to handle a mass of extremely detailed administrative tasks in person.

To return to the alterations in Portsmouth Dockyard, while they may have been momentous, no monument to them will be found there. Some years later, they were considered important enough to be commemorated, at least indirectly, but not in Portsmouth.

Across the Solent on the Isle of Wight these almost unnoticeable blocks of stones set into a garden wall in a pyramid shape are to be found in Bonchurch Village Road, Bonchurch near Ventnor. The inscription reads:

This pyramid of stone was erected in 1773 and is an example of the stone quarried in this vicinity. This stone was at that time shipped for use at Portsmouth Harbour.

A history of the undercliff area explains that the actual monument was erected by a Colonel Hill in or about 1800 to show specimens of the stone which was quarried from The Pitts nearby in Bonchurch to supply to the government for works at Portsmouth. It was thought that the stone was shipped from a jetty which was located on the shore below the Old church at Bonchurch, but is not obvious now.[7]
(AUTHOR'S PHOTOGRAPH, 2004)

The Model Dockyards – Prospects in Three Dimensions

Lord Sandwich was to make a unique contribution to the history of Portsmouth and the Royal Dockyards by commissioning them in model form. The first model originated in Plymouth Dockyard and had actually been made by the foreman on his own initiative. Seeing it on a visit in 1771, Lord Sandwich was so impressed that he ordered similar models of the other dockyards to be made.

They were completed in 1774 and today, the six, Portsmouth and Plymouth, Deptford and Woolwich, Chatham and Sheerness, thanks to the first lord's foresight all that time ago, stand as one of the marvels of the National Maritime Museum in Greenwich. Unfortunately though, the name of the artisan who began it all in the first place is not known for sure and his model no longer exists.

So what was the purpose of the models? Model ships had been made for years of course, but the dockyards were something new. John Graves in his succinct comparative analysis of them[8] emphasises that official approval resulted in a subtle change of attitudes towards them. From being a single model made by an individual with few resources for his own amusement they became a group of splendid presentation pieces for King George III. Their specification was upgraded and they were to be finished as soon as possible.

What was it about them precisely that would have appealed to George III? Today, we find them very perplexing, their status has had an ambiguous and fluctuating history leaving us with the feeling that we cannot quite make up our minds as to which category should they placed in. Are they a toy – a sort of industrial doll's house?

Are they a serious, respectable work of art, but appealing far too much to the child in us for our own comfort or are they the novelty item somewhere in between, such as the model of Westminster Abbey made with thousands of match sticks that is sometimes seen at craft fairs?

The Georgians were untroubled by such intellectual inhibitions. The model dockyard fitted neatly into eighteenth century thought on two levels, firstly, the convention of the prospect and its view and secondly, the broad category of scientific and related apparatus. To the Georgians, function was not enough, an instrument should be a thing of beauty as well, and the three dimensional form of the model fitted this requirement exactly.

Moreover, Lord Sandwich not only brought physical attributes to his post but also the intellectual background of the aristocrat who had been brought up during the period of the Enlightenment. This was a movement of thought and belief which was widely current in Europe during the seventeenth and eighteenth centuries. It was based on that idea that correct reasoning could find true knowledge and lead mankind to happiness. The assumption of a rational and moral order was considered a guide to thought and was based on the philosophy of ancient Greece.

The need for education was very much a part of this movement and was based on the study of classical languages and literature. The grand tour of Europe, for example, in particular Italy and its Roman ruins was an essential part of any gentlemen's education. The study of architectural models of ancient classical ruins was an important aspect of this and a concept that Lord Sandwich would have been very familiar with.

King George III, like his fellow monarch Catherine the Great, took his role as a monarch in the Age of the Enlightenment extremely seriously. He was a energetic patron of both the sciences and the arts but his favourite subject was architectural design in which he had received intensive training. He was an avid collector too and his passion for books led to the creation of the British Library.

This era was also known as the Age of Improvement and the King was a keen supporter of manufacturing developments, the scientific revolution and agricultural innovation, hence his nickname, 'Farmer George'. He could equally well have been known as 'Shipwright George', because one characteristic he shared with the skilled craftsmen of the dockyard, especially the carpenters and joiners who made the models, was a minute attention to detail.

This demonstrated itself in his own hobbies which were watch and clock making and ivory turning. Like them, he knew what it was to spend hours in dedicated, patient and painstaking work and he understood how rewarding, even if sometimes underappreciated, it was too.

In addition, as the first Hanoverian monarch to be born in Britain, King George was very keen to be identified with his adopted country and declared that he, '… gloried in the name of Briton'.[9] However, he was still elector of Hanover and too immersed in military matters at the expense of the Royal Navy for Lord Sandwich's liking. As an island nation, Britain depended heavily on the Navy as an instrument of prestige, deterrence and coercion in her dealings with the rest of Europe – not to mention basic survival.

The model dockyards then, were intended to encourage and foster the King's interest in the Navy in two main ways, firstly, by appealing to his artistic and intellectual interests as a monarch of the Enlightenment. Secondly, to be truly British and retain the support of the British people, a monarch had to be identified with the Royal Navy.

George III was monarch at a time when the country was involved in the Seven Years' War (1756–1763), the War of American Independence (1776–1783) and the French Revolutionary Wars which began in 1793 and led to the Napoleonic Wars. The Navy and the dockyards had an essential role to play which did not decline until the Battle of Trafalgar in 1805. The King's collection of model ships, drawings, plans and its crowning glory, the model dockyards, would have demonstrated and reinforced this identity very strongly.

No doubt too, the possession of the models stimulated the King's acquisitive instincts as a collector – they were unique then and are unique now. Lord Sandwich did not stop there and continued to send him ship models which were supplemented with visits to dockyards. During the course of his research, the earl had probably come across descriptions of Peter the Great's grand embassy to Europe and spotted the similarities between the two men.

Both had a practical bent and enjoyed learning by doing, so he arranged visits to Portsmouth for the King in 1773 and 1778. These were as successful as Peter's visits and the models would therefore serve as a pleasant souvenir of these trips.

To return then to our modern feelings of ambivalence, once the ideas of the Enlightenment fell from fashion the original meaning of the models fell away too. By this time, the Age of Improvement had been supplanted by the Industrial Revolution and the austere, clean lines of neoclassical architecture had been replaced by the intricacies of the Gothic Revival. The models were a phenomenon whose day was done.

As soon as George III died, his son George IV donated them to the Museum of Artillery in 1822. George IV considered himself to be a great connoisseur of the arts but a model dockyard was not his idea of an exquisite sight for the eye. Maybe too, once the Battle of Waterloo had ended the Napoleonic Wars in 1815, the models, like the real dockyards, seemed redundant in a time of peace. The models had served their purpose but times had changed.

In 1914, in line with the thought that the models are toys, the keeper of the Museum of Artillery tried to interest the director of the Bethnal Green Museum of Childhood in them. He grudgingly selected three, Deptford, Woolwich and Portsmouth. Three others were transferred to the Science Museum in London which already possessed over a hundred architectural models.

In Victorian times they were considered to be some of the principal objects in the galleries but by 1912, their artistic respectability had been lost, they were removed from display and considered of little use.[10] It took over half a century before the ideological concept of the model was to be rehabilitated and even longer before all six dockyard models were reunited in one place. They finally became part of the National Maritime Museum's collections in 1996.

The Model Dockyards Today

What is the significance of the models today? Certainly, in Portsmouth, the model shows us Nelson's dockyard miniaturised and frozen at a moment in time in 1774, looking just as if all the shipwrights, carpenters, joiners, officials and other workers had just downed tools and gone home.

For this we have to thank the dockyard carpenters, Nicolas Vass junr and John Doughty. It was Nicholas Vass senr who had designed St George's Church twenty years before. His son was the acting master house carpenter at the dockyard from 1774–1775 and master house carpenter from 1777–1822.

He obviously had an intimate knowledge of the dockyard which he was able to put to good use. This particular part of Nelson's Portsmouth will never be swept away and remains as a monument to all the skilled craftsmen who worked there.

The model is of course, an invaluable window on the past, enabling comparisons to be made not only between the Georgian and Victorian dockyards but their counterpart today. This photograph was taken in black and white in 1914 by the Science Museum and illustrates the model of Portsmouth in its case.

These cases were considered to be an important part of the models and all six were of a similar design. Unfortunately, the originals no longer exist, perhaps as a result of all the moving from one place to another with no one person in charge of them, but they were replaced at some point. The current cases are wooden with a heavy glass lid which has to be propped back to enable the model to be photographed. The picture does give some idea of their sheer size and weight.

This is the Georgian dockyard as it was in 1774. The main gate can be seen at the top right, the long rope house runs across the centre with the three big storehouses at right angles. Slightly to the left of centre we can see the timber berths with the piles of timber laid out. (COURTESY OF SCIENCE AND SOCIETY PICTURE LIBRARY)

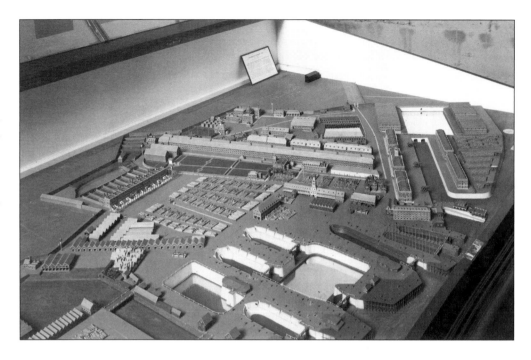

In the Footsteps of King George

Is it possible to identify the buildings on the model? Unlike many of the one dimensional prospects it does not come with a key. In 1754, a detailed plan had been produced by Thomas Milton and dedicated to Lord Sandwich. Milton crammed as much information as possible into a small space which might have appealed to Lord Sandwich but which makes life difficult for us in trying to decipher it all.

The title is, 'A Geometrical Plan and West Elevation of His Majesty's Dockyard near Portsmouth with Part of the Common' and is dated 29 April 1754. As Milton says, the plan of the buildings is shown in the lower half and their elevations in the upper half. Perhaps the most interesting feature of the plan is the ornamental margins and the cherubs with the geometrical instruments on the crest. (COURTESY BRITISH LIBRARY, REF. NO.: KING'S TOP. COLLECTION, vol.43–88, XIV.45–1)

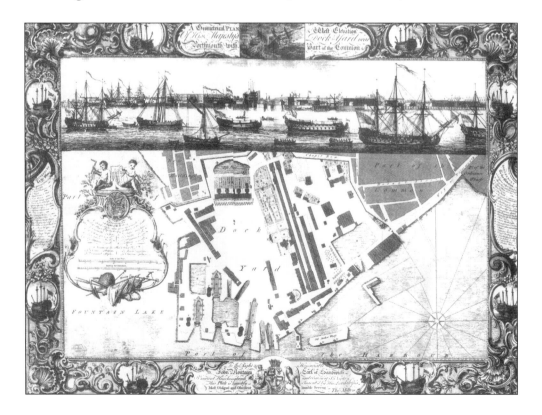

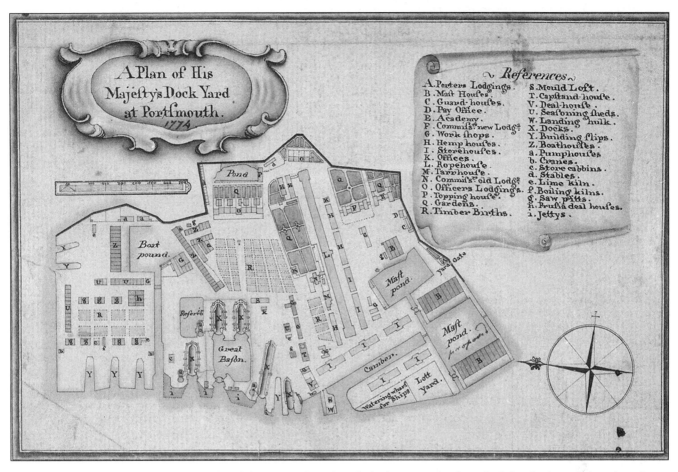

However, in the same year that the model was made a detailed plan was produced of the dockyard that does have a numbered key and is easier to read, so it is possible to identity more buildings.

What the plan essentially reveals is a dockyard in transition, as a comparison of the plan with the model reveals some discrepancies. For example, both the commissioner's old residence built in 1664 and the commissioner's new residence, built in 1785, are shown on the plan, while only the old residence is shown on the model. There is no chapel marked on the plan but it does exist next to the Naval Academy on the model.

The earlier plan drawn in 1754 by Thomas Milton shows a slightly smaller dockyard and included the chapel. A study of the two plans and the model would illustrate very well the changes that took place in the second half of the eighteenth century and how they were recorded.

This plan also illustrates a building which would not been seen today and that is the stables at the left of centre. Presumably, the commissioner and the other officers would need to keep horses and carriages somewhere. Horses were also used as a source of power for some of the industrial processes.

The dockyard gardens are marked clearly at 'Q' and are very similar today. For example, standing in busy Queen Street, one would never guess that there is an attractive secluded garden on the other side of the dockyard wall. (© NATIONAL MARITIME MUSEUM, LONDON, REF. NO.: PU 1077)

The techniques of modern photography have made it possible for us to see the dockyard buildings close-up for the first time. Let us go in and have a look around. This viewpoint today would equate roughly with a shot from the roof of the entrance building of Portsmouth Historic Dockyard and locates us at once.

There is the inside of the main gate, the Porter's Lodge and garden and the inside of the dockyard wall. The Porter's Lodge was built in 1708 and is the oldest surviving building – originally it was in plain brick. (© National Maritime Museum, London, Ref. No.: SLR 2156)

Here we see the three great storehouses, nos. 9, 10 and 11, which were built by the Royal Navy between 1764 and 1784 to store the provisions and equipment needed by Britain's rapidly expanding fleet. Today they house the Royal Naval Museum. This is the route taken by tourists when they visit the dockyard and leads up to HMS *Victory* which now stands in dry dock at the top right corner of the picture. (© National Maritime Museum, London, Ref No.: SLR 2156)

The clock tower on No.10 Storehouse is a most potent symbol of the dockyard. The bell weighed three hundred-weight and sounded the official dockyard time. This was an absolute necessity in an age before wrist watches. The standardisation of time is taken for granted now, but this was not the case in the eighteenth century. The clock was regulated each week by astronomical sights taken from the observatory of the Royal Naval Academy in the dockyard and then later, by time signal from Greenwich.

As the largest industrial enterprise in the country, the dockyard employed thousands of workers and their work times had to be regulated somehow. It is hard to tell now, but it may also have been possible to hear the chimes in Portsea where most of the workers lived.

The clock stood for over 160 years until the Second World War when it was destroyed in the night of very heavy bombing on 11 March 1941 that took most of Nelson's Portsmouth with it. The weather vane is the only surviving part of the original tower as it was rescued from the rubble and taken to Spithead House in the dockyard for safe-keeping. In 1992 the clock tower and weathervane were replaced.

Today, the distinctive chimes of the bell can be heard sounding the hours as in the past. Its melodious ting-tang sound seems to soften the severity of the Georgian buildings and brings the charm and elegance of a vanished age to the dockyard.

The Royal Naval Academy was built in 1733 for the sons of gentlemen to study naval subjects before entering the Navy. Following the visit of George III in 1773, it was granted the title royal. It was probably the most elegant building in the dockyard, and still is. (© NATIONAL MARITIME MUSEUM, REF. NO.: SLR 2156)

This is a most unusual view which is not available to us today and shows the western side of the storehouses, the buildings of Rope Walk and on the far left, the commissioner's residence. On the left side there is timber drying out and in the bottom left hand corner, a wooden fence with some pieces missing; an example of the minute attention to detail of the model-maker. We can also see cannon pointing towards the water which are not there today. (© NATIONAL MARITIME MUSEUM, LONDON, REF. NO.: SLR 2156)

To turn to other buildings, this is the original chapel which was built in 1704. An interesting feature is the flights of stairs on each side leading to the gallery inside. This chapel was demolished in the 1780s when a new residence was built for the commissioner. A new church, St Ann's, replaced it and still stands today. This is the only representation in existence of the original Queen Anne dockyard chapel. (© NATIONAL MARITIME MUSEUM, LONDON, REF. NO.: SLR 2156)

Here we see the original commissioner's residence which was replaced in the 1780s – what a pity we cannot follow George III up the stairs to look inside! (© NATIONAL MARITIME MUSEUM, LONDON, REF. NO.: SLR 2156)

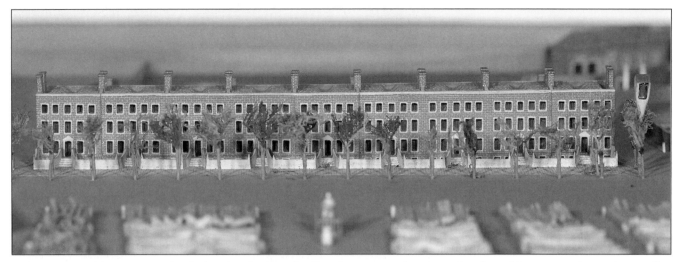

This terrace of houses was built for the dockyard officials, now no longer in brick and known as Long Row. The naval dockyards provided their houses with gardens however small, and these are still there today. Here, all we can see is the row of trees in front which would have made them look very attractive. In the centre lower foreground is the statue of William III which is now at the far end of the Porter's Garden. (© National Maritime Museum, London, Ref. No.: SLR 2156)

This is the statue of William III as it is today at the end of the Porter's Garden. Its inscription reads, *'Gulielmo III optomi regi MDCCXVIII Ricardus Norton, humillime, D.D.'* It was presented to the principal officers of the yard by Richard Norton of Southwick in 1718 many years after William's death in 1702 and dedicated to his memory. Norton was the son of Colonel Richard Norton who was a great friend of Oliver Cromwell: he had become the supplier of oak to Portsmouth Dockyard.

The sculptor was John van Nost the Elder who had originally designed a similar statue in lead for erection in Hampton Court, William's favourite palace, in about 1712. This was never installed but the mould was sold and reused over a long period and perhaps included the creation of this statue, which is bronze gilt.

This time, William is depicted wearing the uniform of a Roman emperor, as opposed to King Neptune, and holding the emperor's baton. This Baroque classical interpretation symbolises William bringing the Rule of Law to England and replacing the concept of the divine right of kings which led Charles I to his death.[11]

Originally, these ships were located in the dry docks on the model. They were repainted at a later date and show one 64-gun ship, two 74s and a frigate in dock, one 74 in frame and the floors of what could be a 64.[12] (PRIVATE COLLECTION)

The Gardens

An unexpected aspect, to us, of the eighteenth century dockyard is the gardens, which we find unlikely on an industrial site with very restricted space. They would, however, have fitted perfectly within the seventeenth and eighteenth century concept of the picturesque. This idea was developed as a reaction to the formal and contrived aspects of the Baroque style and describes a landscape which is arranged by man in a natural way. The concept also includes the principle of incorporating contrasting categories within the same landscape, such as the sublime and the beautiful, the wild and the cultivated, and the general and particular.

There was also the category of the awe-inspiring and the admiration, even fear-inducing: the huge dockyard peopled by thousands of workers labouring away at the many noisy and often dirty and dangerous industrial processes would neatly encapsulate this category. The gardens then would represent a contrast, the contrived works of man in comparison with the natural works of God.

There are different interpretations of the picturesque, town gardens have been categorised as 'metropolitan picturesque', while dockyard gardens could be described as 'industrial picturesque'. Portsmouth itself, as a fortified town, contained many gardens which would also come into this category of thought, perhaps fortified picturesque.

As for the layout of the gardens, both the plan and the model show this very clearly. They run parallel to the ropehouses and behind the Officers' Terrace and were laid out originally in 1692. Gardens are included in the other models too. The Chatham Officers' Terrace and its gardens remain hardly changed today and has been the subject of detailed study.[13]

The model of Chatham Dockyard played an important role in their analysis as it is extremely rare to have the design of an eighteenth century garden reproduced in an accurate model.

In Portsmouth, while the design of the Officers' Terrace gardens or the other gardens has not been analysed to date, the Porter's Garden next to the main gate has been studied. It is interesting to note, though, that the model does not show a garden with plants behind the Porter's Lodge. In 2000, the buildings on the site were demolished and hard landscaping laid down.

The garden could then be laid out and planted on the lines of an eighteenth century garden. This garden is now open to the public, providing a most attractive spot and an insight into the eighteenth century in the part of the dockyard which is accessible to the public.

The Model of Sheerness Dockyard

Lastly, for the purposes of comparison, here is a photograph of the model of Sheerness Dockyard. This was the first model to be finished and is reckoned to be the best in the sense that it is the most detailed with the highest standard of finish. It was also the only model to involve a professional model-maker, George Stockwell, who had also built some of the finest ship models of this period.

While the models were supposed to be constructed to a standard specification, the different personalities of their makers do shine through. This model, for instance, is the only one to include figures, two bullock carts with drivers although they are too minute to be visible in this picture.

Sheerness was different from Portsmouth in that fortifications instead of a brick wall protected the dockyard, and these stand out well in the centre. There was also no equivalent of Portsea for the workers who had to make do with the hulks on the left for their accommodation.

One final question then, did Nelson ever see these models? As far as is known, they went straight into the royal collection and were probably kept at Windsor Castle. In spite of his achievements and immense popularity, Nelson was never intimate with George III and Queen Charlotte so it can be assumed that he did not. (© National Maritime Museum, London, Ref. No.: D7824)

A Naval Artist Sketches Portsmouth: Gabriel Bray RN (1750–1823)

Somewhat of an anticlimax after the intensities of the model dockyards, this sketch is one of a number drawn by Gabriel Bray, who was a second lieutenant on the frigate HMS *Pallas* during two voyages in 1774–75 and 1775–76. While it was not unusual for men to produce sketches at sea, Bray's work is unique, firstly, because it survived; secondly, because he recorded the everyday life on board ship as opposed to other ships or scenery and thirdly, because his sketches in Portsmouth can be accurately dated to between October and early December 1774.[14]

This sketch is entitled, 'A View of the Dock Gates at Portsmouth taken from the Navy Coffee House Window Dec. '74.' We sense Bray sitting in the coffee house, drinking his coffee and observing the activities outside, the vegetable stalls alongside the dockyard wall, two boys playing marbles in the street and a driver trying to manoeuvre his over-loaded horse and cart along the narrow street.

The smoking chimney of the tavern in the background is a rare sight in our post-Second World War era of smoke-less zones. The dockyard gateway and the side of the Porter's Lodge is quite recognisable today although we would be surprised to see the sentry on guard duty. A similar viewpoint today would locate us in the middle of Queen Street. (© NATIONAL MARITIME MUSEUM, LONDON, REF. NO.: PT 1994)

Opposite page, top: This sketch is entitled, 'A Shop on Portsmouth Point Nov. 74'. Out front there is a good selection of veg. on sale – cabbages, leeks, carrots, possibly celery and on the shelf, baskets of fruit. However, inside the window there is something even more interesting and that is a pile of clay pipes.

Clay pipes were the eighteenth century's equivalent of cigarettes, which are a late-Victorian development and were not only very popular but were manufactured in Portsmouth just down the road from this shop. Archaeological excavations in 1968–71 revealed the remains of a complex of tobacco-pipe kilns located on the west side of what is now Oyster Street and its junction with White Hart Lane.[15]

Portsmouth has a continuous history of pipe making from about 1620 until 1932 for two reasons. Firstly, a garrison town full of soldiers and a dockyard and harbour full of sailors and other workers would guarantee plenty

of demand for them. Secondly, the pipe-clay deposits needed for their manufacture were easily accessible on the Isle of Wight in the Alum Bay and Freshwater area.

The excavations also turned up the remains of a large number of different designs of pipes, so much so that a detailed study could be made of their types and dates in 1979.[16] Pictures of the excavations and some of the clay pipes are also on show at Portsmouth City Museum. Gabriel Bray's affectionate vignette of Portsmouth life has given us a glimpse of the pipes on sale too.

The use of clay pipes is a good example of a day-to-day facet of eighteenth century life which would have been so familiar to Nelson but which is completely lost to us now. He might have even have known the proprietress of the shop and bought one of her clay-pipes.

It is not known whether or not Nelson smoked as an adult, but he may well have tried a puff or two as a youngster. A nice little greengrocer's like that on Point today would not come amiss either. (© NATIONAL MARITIME MUSEUM, LONDON, REF. NO.: PT 2014)

Another part of Portsmouth harbour life which would have been familiar to Nelson is the role of waterman – one

is shown here drawn in November 1774. The job of waterman has been described as the second oldest profession and certainly, their work is essential. They ferried people across the harbour and rowed out supplies and sailors to the ships.

The watermen were described by Major General John B. Richardson who visited Haslar Hospital in 1916,

...A curious race of boatmen existed – hard, weather-beaten longshoremen, with a conversation largely enlivened by strange oaths and chewed tobacco. They possessed an extraordinary acquaintance with the weather, tides and currents of the locality, and the methods of saving themselves all possible exertion.

I have known boatloads cross to Gosport worked entirely with one oar, but, generally, on the mere suspicion of a breeze, up went mast and sprit sail, and most cleverly the boats were managed. There was great touting for passengers as far back as the High Street, in Portsmouth.

A tariff was supposed to exist, but the boatmen invariably grumbled at it. If bad weather came on, a ball was hoisted at the Point, and the tariff doubled. I think the ordinary fare to Haslar was 9d., though it generally cost a shilling. It took quite half an hour to arrive at Haslar jetty...[17]

(© NATIONAL MARITIME MUSEUM, LONDON, REF. NO.: PT 1990)

A second waterman, also drawn in November 1774. These two watercolour sketches contrast strikingly with the formal, posed portrait of Captain Suckling in oils.

The job of waterman still exists today providing a specialised service for ships in the harbour alongside the conventional ferry services. In 1804, the Watermen's Acts were introduced which regulated the profession and fixed fares were laid down. Today, Portsmouth Harbour has 19 qualified watermen who are entitled to fly their own blue and yellow flag, wear the waterman's badge and carry a licence plate.
(© National Maritime Museum, London, Ref. No.: PT 1991)

1776 – A New Lieutenant Arrives

To return to the career of Captain Suckling, on 12 April 1775 Lord Sandwich had chosen him to be Comptroller of the Navy Board. This was a very important position as he was head of the Navy Office and responsible for the dockyards, ships and warrant officers such as masters, pursers, surgeons and boatswains.

The captain had become a man of prestige and patronage and to add to this on 18 May 1776, he became MP for the borough of Portsmouth. Also in 1776, came the War of American Independence and for the next seven years, the West Indies would be the most active theatre of this war.

Unfortunately, neither Maurice Suckling nor his young protégé Nelson were to enjoy the benefits of this promotion for very long. He survived for only two more years, but during that time his influence ensured that he was able to obtain promotion for his nephew and introduce him to Portsmouth. On 26 September 1776, Nelson received an order from Sir James Douglas, the Port Admiral of Portsmouth, which appointed him as acting lieutenant of the *Worcester* which was preparing to sail for Gibraltar.

On 8 October 1776 Nelson arrived on board and was rated fourth lieutenant. His captain was Mark Robinson, a friend of his uncle's who took a special interest in him. On 10 October 1776 he was invited to dine at the captain's table with the Mayor of Portsmouth, Philip Varlo (1722-1778). Before the ship left for Gibraltar, Nelson accompanied the captain ashore to dine with the mayor on at least two occasions.[18]

The local press reported the shipping movements just as it does today and in the *Hampshire Chronicle* a report reads:

A Captain, two lieutenants and 90 marines are embarked on board the Worcester, *of 64 guns, Capt. Robinson, who is ordered to take on board a 74 gun ship's complement.*

Presumably one of the lieutenants could have been Nelson although it is interesting to note the difference in dates as the newspaper report is dated 5 October.

As to the purpose of the voyage, the report continues:

She is to go on a secret expedition, as is likewise the Reasonable, *from Plymouth, and the two frigates. The report is, that they are to convey the merchantmen to Lisbon and from there proceed to the Brazils, to watch the motions of the Spaniards, who are reported to be gone to that quarter.*

Invitations to Dine in the Town

As to Nelson's trips ashore with the captain, the obvious questions to ask are where did they go to dine and do the buildings exist today? Assuming that they went to private houses and not to a public eating establishment as mayor, Philip Varlo could have invited them to dinner at the mayor's parlour in the Town Hall.

This is an artistic impression on a postcard of the building by Martin Snape (1852–1930), who painted many scenes around Gosport and Portsmouth and is regarded as Gosport's finest artist. The card was produced by Charpentier & Co., a very well-known firm of printers and publishers whose premises were at 46, High Street, Portsmouth.

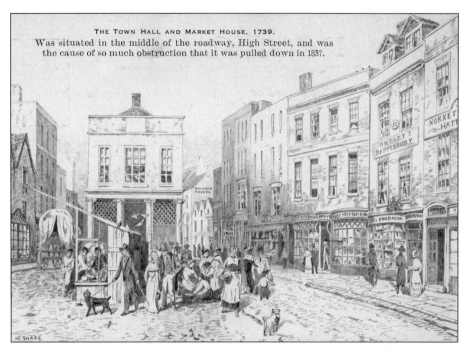

THE TOWN HALL AND MARKET HOUSE, 1739.
Was situated in the middle of the roadway, High Street, and was the cause of so much obstruction that it was pulled down in 1837.

In 1776, Portsmouth Town Hall would still have been a relatively new building, having been constructed in 1739. Amazingly to us, it stood in the middle of the High Street near the junction with Lombard Street opposite the George Inn. Resembling a municipal building in a market town, it consisted of a ground floor market place enclosed by arches with the council chamber and offices on top.

This building lasted less than a century. Its facilities may have been sufficient for Georgian Portsmouth, but by the end of the Napoleonic Wars the town had expanded, it had grown too small and its situation in the centre of the street blocked the flow of traffic. In 1837 it was demolished to make more room for the traffic. A new Town Hall was built on the east side of the High Street and opened in 1838.

Portsmouth has had at least three Town Halls throughout its history but the building which lasted from 1739 to 1837 most symbolises Nelson's Portsmouth – he would have last seen it in 1805. The Town Hall in the middle of the road with all its surrounding market stalls cluttering up the street would have been the first thing to greet anyone arriving from London on the stage coach through the fortifications at the Landport Gate and turning down into the High Street.

Its demolition represented the sweeping away of the Georgian era with its continual wars and the beginning of the Victorian age and its long period of peace. (AUTHOR'S COLLECTION)

✳✳✳

Where else could Philip Varlo have taken Nelson and his captain? He could have invited them to dine at his own house but where was this? According to the historian Henry Slight, Philip Varlo lived in a house at No.111 High Street. He described Varlo as a man of much celebrity in the political history of the town and his house reflected this status.

Originally, the entrance to the house was in the centre up a flight of stone steps. To the left of the mansion was the carriage entrance to the gardens which contained a large rookery. On the opposite side, where the entrance can be seen, stood a high wall with a small gateway.

However, it was not his house for long after 1776. On his death in 1778 it was let to pay taxes and during the command of Admiral Parker was purchased by the government for £2000 as the residence of the port admiral. Previously, this had been at No.106 High Street. This photograph shows it to be a most imposing residence and it is fascinating to think of Nelson as dining there.

In 1826, on the demolition of the Government House complex at Domus Dei, it then became the residence of the military governor and was known as Old Government House. In 1882 a new Government House was built in Cambridge Road adjacent to Landport Terrace and in 1886 Kelly's *Directory* described the old building in the High Street as the Garrison Office.

The date of this photograph is not known but judging by the sentry on duty it is probably before 1882. Had it not been for the Second World War, Old Government House might still be in existence, but sadly, it was destroyed during the bombing and has been replaced by a block of flats. (COURTESY PORTSMOUTH CITY MUSEUM AND RECORDS OFFICE)

The Worcester Sails

The *Hampshire Chronicle* continued to report the shipping news and realities of life in a naval town. A report dated 21 October reads, 'On Wednesday a sailor fell off from the head of the *Worcester* and was drowned.' On 2 November the following was reported:

On Wednesday last press warrants were received here, and the same night a very hot press ensued; all the lieutenants in commission were upon that duty (presumably including Nelson) with their respective gangs, and we are told they collected about 150 men from the merchants' ships and on shore. Not a man was detained from the outward bound ships, though there are near 90 sail of them at this port, bound to different places, all waiting for convoy, as they are afraid of the Provincial privateers.

The Worcester *has received orders not to sail till the arrival of two ships from the river laden with stores of all kinds, which are to go under her convoy.*

On account of this great disturbance in pressing very few people are to be seen about the streets, and it is with the utmost difficulty a seaman can be got to carry people over the ferries.

On 9 November the following was reported:

The press[gang] is so very hot here that there is not a seaman or even a landsman to be seen, and as the fishermen are afraid to stir, scarce a fish or even an oyster is to be got.

This report gives us an insight into the effect the pressgang's activities had on the daily life of Portsmouth's citizens. While the watermen, such as the two sketched by Gabriel Bray might have considered it to be an occupational hazard, local shopkeepers like the one on Point cannot have been very pleased to have their trade continually disrupted.

At last, on 30 November, Nelson's ship gets under way and he leaves Portsmouth:

His Majesty's Ship Worcester, *Captain Robinson, and* Thames, *Captain Howe, sailed from Spithead to cruize off Lisbon to intercept the American privateers on that coast, having about 25 sail of merchant ships under their convoy.*

Then on 5 December, 'On Thursday *Worcester* sailed for Lisbon to intercept American privateers on that coast having about 50 sail of merchantmen under their convoy.'

Ornamental Gates for the Camber, the Landport and Portsea: 1760–1779

Four more ornamental gates were built in Portsmouth during the eighteenth century as part of the programme of extending the fortifications around the Camber and Portsea. They were all designed in a late Baroque style of architecture with classical features but only the two latest ones were to have carvings.

The Landport Gate

The next gate to be built was the Landport Gate in St George's Road which is familiar to us as it still exists. It was built in 1760 to a design which is still Baroque style but with the classical details much more muted. There is also a stone octagonal turret with openings and a globe finial.

The Landport Gate was the principal entrance into Portsmouth until 1875 when the fortifications were demolished. Not only was it then made redundant as part of the defence system but its function as a gate disappeared.

Today, to understand what the gate would have looked like originally, we need to mentally separate it from its surroundings. Firstly, the façade accessible to the public is actually its rear. While the gate may be in the same place, the road which it led to, the London Road out of Portsmouth, has been rerouted. This was done when Cambridge Road and Alexandra Road were laid out in the 1870s.

The gate had its function taken from it as instead of forming an important focal point in the main road into Portsmouth and a link between the High Street and the other side of the fortifications, it now overlooks the United Services Recreation Ground. Not only is it never approached from that direction but there is not even public access to the front façade.

Secondly, it did not stand in isolation as it does today but was part of a complex defence system of curtain walls, a moat and a bridge. Now, Landport Gate is Crown property and owned by the Ministry of Defence but is in the care of English Heritage. Regarding its listing status, for many years it had a dual listing as it was both a scheduled ancient monument and Grade I listed. However, on 2 April 2001 it was descheduled, in common with many other monuments, as the Grade I listing was deemed to be sufficient for its care. (AUTHOR'S PHOTOGRAPH, 2003)

Below left: This photograph shows a plaque on the wall which reads, 'The old 'Land-Port' the Principal Entrance Into Portsmouth Previous to the Demolition of the Fortifications 1875'. (AUTHOR'S PHOTOGRAPH, 2003)

Below right: Lastly, a stone crown just above the central arch which is unusual in two respects. Firstly, the design is shown in a slightly different form although it does represent the British crown. Secondly, it is odd that this crown should be on the rear façade and not the front of the gate.

Henry Slight gives a possible explanation for this when he notes that when earth was removed for repairs in about 1788, the crown was discovered in the rubbish above the arch. In his view, it formed the keystone of the ancient gate and had been removed during the Commonwealth (the Protectorate of Oliver Cromwell 1649–1658). He noted that it was recut and placed in its present situation by the late Mr James Hay, of Queen Street, Portsea.

Landport Gate was also the site of the ceremony of the keys, whereby whenever the monarch visited Portsmouth, he was presented with the keys of the garrison; these were the key of the Landport Gate and King George's or Town Gate. For example, when George III came to the town in 1773, his entrance was preceded by the ceremony of the keys and a salute of 132 guns. (AUTHOR'S PHOTOGRAPH, 2003)

King George's Gate

The next gate was King George's Gate at the entrance to the Camber which was situated roughly where the junction of Lombard Street and King Charles Street is today. Henry Slight gives its date of construction as 1768 and describes it as a 'noble structure, in the rustic style, adorned with massive pillars and entablature of grand proportions.'

Its design separates it stylistically from King James's Gate and the Landport as the classical details are very prominent and more austere. It had Tuscan columns and rusticated, vermiculated masonry with the scrolls and globes on either side lightening the severe effect.

Above the gate were various apartments which were formerly the offices of the governor and inside was a large guardhouse. Unfortunately, the gate was demolished when the rest of the fortifications went in the 1860s, so it is easy to forget how imposing it must have looked to anyone landing at the Camber for the first time.

A telling detail is the wooden cart in the lower right hand corner. These are so often seen in old photographs and were as common as the parked motor car is in photographs today. They remind us of what it must have been like to live in an age when the only means of transport was the horse and cart or just the handcart on its own. (AUTHOR'S COLLECTION)

The Lion Gate

Now we come to the last two gates to be built in the eighteenth century. The first, the Lion Gate was constructed in 1778 at the east end of Queen Street to form the main gate through the defences into Portsea. Again, the design has prominent classical features including Tuscan pilasters, rusticated masonry and a sharply defined complete pediment as opposed to the broken one of King James's Gate. There are no attempts here to soften its imposing impression and indeed, this is actually reinforced by the sculpture of a lion couchant within the pediment.

The lion represents the lion of England and it is shown supporting a standard, presumably the Union Jack, but unlike the very stylised lions of royal coats of arms, this lion is shown in a naturalistic pose. Certainly, this is a very different design from all the other coats of arms on buildings in Portsmouth.

When shown with the royal arms, the supporters, the lion and unicorn, are more usually shown as rampant. However, it became common in the eighteenth and nineteenth centuries to show them lying down. This indicated symbolic official, as opposed to royal, status while at the same time symbolising Britain.

Right: Looking through the gate towards Queen Street, the over-loaded horse and cart makes another appearance. (AUTHOR'S COLLECTION)

The Lion Gate was given a new lease of life just after the First World War. When the fortifications were demolished it was moved from Queen Street and stored. In 1913, the Semaphore Tower in the dockyard was destroyed in a major fire. When it was rebuilt in 1929, the Lion Gate was constructed as its entrance on to South Railway Jetty facing the sea. On the right side of the central arch is a block inscribed, 'The Lion Gateway Portsea. Built 1778. Incorporated in this building in the year 1929.'

Now, dwarfed by the building and tower superimposed on top of it, naval base security means that the gate can only be seen from a distance by yachtsmen entering and leaving Clarence Marina. It is Grade II listed. (COURTESY BASE SECURITY OFFICER; AUTHOR'S PHOTOGRAPH, 2004)

Right: This photograph shows the lion and flag in close-up. (COURTESY BASE SECURITY OFFICER; AUTHOR'S PHOTOGRAPH, 2004)

The Unicorn Gate

The mythical medieval unicorn of western Europe is depicted as an elegant and beautiful animal. It is similar to a horse but with cloven feet, a lion's tail, a goat's beard and a delicately spiralling horn on its forehead. The attributes of purity and virtue were ascribed to it and it became a symbol of Christ. Its distinctive horn was thought to have the medicinal powers of healing and purification. When James VI of Scotland came to the throne of England in 1603, he adopted the unicorn as one of the supporters of his royal coat of arms, the other being the lion of England.

The Unicorn Gate was built in 1779 as a second entrance through the fortifications into Portsea. When they were demolished it was re-erected in 1865 on Anchor Gate Road as one of the principal entrances to the dockyard. The design is similar to the Lion Gate but the classical details are more pronounced with pairs of flat pilasters on each side. Again, there is a sharply defined complete pediment in which a unicorn couchant bears a Union Jack.

Looking through the arch a group of soldiers stand at ease and in the far distance, another handcart. (AUTHOR'S COLLECTION)

Left: The Unicorn Gate has since been reset on the alignment of the dockyard extension wall in Circular Road and additions made to the original design which dilute its classical line. Smaller round pedestrian archways in Portland stone descend in concave curves to flanking pillars topped by stone balls on cushion finials. However, its function is less of a gate than a traffic roundabout, as traffic is not routed under the arch. It is Grade II listed. (COURTESY BASE SECURITY OFFICER; AUTHOR'S PHOTOGRAPH, 2004)

Right: A close-up of the unicorn itself which is indeed depicted as a beautiful animal. It also wears a very elegant collar and chain which shows that it is intended to be seen as a royal supporter. (COURTESY BASE SECURITY OFFICER; AUTHOR'S PHOTOGRAPH, 2004)

Left: The façade of the gate not normally seen by the public. (COURTESY BASE SECURITY OFFICER; AUTHOR'S PHOTOGRAPH 2004)

Right: Another view. (COURTESY BASE SECURITY OFFICER; AUTHOR'S PHOTOGRAPH, 2004)

The Unicorn Gate photographed on 7 August 1973 by the City Engineers' Department of Portsmouth City Council. Here the gate is still in use as a gate. This shot also shows up the immense wooden inner doors which were common to all the gates and which now only two gates possess, the Landport Gate and the main dockyard gate, now the Victory Gate. The up-ended cannon at each side were also a feature of the gates. A recreation of the Unicorn Gate may also be seen in the Royal Naval Museum complete with a soundtrack of the dockyard employees passing through it.

The great gates of Portsmouth are a most fascinating part of its Stuart and Georgian history. As far as Nelson was concerned, he would have been familiar with King James's Gate, King George's Gate and the Landport. The Lion Gate and the Unicorn Gate would have been constructed during his time in the Navy. The combination and cumulative effect of all five of them would have created a very strong impression, giving Portsmouth a most distinctive character.

As for their demolition or resiting, William Gates aptly described all this as the symbolic emasculation of Portsmouth. Today, they certainly are a muddled collection with no unifying purpose: it is very sad to see the wonderful King James's Gate sitting forlornly by the road side.

The four remaining gates are all owned by the Ministry of Defence and two, the Landport and King James's, are also in the care of English Heritage. None has complete public access. If the Victorians had only had left them intact, Portsmouth would be unique with its walled, fortified town and set of five Baroque gates with their classical designs. As it is, at least the development of photography meant that they were captured just before they disappeared. (COURTESY OF PORTSMOUTH CITY MUSEUMS AND RECORDS SERVICE)

The Death of an Uncle and a Mayor

The death of Maurice Suckling occurred on 14 July 1778. He had attended his last meeting of the Navy Board on 4 March and died in London four months later at the age of fifty-two. He was taken back to Suffolk and buried in the chancel of Barsham church near his parents. The captain had been ill for some time but what effect did his death have?

N. Rodger, in his book on the Earl of Sandwich published in 1993, points out that no serious study has ever been made of Suckling's period of office at the Navy Board, perhaps because it only lasted three years. His time as an MP for Portsmouth was even shorter, just the two years, and he never took his seat in the House of Commons.

Twelve years later, at the time of writing, there is still no biography of him so it is very difficult to assess his role. N. Rodger sums him up:

He seems to have been another of Sandwich's favourite type of sea officer: able, hard-working and somewhat obscure, capable of doing the job, and not closely linked with any obvious political rivals.

Suckling had functioned not only as the head of the Navy Board but also as a professional advisor to Lord Sandwich.

The experience gained from his naval career must have been of great advantage especially during Lord Sandwich's reforms. Like the earl, Captain Suckling had a capacity for hard work allied with attention to detail, but unlike his patron, was able to remain out of the limelight. Today perhaps, we would see him as a professional civil servant. As for

Nelson who had just joined the crew of the *Bristol*, he was to feel the loss of his uncle and patron profoundly.

Concerning Captain Suckling's connection with Portsmouth, there has been no analysis of his role on the Navy Board or his relationship with the mayor Philip Varlo. Indeed, there is no current published work which does full justice to the Byzantine complexities of all the vested interests which affected political life in eighteenth century Portsmouth. As Dr James Thomas points out, while the relationship between town and dockyard appeared on the surface to be straightforward, in reality it was anything but.

At work was a combination of the interests of the Admiralty, the Army, the urban authorities as they were prior to the Great Reform Bill of 1832 and the religious authorities. Land ownership issues underlay everything on Portsea Island, in particular, the role of the institutional landowners such as Winchester College and the Dean and Chapter of Windsor and their interaction with the individual landowners.

As for commercial interests, the very powerful trading ventures such as the East India Companies of England, the United Provinces and Sweden had an influential role which requires further exploration. Overall, the demands of the state took priority, especially during war time and commercial interests, such as those of banking and trade had to operate within those limits.[19]

Regarding the social history of Portsmouth, Peter Guillery in his book on the small house in eighteenth century London, has set Portsmouth in the context of the other model dockyard towns. He examines Greenwich, Deptford and Woolwich in particular, which he describes as military-industrial satellites of London, neither suburbs of the capital nor independent towns. These three, while linked closely to London, had a distinctive collective identity as self-contained and self-sustaining maritime places.

Portsmouth was too far away to be considered as a satellite, besides which of course, it had been an independent town in its own right since medieval times. Nevertheless, to study it entirely in geographic isolation overlooks its role as a military-industrial colony of London and any affinity it might have with the fortified maritime towns of western Europe such as Amsterdam.

To return to Captain Suckling, he and Varlo were contemporaries and by the time Suckling became an MP, Varlo had been mayor on five occasions (in 1764, 1768, 1770, 1775 and 1776). Philip Varlo was also to die at a relatively young age, even for the eighteenth century. At the age of fifty-six, just three months before the captain, he died on 6 April 1778.

A Family Remembered

The *Hampshire Chronicle* announced on 11 April 1778, 'This week died, greatly lamented, Philip Varlo Esq., one of the Alderman of this Borough': there was to be no such tribute to Captain Suckling on his death. There is also a memorial to the memory of Philip Varlo in Portsmouth cathedral on the wall near the Navy aisle.

Easily the most stylish memorial tablet in the cathedral, it is a very elegant, triangular monument in a simple yet imaginative and artistic design. Its colour scheme of a light and dark marble set on a darker stone base lends it depth and perspective.

The tablet commemorates three people: Philip Varlo; his uncle, also Philip Varlo (1695–1749); and his wife Mary, who died on 6 November 1795 aged 68. Like the memorial to the Duke of Buckingham, it is in a Baroque style but much later, presumably dating from the death of Mary in 1795.

The design includes Baroque details such as the cherub at the top, the flowers and the ornamental scrolls under the supporting shelf. The background is a flattened obelisk giving the tablet a pyramidal shape which is typical of Baroque funerary monuments. By the end of the eighteenth century though, tastes have changed, the momento mori has become unfashionable and there are no gruesome skulls to be seen here.

Its main feature, however, is the suspended disc. These discs were frequently seen on seventeenth and eighteenth century memorials, often with the face in relief of the person commemorated.

In this case, the exquisite calligraphy sets out a large amount of information in a tiny space, unifying a memorial to three people, two of them with the same name, who died nearly half a century apart. The same name set out three times is an interesting feature and ensures that the name of Philip Varlo will not be forgotten in Portsmouth.

The rectangular piece of column in a darker coloured marble reinforces the scrolled support without impeding the curves. It appears to counteract the weight of the suspended disc and its solidity contrasts with the ephemeral flowers and cherub above, giving the whole design balance and harmony.

To sum up then, for just three years, from 1775 to 1778, Nelson was connected to Portsmouth by a close family relationship. Had the captain and Mr Varlo lived longer and remained in office, it may well have been that Nelson would have been motivated to develop closer personal links and a political foothold within the town.

As it was, he was never given the Freedom of the Borough although he did receive the Freedom of London, Bath, Bristol, Norwich and Plymouth. He was never to buy a house in the town unlike other famous naval officers. Things might have been different had Captain Suckling lived.

As an afterthought, one wonders if the survivor of this group, Philip Varlo's wife Mary, who lived on until 1795 ever met Nelson: if so, did she ever think about the young lieutenant on the threshold of his career who had dined with them at their house in Portsmouth in 1776? (COURTESY PORTSMOUTH CATHEDRAL; AUTHOR'S PHOTOGRAPH, 2005)

References

[1] *Spreading the Word*, p.93.

[2] The popularity of these prospects can be gauged by the fact that in the volume of the *Universal Magazine* I consulted in the British Library, they are all missing!

[3] *The Book of Gosport*, p.56.

[4] *The History of the Foundling Hospital*, p.42.

[5] I am indebted to Dr James Thomas for this reference.

[6] The abbreviation O. S. stands for Old Style which indicates that the date is given in the Julian calendar. This was in use in Russia in the eighteenth century and was eleven days behind the Gregorian calendar which had been introduced in Europe in 1752, remains in use today and is known as New Style.

[7] *The Undercliff of the Isle of Wight: Past and Present*, p.79. I am indebted to Dr Robin McInnes, historian and Coastal Manager of the Isle of Wight Council for this reference.

[8] *George III's Miniature Dockyards*, pp.15–17.

[9] *The Architect King*, p.80.

[10] *Inside Outside: Changing Attitudes Towards Architectural Models in the Museums at South Kensington*, p.157.

[11] *Wrest Park 1686–1730s: Exploring Dutch Influence*, p.145.

[12] *The Dockyard Models of George III*, p.9.

[13] *The London Town Garden*, p.103.

[14] *An Album of Drawings by Gabriel Bray, R.N., HMS Pallas, 1774–1775*, p.37.

[15] *Excavations at Oyster Street, Portsmouth, Hampshire 1968–71*, p.65.

[16] *The Clay Tobacco Pipes of the Portsmouth Harbour Region*.

[17] *A Visit to Haslar 1916*, p.8.

[18] *Nelson: A Dream of Glory*, p.108.

[19] *Dockyards*, vol.10, Issue 1, February 2005, p.2.

Chapter III

1782–1783:
'I WANT MUCH TO GET [OFF]
THIS D....D VOYAGE'

Since the death of his uncle in 1778, Nelson's career had continue to progress, in the December of that year he had been promoted to master and commander, and in June 1779 he had made post-captain. However, during the Nicaraguan campaign of 1780, he had caught yellow jack fever and had been invalided home to recover. From October 1780 to October 1781 he was in England on half pay.

Eventually, he was given a command as captain of the *Albermarle*, which lasted from 1781 to July 1783. From 1782 onwards, we can hear Nelson's own voice through the medium of his letters and do not just have to read about his ship in the newspapers. He wrote to colleagues, family and friends while ashore in Portsmouth or aboard ship anchored at Spithead or St Helen's. Here he is:

1782

To Philip Stephens, Esq., Secretary to the Admiralty.

Albemarle, at Spithead, 2nd February, 1782.

Sir,
I am to acquaint you, for the information of my Lords Commissioners of the Admiralty, that I arrived here this morning in His Majesty's Ship Albemarle, *under my command; and inclosed I transmit you her State and Condition.*

I am, Sir, &c.
Horatio Nelson.

To William Locker, Esq., Gray's Inn.

Portsmouth, February 5th, 1782.

My dear Sir,
Since I received yours, the Albemarle *is much altered for the worse. An East India Store-ship came on board us in a gale of wind, and carried away our foremast, bowsprit, head, and quarter gallery, and done considerable damage to her hull. We arrived here two days ago, and are now coming into the harbour to be docked. I was ordered for Foreign service. Charles Pole is here: he is going to Gibraltar with a large Cutter, laden with Gun-boats; I wish he was safe back. I think he runs great risk of going to Cadiz. Sir Richard Bickerton is here; - a great man, he seems to carry it pretty high with his Captains. Jack Moore is with him, and I heard him tell Captain Robinson, who was Admiral Parker's Captain in the* Fortitude, *he would certainly provide for him. I shall certainly see you in Town before the* Albemarle *gets out of the harbour. Mr. White, the builder, has inquired after you. Farewell, my dear Sir, and believe me to be,*

Faithfully yours,
Horatio Nelson.

Compliments to the Bradleys, and all that ask after me.

This gossipy, intimate letter to William Locker, (1731–1800) is a great contrast to the formal missive to the secretary of the Admiralty. Locker joined the Navy in 1746 and was promoted to his first command in 1762. In 1777, Nelson, just 19, joined his ship the *Lowestoffe*, which was bound for the West Indies, as one of his lieutenants. He remained on board for just over a year, during which time he was, of course, to lose his uncle, Captain Suckling.

Locker was invalided out of the Navy in 1779 and became lieutenant governor of Greenwich Hospital in 1793, where he died in 1800. Locker's son wrote later of the relationship between his father and Nelson:

> *...Captain Locker, who soon perceived the defects as well as the merits of his character, watched over him with a father's care, and well supplied to him the place of his distinguished uncle, Maurice Suckling Comptroller of the Navy, under whom he had first embarked at sea, and from whom he received the first and most important part of his naval education while a midshipman.*[1]

This portrait of Captain Locker is an engraving by H. T. Ryall after an oil painting by G. Stuart painted about 1785, three years after this letter was written. It was presented to Greenwich Hospital by his family and published in 1832. It is easy to see why he appealed to Nelson as his warmth of character and intelligence shine out from the page. He comes over too, as very human and probably made a very successful hospital governor. (COURTESY ROYAL NAVAL CLUB & ROYAL ALBERT YACHT CLUB)

❋ ❋ ❋

To the Reverend Mr. Nelson, Burnham

Portsmouth, February 8th, 1782.

Dear Brother,

Your letter of January 30th I received two nights ago; and am much obliged to you for it; I should have wrote before I did from the Downs, only I expected my orders every day, when I could have told you where I was to have been stationed. You have heard of the accidents that have happened to the poor Albemarle, *both by my letter and the Papers long before this. I was under orders for Foreign service, and I fancy was going with dispatches to North America. I am now waiting at Spithead for a wind to bring me into the harbour to be docked and repaired; what will become of me afterwards I know not. If I should touch at any wine Countries, you may assure Lord Walpole I will purchase some of the best wines for him. I beg you will make my best respects to him and Lady Walpole, with many thanks for their kind inquiries after me. I regret very much I had not the pleasure of receiving Mr. Walpole on board the* Albemarle, *or if he had been in Yarmouth, I should certainly have paid my respects to him. Apropos of wine:- in my opinion, the expense of sending a cask of wine from this place to Burnham is almost the original cost; but there it is, if you please to have it; only send word. Charles Boyles sailed from here the day before my arrival.*

Whatever may be the opinion of the Wells people respecting Captain Gardner's behaviour in the matter of his Lieutenants quitting his ship, I will answer he was right. There is not a better Officer, or more of a gentleman, this day in the Service. I am much afraid poor Charles will wait a long while with Mr. R-------- before he gets promotion, for he is a great liar. Sir Richard Bickerton, with the East India Fleet, sailed yesterday afternoon with six Sail of the Line for India, and three Sail of the Line and two Fifties, to go part of the way with them. The West India Fleet is not yet ready: they will sail Saturday or Sunday, if the wind is fair.

I wish I could congratulate you upon a Rectory instead of a Vicarage: it is rather awkward wishing the poor man dead, but we all rise by deaths. I got my rank by a shot killing a Post-Captain, and I most sincerely hope I shall, when I go, go out of [the] world the same way; then we go all in the line of our Profession... a Parson praying, a Captain fighting. I suppose you are returned from Hilborough before this, and take Miss Ellen and the Living. As Miss Bec takes so much notice of my respect to her, tell her I think myself honoured by being in her favour. Love to Mrs. Bolton and Mun, not forgetting little Kate. You have wrote so long a letter, that I must get another half sheet to work. [The conclusion is missing.]

❊❊❊

To William Locker, Esq., Gray's Inn

Portsmouth, March 10th, 1782.

My Dear Sir,
Your favour I received last night inclosing a letter from Ross, of December the 31st. He has twice been on his passage for England, was once drove back by the French Fleet, and the other time shipwrecked; but he is going to make another trial, and I suppose will arrive in this Convoy. He desires his particular compliments to you: it is as friendly a letter as I ever received. I dare say you will see him very soon. In his postscript he mentions having received a letter from Mr. Higgins, saying that I was going to pay for a pipe of Madeira wine. He desires me, if I have paid it, to send for the money again, as there is no error existing but in Mr. Higgins' accounts; but, if you remember the circumstance, I did not pay for the wine.

All the Admiral's family are well, enjoying the mountains, and daily increasing in wealth. General Dalling landed here last night; he came home in the Ranger Armed Ship; one or two of the Convoy are also arrived. The **Jupiter** arrived yesterday morning, with a brig from St Domingo, and a French privateer. I have just learnt that the Ranger's Convoy were most of [them] taken in the Gulf of Florida, by two Line of Battle Ships, and six armed Schooners, so I suppose Ross is carried into the Havannah. Adieu, my dear Sir and assure yourself I am your

Most obedient Servant,
Horatio Nelson.

❊❊❊

To the Reverend Mr. Nelson, at James Coldham's, Esq., Bircham, Norfolk.
Portsmouth, March 29th, 1782.

Dear Brother,
Yours of the 24th I received last night, as well as two letters you wrote before to me. I have had so much business upon my hands in fitting the old **Albemarle** once more for service, that you must excuse my not having wrote. I shall sail, if the weather is moderate, in the first week of April, from Spithead to Cork, where I am to take a Convoy, and carry them to Quebec. Whether I am [to] come home in the autumn or not is uncertain. Perhaps, and I believe, your reasoning upon giving up the money to Mr. Bolton is very just; but yet I shall sign the power of attorney, if it is sent me. If the children have nothing else I am sure that is no object. Your argument that, if his trading schemes should fail, our family must maintain her, and his children, I deny; I don't think myself obliged to do any such thing. Perhaps our denying the money to Mr. Bolton, may bring on a disagreement between him and his wife: it is better for us to run the risk of the sum, than such a thing should happen. I beg we may not interfere about the houses at Wells: if he don't do it let it rest. I have burnt our letter. Oliver is still on board the **Albemarle**, and well: he has wrote several times to his wife, but has had no answer. I would, with great pleasure, have sent you the wine, but a quarter cask cannot be entered at the Custom House. I am very sorry you have not got Newton Living: I hope, now, Lord Walpole will look out for something for you. Make my compliments to all at Wells, &c., and give my love to Mun. Adieu, dear Brother, and believe me to be

Yours affectionately,
Horatio Nelson.

Lord Howe is to command the Fleet.

To William Locker, Esq., Gray's Inn.

Portsmouth, April 2nd, 1782

My dear Sir,
I ought to [be] scolded for not having wrote to you for this long time past: I cam make but very lame excuses. The weather has been so bad for these ten days, and Southerly winds, that I have not been able to get the old Albemarle out of the harbour. I am ordered to Cork to join the Daedalus, Captain Pringle, and go with a Convoy to Quebec; where, worse than all to tell, I understand I am to winter. I want much to [get] off from this d----d voyage, and believe, if I had time to look a little about me, I could get another Ship. Mr. Adair, who attends on Mr. Keppel, might tell him, that in such a country I shall be laid up: for he has told me, that if I was sent to a cold damp climate, it would make me worse than ever. Many of my Navy friends have advised me to represent my situation to Admiral Keppel, and they have no doubt but he would give me other orders, or remove me; but as I received my orders from Lord Sandwich, I can't help thinking I wrong to ask Mr. Keppel to alter them.

Charles Pole tells me he wrote you yesterday, I am exceedingly happy at his success: in his seamanship he showed himself as superior to the Don, as in his gallantry; and no man in the world so modest in his account of it. Admiral Pye hoisted his flag to day. Admiral Barrington hoists his after the Court-Martial is assembled to-morrow, on board the Britannia. Lord Longford introduced me to him this morning, and told him who I was: it is from that quarter, could I stay long enough in Port, that I expect a better Ship. Admiral Barrington takes twelve Sail of the Line, as soon as ready; he is in very good spirits; he gets amongst all the youngsters here, and leaves out the old boys. We are all alive here: I hope to hear, by next [post], you have a Ship. Farewell, my dear Sir, for I have been so idle, that I have not had ten minutes to spare for this.

Yours most sincerely,
Horatio Nelson.

❈ ❈ ❈

Pringle would not have gone this voyage, but for a hundred thousand pounds going out to Quebec, and he's got it all. See what it is to be a Scotchman. I hope their times are over. Sandys desires his compliments. Ferguson of the Berwick was honourably acquitted, as also Thompson of the Hyaena.

Nelson's mention of Lord Sandwich probably refers to that fact that the earl was no longer first lord of the admiralty. Lord North had resigned on 20 March 1782 and the earl went with him. Lord Sandwich never again held high office although he continued in public life until his death in 1792.

In him, Nelson had lost a patron and the Navy a champion and a worthy successor to Samuel Pepys, who was known as the father of the Royal Navy. Lord Sandwich had laid the administrative foundations for Nelson's victory at Trafalgar in 1805 and his enthusiasm and support for the Navy was never to be replaced. Henry Slight pays tribute to his connection with Haslar Hospital:

...To thee,
Illustrious SANDWICH! whose humanity
Snatched from the deadly fang the sinking man,
To give him back to happiness and joy,
The Muse must pay the tribute of her praise,
Long as our fleets shall rule the tribute main,
And distant nations tremble at our power,
So long thy name shall be by Britain blessed,
Thy naval ministry immortalized –
Thy envied title still – the Sailor's Friend!

To William Locker, Esq., Gray's Inn.

Portsmouth, April 16th, 1782.

My dear Sir,
I am very much obliged to you for the great trouble you have given yourself, in trying to alter my destination. Tomorrow I sail, if the weather is moderate. If I can get home in the autumn I hope I shall get a better Ship and a better station. Pringle, in the Daedalus, *is going to Newfoundland, after having seen the Convoy to Quebec. God bless you, and assure yourself*
I am ever faithfully yours,
Horatio Nelson.

Remember me to the Bradleys. Charles Pole desires his compliments: his Ship is in the harbour. He is coming soon to London.

1783

To Philip Stephens, Esq., Secretary to the Admiralty.

Albemarle, *Spithead, June 25th, 1783.*

Sir,
I beg you will acquaint my Lords Commissioners of the Admiralty of my arrival at Spithead, with his Majesty's Ship under my command. I parted with the Fleet under the command of Lord Hood, on the 14th of May 1783, in latitude 30 Degrees North, and longitude 80 Degrees West of London. Inclosed is the state and Condition of his Majesty's Ship under my command, and a copy of Lord Hood's Order for my proceedings.
I am, Sir, &c.
Horatio Nelson.

✻✻✻

To William Locker, Esq., West Malling, Kent.

Portsmouth, June 26th, 1783.

My dear Friend,
After all my tossing about into various climates, here at last am I arrived, safe and sound. I found orders for the Albemarle *to be paid off at this place. On Monday next I hope to be rid of her. My people I fancy will be pretty quiet, if they are nor set on by some of the Ships here.*
I have on board for you, drawn off, twelve dozen of rum: I intend to put it for the present under Mr. White's care, as I dare say he will take care of it, (provided the Custom House do not seize it) for I do not think rum is worth the expense of the duty. I hope this will find you in perfect health. Captain Gardner tells me you still live at Malling. Farewell, my dear Sir, and assure yourself,

I am your affectionate Friend,
Horatio Nelson.

I suppose you have heard from Charles Pole; I left him exceedingly well, and very anxious to get Home. Make my compliments to all my acquaintance in your part of the world. Lord Hood's Fleet is just heaving in sight round St Helen's.

The Story of Nelson's Initials

The American War of Independence came to an end in 1783 and Nelson was to spend the next few months on half-pay in France and England.

This photograph shows a window which was removed from the Star and Garter pub at Point when it was demolished in 1954. It was then put on display on the wall in the Dolphin pub in the High Street where it can be seen today, as legend has it that the initials, 'H' and 'N' were scratched on it by Nelson on his last visit to the pub.

Next to it is part of a quotation from a book by Marguerite Steen entitled, *A Pride of Terrys: Family Saga*, which is a history of the famous acting family, the Terrys. They originated in Portsmouth, and Ellen Terry (1848–1928) was their most famous member.

The full quotation reads:

He took the boys to the Sally Port, where the little, dark, unhappy bride of Charles II landed nearly two hundred years before; and showed them King James's Gate and the old Star and Garter from which Franklin sailed, with Erebus *and* Terror, *to seek the North-West Passage, and never returned.*

Young Ben could remember that; but he was too young to be suitably impressed by the initials 'H.N.' scratched on a seaward window, between 'Dot' and 'Flora', Nelson's last record on his last visit to the famous inn.

(Courtesy Anthony Triggs)

The Meeting House Square Tablet

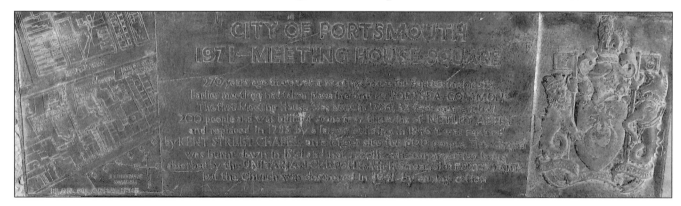

This tablet commemorates the first Meeting House for Baptists in Portsea and was originally set up in 1971 in Kent Street, Portsea. When the area was redeveloped its condition had deteriorated so it was taken down and placed in the care of the City Museum.

The inscription reads:

270 years ago there was a meeting house for Baptists on this site. Earlier meetings had taken place in a barn on Portsea Common. The first Meeting House was built in 1704, 32 feet square, it held 200 people and was built of stone from the ruins of Netley Abbey and replaced in 1783 by a larger building.

In 1846 it was replaced by Kent Street Chapel on a larger site for 800 people. This Chapel was burnt down in 1891 and not rebuilt – the congregation being absorbed by the Unitarian Church in High Street, Old Portsmouth, but the church was destroyed in 1941 by enemy action.

(Courtesy Portsmouth Museums and Records Service)

References
[1] *Memoirs of Celebrated Naval Commanders*, p.23.

Chapter IV

1684–1787:
'I AM FONDER OF THE SEA THAN EVER'

In March 1784 Nelson was given command of the Boreas, a 28-gun Sixth Rate frigate in which he was to stay for three and a half years.

To Philip Stephens, Esq., Admiralty.

Boreas, Spithead, April 18th, 1784.

Sir,
I have the honour to acquaint you, that his Majesty's Ship under my command, arrived at this place yesterday, and enclosed is her State and Condition. Your answer to my last letter of the 14th, I received yesterday evening. I have therefore to suppose that my first of that day did not come to hand.

I am Sir, &c.,
Horatio Nelson.

❋❋❋

To William Locker, Esq.,

Portsmouth, April 21st, 1784.

My dear Sir,
Since I parted from you, I have encountered many disagreeable adventures. The day after I left you, we sailed at daylight, just after high water. The d----d Pilot – it makes me swear to think of it – ran the Ship aground, where she lay with so little water that the people could walk round her till next high water. That night and part of the next day, we lay below the Nore with a hard gale of wind and snow; Tuesday I got into the Downs: on Wednesday I got into a quarrel with a Dutch Indiaman who had Englishmen on board, which we settled after some difficulty. The Dutchman has made a complaint against me; but the Admiralty fortunately have approved my conduct in the business, a thing they are not very guilty of where there is a likelihood of a scrape. And yesterday, to complete me, I was riding a blackguard horse that ran away with me at Common, carried me round all the Works into Portsmouth, by the London gates, through the Town out at the gate that leads to Common, where there was a waggon in the road, – which is so very narrow, that a horse could barely pass. To save my legs, and perhaps my life, I was obliged to throw myself from the horse, which I did with great agility: but unluckily upon hard stones, which has hurt my back and my leg, but done no other mischief. It was a thousand to one that I had not been killed. To crown all, a young girl was riding with me; her horse ran away with mine; but most fortunately a gallant young man seized her horse's bridle a moment before I dismounted, and saved her from the destruction which she could not have avoided.

Kingsmill came to Town on Sunday, and has taken possession of his Ship and Land Frigate again. At Maidstone I see by the Papers, you have returned the old Members: how consistently Mr. Marsham has behaved to support Mr. Fox, and then thank the King for turning him out. There can be no good at the bottom, I am afraid. Lady Hughes is here, but I have not received my orders. Give my compliments to Madam Bradley, &c. and rest assured

I am yours, most sincerely,
Horatio Nelson.

Give my best compliments to George Smith: you can vouch for my intention to have visited him. Kingsmill desires his compliments. What inquiries you wish me to make about your land in Dominica, pray put upon paper.

The Runaway Horse

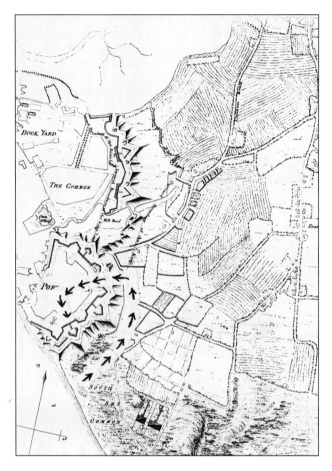

Nelson's escapade with the runaway horse has been reproduced many times in biographies, but where did the horse actually take him? This segment of map taken from a plan of the encampments on Southsea Common and dated 1778 gives an overall view of Portsmouth and the works – by works Nelson means the fortifications.

Nelson describes in his letter the route that the horse took and it seems straightforward enough. They galloped around from Common to Common, but in 1784,[4] there were two areas known as Common, Portsea which was on one side of Portsmouth and Southsea Common, which was on the other.

It does seem strange to associate Nelson with a horse, but riding was not only a means of transport but a popular activity. G. Marcus in his book on the Georgian Navy describes the latest fashion at the time which was for young men to hire carriages and drive around loaded up with women. Nelson says that he was accompanied by a young girl. So where would they do all this riding? Southsea Common is the most likely place. Southsea as we know it today did not exist then and its large expanse would provide plenty of room.

The route indicated on the map, takes us from Southsea Common, round to the Landport Gate, through the gate, probably along High Street, turning left into what was then Fighting Cock Lane and is now Pembroke Road and along to the fortifications. There was no large gate there, as King William's Gate was not built until 1833, but there was some sort of exit through the fortifications out on to the common.

Presumably, this is where Nelson has the encounter with the loaded wagon and threw himself off his horse. The gateway would certainly have been narrow and we know from previous pictures how much room a loaded wagon would take up. Is it possible to walk the route today? Southsea Common is still an open space of course, but the rest of the way is so built up that it is almost impossible to visualise. Nevertheless, a fascinating story. (Courtesy Portsmouth City Council)

To the Reverend Mr. Nelson, Burnham.

Boreas, Portsmouth April 23rd, 1784.

Dear Brother,
Come when you please, I shall be ready to receive you. Bring your canonicals and sermons. Do not bring any Burnham servants. I cannot say more, being much hurried.
Yours affectionately,
Horatio Nelson.

In less than a fortnight my Ship will not sail. I have a fine talkative Lady for you to converse with.

❈ ❈ ❈

To Philip Stephens, Esq., Secretary to the Admiralty.

Boreas, Spithead, April 29th, 1784.

Sir,
Be pleased to state to their Lordships, that William Bell, Gunner of his Majesty's Ship Medea, *who has formerly sailed with me, and for whom I have an esteem, and Thomas*

Harries, at present gunner of the Boreas, *who is in a very bad state of health, are desirous of exchanging Ships; and I shall deem it a particular favour, if their Lordships will approve of the exchange, and to appoint them accordingly. Inclosed is their joint letter, and*

I am, &c.,
Horatio Nelson.

✿✿✿

To Philip Stephens, Esq., Admiralty.
Boreas, *Spithead, May 10th, 1784.*

Sir,
Their Lordships' orders of the 6th instant I have received; and as soon as the Ship's company are paid their advance, shall put their Orders in execution with all possible dispatch.

I am, Sir, &c.,
Horatio Nelson.

✿✿✿

To William Locker, Esq.,
Boreas, *Spithead, May 14th, 1784.*

My dear Friend,
The Commissioner is now paying my Ship, and I am making use of the time that I may be able to save Post, as none goes out to-morrow. I was agreeably surprised by your letter, as I did not expect to hear you was in London. I thank you much for your news, which if true, hostilities must commence soon again with the French: God send, I say. But if Cornwallis is going out, I shall be a little vexed that I am not to be one of the Ships. Whenever I go to Dominica, you may as assured that every circumstance relative to your estate shall be inquired into. Jamaica is the place I wish to go to. I have not time scarcely to say, how much I am your devoted,

Horatio Nelson.

I will write more by Sunday.

Here, Nicolas adds an appendix:

Walking the Boreas' Quarter-Deck on the 30th May 1784, at 7 in the Evening.

Editor's note: The great number of passengers and officers on the *Boreas* seems to have induced Captain Nelson to make the following list:

1. *Lady Hughes*
2. *Miss Hughes*
3 *Captain Nelson*
4. *Lieutenant Wallace, [Lieutenant James Wallis, who was appointed by Nelson, Commander of the* Rattler *in May 1787, but was not confirmed until 1794. He was Posted in 1797, and died between 1806 and 1809.]*
5. *Lieutenant Dent, [Lieutenant Digby Dent, made a Commander in 1797.]*
6. *Jameson M. [James Jameson, Master of the* Boreas.]
7. *R. Mr. Nelson [Afterwards Earl Nelson.]*
8. *Masters Mate Bromwich, [Joseph Bromwich; made a lieutenant in 1793, and afterwards]*
9. *Warden of Portsmouth Dock Yard.*
10. *Masters Mate Powers [He was discharged in the West Indies, and went to America.]*
11. *Masters Mate Graham [Surgeon of the* Boreas.]
12. *Masters Mate Peers and Mrs. Peers, [The Purser and his wife.]*
13. *Mr. Lane, Marines*
14. *Mr. Oliver [Mr. Oliver was discharged from the* Boreas, *for being concerned in a duel.]*
15. *Mr. Hughes [Richard Hughes, eldest son of Rear-Admiral Sir Richard Hughes: he was*

made a Lieutenant in November 1790, and died a Post-Captain in 1810.]
16. Mr. Jones.
17. Mr. Bremer [James Bremer, who afterwards commanded the **Berbice** *Schooner, (so often mentioned in Captain Nelson's letters) Tender to the Flag Ship: he was made a lieutenant in November 1790, and a Commander in August 1811, in which rank he died.]*
18. Mr. Beale.
19. Mr. Bayntun.
20. Mr. Talbot, [Now Admiral the Hon. Sir John Talbot, G.C.B.]
21. Mr. Boyle, [The late Vice-Admiral the Hon. Sir Courtenay Boyle, K.C.H.]
22 Mr. Purefoy.
23. Mr. Batty [Mr. William Baty.]
24. Mr. Parkinson, Senior.
25. Mr. Parkinson, Junior.
26. Mr. Suckling [Maurice William Suckling, a distant relative of Captain Nelson, son of Mr. Suckling, of Wooton near Norwich. He was made a lieutenant in 1790, succeeded to the estates of his family, and died without issue in 1820.]
27. Mr. Nowell.
28. Mr. Stainsbury [He was discharged because he had wounded Mr. George Andrews, a young Midshipman of the Boreas, in a duel.]
29. Mr. Brown.
30. Mr. Tatham, [Apparently William Tatham, who was made a lieutenant in 1794.]
31. Mr. Lock, [Charles Lock. He was made a lieutenant on the 22nd of November 1790, a Commander in 1796, and appears to have died Captain of the Inspector in February 1800.]
32. Mr. Morgan.
33. Mr. Bishop.

Portchester Castle

Portchester Castle lies on the north shore of Portsmouth Harbour at the south end of Portchester village. It is a Roman fort dating from AD3–4 and was built to protect the coast from Saxon pirates. In medieval times, its position at the head of Portsmouth Harbour made it a convenient stopping point for monarchs on their way to the continent but by the time of the Stuarts, it was no longer a royal residence and had become a military prison and hospital.

This print by S. Hooper and Sparrow is absolutely contemporary with Nelson as it was published on 30 June 1784 while he was on the *Boreas*. The sentry and the sentry box at the postern gate in the castle's north wall indicates its use as a military prison.

However, the two figures on the bridge taking in the view emphasise the castle's attraction as a romantic ruin in the picturesque style. Not only does this make a pleasing picture, but the figure pointing out the great Keep and Assheton's Tower with his stick, reminds us of its antiquity too.

A phenomenon of the late eighteenth century was the many thousands of prisoners taken as a result of the Napoleonic Wars. The main question of the time was how and where to accommodate them – a problem which was not to occur again for another 150 years when vast numbers of American and Canadian troops had to be quartered on the south coast prior to D-Day in 1944. One solution to the problem of the French prisoners would be to put them in Portchester Castle. (AUTHOR'S COLLECTION)

The Portsmouth Beneficial School, Portsea

Other developments were happening in Portsmouth while Nelson was on the *Boreas* although it was unlikely that he would have been aware of them. Back in 1754, the Beneficial Society had been formed by a group of eight local men who were concerned at the lack of education for poor boys in Portsea.

Their foundation was intended to provide schooling for them and thirty years later, this building was constructed in Kent Street, which was then known as Old Rope Walk: the architect was William Hay. The plaque on the gable reads 'This building was erected in 1784 by the Beneficial Society for their Free School for boys established 1755', and the wording over the portico, 'Beneficial School Established 1755'.

This is another atmospheric photograph by W. J. Lawrence taken in 1937. It shows an elegant Georgian building, the only remaining example of a Georgian charitable school in Portsmouth which is still in use. Fortunately, it survived the bombing which destroyed most of Portsea. The school used the ground floor which was a large open hall and the members of the Beneficial Society held their meetings on the upper floor denoted by the large Venetian-style Palladian window.

However, the Beneficial Society School was more than just a place of education, important though that was. Its significance in the eighteenth century history of Portsmouth lies in the fact that it was a very popular venue for functions and entertainments. In 1805, celebratory dinners following the Battle of Trafalgar would be held there.

Another glance at the photograph reveals details which are almost more interesting than the building itself. The small houses next door were swept away long ago. In the bottom left hand corner we see a handcart, this time joined by a bicycle. (Courtesy J. C. Lawrence)

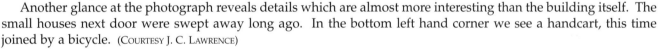

1787

Nelson has returned to England after having served as commander of the Leeward Island squadron, a group that had as its home port English Harbour on Antigua.

To Philip Stephens, Esq.,

Boreas, Spithead, July 4th, 1787.

Sir,

I have the honour to acquaint you of he arrival of his Majesty's Ship under my command, in obedience to orders from Commodore Parker.

I am much distressed that their Lordships should think I had directed the Prince not to do what was right in respect to the Muster-Book for the Clerk of the Cheque at Antigua. I assure the Board that I was guided, when his Royal Highness did me the honour of asking me relative to the Book, by the eleventh and fourteenth of the Captain's, and thirteenth Articles of the Purser's Instructions. If I have erred, I fear it has been by too strict a compliance with those Articles.

As I have been under the necessity of mentioning his Royal Highness's name, I feel I should be remiss in my duty did I neglect to acquaint their Lordships that the Pegasus is one of the first disciplined Frigates I have seen; and his Royal Highness the most respectful and one of the most attentive obedient Officers I know of.

I trust their Lordships have done me the honour of confirming the Appointments to the Rattler *and* Boreas, *which were made thirty days before Commodore Parker arrived at Barbadoes, as they were made agreeably to the Board's Instructions left with me by the late Commander-in-Chief at the Leeward Islands.*

Having given Commodore Parker a Return of the Squadron, and the services they were employed upon, which doubtless he has transmitted, it is needless for me to trouble you with a repetition.

I have the honour to be, &c.,
Horatio Nelson.

Herewith I transmit you the State and Condition of his Majesty's ship Boreas *under my command.*

The prince mentioned in this letter is Prince William Henry (1765–1837). He was the third son of George III and seven years younger than Nelson. He had made the Navy his career and was created Duke of Clarence in 1789. He was eventually to become King William IV on the death of George IV. As a naval man with an energetic love life he was familiar with Portsmouth, writing in 1790 to the Prince of Wales, that in Portsmouth there, '...was not a woman fit to be touched with tongs'.[1]

To William Locker, Esq., Kensington.

Portsmouth, July 9, 1787.

My dear Sir,
You truly kind letter I received last night: you are as ever, too kind. What is to be my immediate destination I know not, but I rather think I shall go out with the Fleet now at Spithead. We are ultimately to be paid off at Woolwich, I have rum and tamarinds for you, and in what quantity you wish, for I have abundance. My dear wife is much obliged by your kind inquiries. I have no doubt but you will like her upon acquaintance, for although I must be partial, yet she possesses great good sense and good temper. We are at a Court-Martial.

Ever yours truly,
Horatio Nelson.

Charles Pole desires me to say everything kind for him.

This is the first mention of Nelson's wife, Frances (Fanny) Nesbit (1761–1831), a young widow whom Nelson had first met in 1785. Fanny had been born on the island of Nevis, which is located in the northern part of the Leeward Island in the eastern Caribbean. Now, it is known as the Federation of St Christopher (St Kitts) and Nevis. In Nelson's time, Nevis had become very prosperous from its sugar industry and her family were originally part of the colonial elite. Fanny was heir to her uncle who was not only the president but was also the richest and most powerful man on the island.

After a courtship of two years, Nelson and Fanny were married on 11 March 1787. Prince William Henry was in the area at the same time, so Nelson took the opportunity to have a member of the royal family involved in his wedding. The prince gave the bride away and acted as witness.

Nelson also mentions the tamarind which seems an exotic delicacy for the time. According to *Law's Grocer's Manual* published in 1895, the tamarind was a preserved fruit, resembling jam and consisting of the pods, pulp and seeds of the tamarind tree. They were imported from India, Africa and Central America in casks forming a reddish-brown moist sugary mass containing strong fibres and brown shiny seeds. These were enclosed in a tough, papery membranous coat with a fine juicy acid pulp.

Generally, they were used for making sauces by being boiled in water or vinegar. A specific eighteenth and nineteenth century use for them was as a cooling and refreshing fever drink once they had been boiled in water and strained. Nowadays, the tamarind is used as a fruity-sour seasoning and can be bought in many forms, raw, powdered and in concentrate. It is also referred to as an Indian date.

To Philip Stephens, Esq., Admiralty.

Boreas, Spithead, July 10th, 1787.

Sir,

As I understand that no official accounts are yet received by their Lordships of the reasons why his Majesty's Ship Pegasus, commanded by his Royal Highness Prince William Henry, proceeded by the way of Jamaica to Halifax in Nova Scotia, I think it my duty to acquaint the Board that on the 23rd of January last, Lieutenant Isaac Schomberg, first Lieutenant of his Majesty's Ship Pegasus, wrote me a letter of which No. I. is a copy. From his Royal Highness having but a few days before released Lieutenant Schomberg from Arrest, and from other antecedent circumstances, together with the extraordinary attack of accusing his Royal Highness of having put his name to what had not happened, I judged it proper to suspend him from duty, and directed his Royal Highness, as by No. II. Other reasons which influenced my conduct were, by being convinced that it was impossible Lieutenant Schomberg could ever serve properly after what had happened; and I was not without hope that when a Commander-in-Chief arrived, some mode might be adopted by him to prevent a Court-Martial, and to get Lieutenant Schomberg removed from the Pegasus. His Royal Highness also acquainted me that Lieutenant Schomberg had told him before the Officers of the Pegasus, that his Royal Highness was now grown so very particular that no Officer could serve under him, and that sooner or later he must be broke; therefore he should stand a Court-Martial, and if they did not break him, he should apply to quit the Ship. This, I hope, their Lordships will consider a sufficient reason for my suspension of Lieutenant Schomberg. Indeed I was so much inclined to think that some other Officers would write for Court-Martials to vindicate their conduct, that I thought it proper to give our the Order No. III; and I was convinced from appearances that if I had not suspended Mr. Schomberg, I should soon have had an application from another quarter.

On the death of Captain Wilfred Collingwood, I sent a blank Commission to his Royal Highness, which he filled up. I thought it was the least compliment I could possibly pay him. By return of the Rattler his Royal Highness acquainted me that Lieutenant Hope wished to exchange out of the Pegasus into the Boreas. This request I thought proper to comply with.

I transmitted to Commodore Gardner by his Royal Highness their Lordships' secret orders. I also desired H.R.H. to give Commodore Gardner a copy of Commodore Sawyer's orders. If there were Ships enough assembled a Court-Martial might be held, the prisoner released, and H.R.H. made easy in his mind. If the Ships could not be assembled, H.R.H. had ample time to comply with Commodore Sawyer's orders. My reason for attending to the Commodore's order, although it was in some measure contrary to their Lordship's orders, was, that had the Pegasus fell in with the ice, and any unfortunate accident happened, it might have been said Captain Nelson should have paid more attention to what an old Officer and Commander-in-Chief directed. Their Lordships will not impute an other reason for my not sending the Pegasus away agreeable to their orders, as she sailed completely refitted for her voyage to North America, and every object of his Royal Highness's visit to this station was accomplished. Numbers IV. and V. are my letters to Commodore Gardner, and his Royal Highness's order. I have the honour to remain, Sir,

Your most obedient Servant.
Horatio Nelson.

No.VI. are Extracts from his Royal Highness' letters to me.

❋ ❋ ❋

To Philip Stephens, Esq., Admiralty.

Boreas, Spithead, July 11th, 1787.

Sir,

I am just honoured with your letter of yesterday's date, wherein you inform me that as I was not duly authorised by their Lordships to fill up appointments, they cannot by the rules of the Board be confirmed.

When Sir Richard Hughes, Baronet, resigned the Command of the Leeward Island Station in July 1786, which he informed me (by his order) was in obedience to the directions of the Admiralty Board, he left me the instructions of their Lordships to him, countersigned by himself, and, amongst others, the power of giving Commissions; also the power of holding Court-Martials, and directing them to be held; and also their Lordships' orders relative to improper Appointments. I therefore could not but suppose myself duly authorised, and with the sanction of their Lordships; or, otherwise, I should during the time of my command have been informed to the contrary.

If from this, what I supposed full, authority, my Appointments are not confirmed, I shall be looked upon in the Service as an Officer who arrogated to himself powers with which he was not invested, for the Service can never know what Sir Richard Hughes left me. Indeed the most serious consequences might have happened, and what might have embittered my future days. Had there been Ships enough on the Station, I should not have sat at Court-Martials, and consequently the Courts would have been illegal.

A man belonging to the Rattler *was sentenced to death. As Senior Captain of five Ships, or as an Officer detached from the Fleet by a Commander-in-Chief, I had not leave to carry a sentence of death into execution. Sir Richard Hughes's Flag was struck, and I was only under the orders of their Lordships; therefore I felt myself empowered to carry any sentence of death into execution; which would have been the case of the unhappy man belonging to the Rattler, had not his Royal Highness interceded for pardon. Thus as I near, if not cutting the thread of life, at least of shortening a fellow-creature's days. The Law might not have supposed me guilty of murder , but my feelings would nearly have been the same. I had always been bred up with the idea of obeying my Commanding Officer most correctly; and what must I feel at finding the Commander-in-Chief's directions a mere nullity?*

I have heard that reports are circulated that I knew Commodore Parker was near the Station when I sent the Pegasus *and* Rattler *away, and that I knew he had been at the Island of Madeira. I assure the Board the report is false. Indeed, on the day the Pegasus sailed, a report came from Antigua, (said to be brought by a Ship that arrived there eleven days before,) that the* Jupiter *sailed from Spithead the latter end of March, but there appeared to me no foundation for it. Indeed, since November last, I had almost always a Ship at Barbadoes, to look out for a Commodore, but I never had the idea of the arrival of one about this time.*

Their Lordships may be assured that one of the happiest acts of life would have been to have resigned the Command before the Pegasus *left the Station.*

I have the honour to remain, &c.,
Horatio Nelson.

✻✻✻

To the Earl of Cork.

Portsmouth, July 15th, 1787.

My Lord,
I am this moment honoured with your letter. I have great pleasure in doing what I know will give our dear Courtenay so much happiness. He is amiable in the truest sense of the word; and I feel real regret in parting from him. In his professional line he is inferior to none: his virtues are superior to most.

I am, &c.,
Horatio Nelson.

✻✻✻

To Philip Stephens, Esq., Admiralty.

Boreas, Spithead, July 18th, 1787.

Sir,
I am this day honoured with your letter of yesterday's date. I beg you will inform their Lordships that I duly observe the contents of it; and they may be assured that in future no consideration shall ever induce me to deviate in the smallest degree from my orders.

I have the honour to remain, &c.,
Horatio Nelson.

✻✻✻

To Philip Stephens, Esq., Admiralty.

Boreas, *Spithead, 20th July, 1787.*

Sir,

Inclosed I have taken the liberty to transmit you a Passing Certificate, with two Warrants, for Mr James Ballentine, Gunner of his Majesty's Ship under my command. I beg leave to recommend him as a sober, diligent and careful man, and worthy of their Lordships' confirmation.

I have the honour to be, &c.,
Horatio Nelson.

❀❀❀

To the Reverend Mr. Nelson, Hilborough.

Portsmouth, July 21st, 1787.

My dear Brother,

Your kind letter of the 15th I have received; and indeed, I have been so very unwell, with a violent cold, that I have scarcely been able to hold my head up till yesterday. What is to become of the Boreas, *seems as yet uncertain. A Fleet seems necessary, and we are all ready to sail at a moment's warning. However, in my humble opinion, we shall not go to Sea this summer. The French have eight Sail in Brest Water, and we shall not be in a hurry to force them to Sea; but next summer I fear will involve this Nation in a War: it seems almost unavoidable. Although we are in a bad state for it, yet, thank God, the French are worse. So much for politics. Your Warrant I have safe: what may arise from it, or if anything I can't tell. I shall give it to my Agent when the Ship is paid off, and he will do what is proper. All on board are well, and desire their compliments. When I know what is to be our destination I will tell you. Adieu.*

Ever yours,
Horatio Nelson.

❀❀❀

To the Earl of Cork.

Portsmouth, July 22nd, 1787.

In the first place, my Lord, it is necessary that he should be made complete in his Navigation; and if the Peace continues, French is absolutely necessary. Dancing is an accomplishment that probably a Sea Officer may require You will see almost the necessity of it, when employed in Foreign countries; indeed, the honour of the Nation is so often entrusted to Sea Officers, that there is no accomplishment which will not shine with peculiar lustre in them. He must nearly have served his Time, therefore he cannot be so well employed as in gaining knowledge. If I can at any time be of service to him, he may always call upon me. His charming disposition will ever make him friends. He may as well join the Ship, when his brother goes to the Continent.

I have the honour to be, &c.,
Horatio Nelson.

❀❀❀

To Philip Stephens, Esq., Admiralty.

Boreas, *Spithead, July 26th, 1787.*

Sir,

Inclosed I transmit you the Warrant of Charles Green, Boatswain of the Boreas, *with the Certificates of his good character from others, his Captains; and I beg leave to recommend him to their Lordships as worthy of having a confirmed Warrant.*

I am, sir, &c.,
Horatio Nelson.

❀❀❀

To H.R.H. Prince William Henry.

Portsmouth, 27th July, 1787.

If to be truly great is to be truly good, (as we are taught to believe,) it never was stronger verified than in your Royal Highness, in the instance of Mr. Schomberg. You have supported your character, yet, at the same time, by an amiable condescension, have saved an Officer from appearing before a Court-Martial, which ever must hurt him. Resentment I know your Royal Highness never had, or I am sure ever will bear any one: it is a passion incompatible with the character of a Man of Honour. Schomberg was too hasty certainly in writing his letter; but, now you are parted, pardon me, my Prince, when I presume to recommend, that Schomberg may stand in your Royal Favour, as if he had never sailed with you; and that at some future day, you will serve him. There only wants this, to place your character in the highest point of views. None of us are without failings: Schomberg's was being rather too hasty; but that, put in competition with his being a good Officer, will not, I am bold to say, be taken in the scale against him.

I wish this matter could have settled on my Station, and I am sure your Royal Highness will join me when I acquaint you, that I have been reprimanded by the Admiralty for allowing your Royal Highness to proceed to America by way of Jamaica. More able friends than myself your Royal Highness may easily find, and of more consequence in the State: but one more attached and affectionate, is, I am bold to say, not so easily met with. Princes seldom, very seldom, find a disinterested person to communicate their thoughts to. I do not pretend to be otherwise: but of this truth be assured by a man who, I trust, never did a dishonourable act, that I am interested only that your Royal Highness should be the greatest and best man this Country ever produced. In full confidence of your belief of my sincerity, I take the liberty of saying, that having seen a few more years than yourself, I may in some respects know more of mankind. Permit me then to urge, a thorough knowledge of those you tell your mind to. Mankind are not always what they seem. Far, very far, be it from me to mean any person whom your Royal Highness thinks proper to honour with your confidence; but again let me impress on your Royal mind what I have before mentioned.

As to news; from a much better quarter, most probably you will be furnished with that. However, **Boreas** *is not paid off; but is kept in readiness to go to Sea with the Squadron at Spithead: but in my poor opinion, we shall go to no farther at present. The French have eight Sail in Brest Water, ready for Sea: therefore I think we shall not court the French out of Port. The Dutch business is becoming every day more serious; and I hardly think we can keep from a War without giving for ever the weight of the Dutch to the French, and allowing the Stadtholdership to be annihilated, – things which I should suppose hardly possible. I wrote to your Royal Highness, and sent a number of letters to Jamaica: Gardner, I am sure, will forward them. When I go to Town, I shall take care to be presented to his Majesty and the Prince of Wales, that I may be in the way of answering any question they may think proper to ask me. Nothing is wanting to make you the darling of the English Nation, but truth Sorry I am to say, much to the contrary has been dispersed. Lord Hood and the good Commissioner have made many inquiries about you.*
Permit me to subscribe myself,

Your Royal Highness's attached and affectionate,
Horatio Nelson.

❀ ❀ ❀

To William Locker, Esq., Kensington.

Portsmouth, August 12th, 1787.

My dear Sir,
It is not kind in one's Native air to treat a poor wanderer, as it has done me since my arrival. The rain and cold at first gave me a sore throat and its accompaniments: the hot weather has given me a slow fever, not absolutely bad enough to keep my bed, yet enough to hinder me from doing anything; and I could not have wrote a letter for the world; now the wind had set in to the Westward, and the air is cool, I am quite well again.

You have but too much cause to scold me for not writing, but all my other friends have the same cause, if that is any excuse. However, be assured that the things I have for you are perfectly safe, and although I may be careless in not writing, yet your former kindness to me is never out of my mind. Your sixty-gallon cask of rum is ready to go to the Custom-house whenever **Boreas** *goes up the River. I have a hogshead of Madeira, which I intend you shall have half of as soon as it can be drawn off. Tamarinds and noyeau I must get smuggled, for duty on the former is so enormous, that no person can afford the expense. The latter is not* *enterable. I shall send up by Clarke's waggon a dozen bottles of Veritable, for when we get to Woolwich, the Custom-House people will be so thick about us, and our time so short, that most probably I shall lose it – and it's invaluable. I will send you a line when it sets off, and it must take its chance. Kingsmill came, and staid a day or two here. I have not heard of him since he went away. He was fortunate in his wine; and I have given him a stock of rum, and a dozen noyeau.*

When Boreas *is to be paid off, seems as uncertain as ever. If we are to have a Bustle I do not want to come on shore; I begin to think I am fonder of the Sea than ever. Mrs. Nelson returns her best thanks for your kind inquiries; I shall have great pleasure in making her known to so valuable a friend, but she knows you already most perfectly. Charles Pole is gone to Southampton; he is perfectly well. I beg my compliments to the Bradleys, and my kind remembrances to your sons, and believe me to be ever,*

Your most affectionate,
Horatio Nelson.

❄❄❄

Poor old Nelson was feeling poorly – this is his second reference within a month to feeling ill. While the first mention was of a violent cold, this second is to a slow fever. This could have been an ague which was very common in Portsmouth because of the poor sanitation. Also known as intermittent fever, the symptoms of the ague were stages of feeling hot, then cold, then sweating, then a stage of remission.

A medical dictionary published in 1811 devoted two whole pages to the details of these fevers which were caused by, 'marsh miasma arising from stagnant water or marsh ground'. The dictionary adds that the putrefaction of vegetable and animal matter made the effluvia worse.

Brian Patterson in his work on the fortifications noted that, by the 1840s, Portsmouth was notorious for its poor sanitation which was partly caused by its being a fortified town. The town gates were closed from midnight until four in the morning forcing the night wagons full of the soil from the pits and cesspools of the town to wait several hours before they could leave. In addition, the effluvium from the moats, the Mill Dam and the Camber was very offensive, especially on warm nights.

Agues were very frequent: Dr Quarrier, the inspector general of naval hospitals was quoted as saying, '…recruits of the Royal Marines doing drill on Southsea Common would suddenly be seized with ague, and their firelocks (a type of musket) would fall from their uncertain grasp.'[2]

Portsmouth itself was not the only problem. J. R. Western in his study of the English Militia in the eighteenth century, described Hilsea Barracks in the north-west corner of Portsea Island as a veritable deathtrap. The barracks were low-lying and surrounded by salt springs. Further, in 1779, stagnant water covered most of one side of the buildings and only one of the two pumps produced water fit to drink.

It was said that better drains would make the place healthy, but a government surgeon admitted that everyone thereabouts was subject to intermittent fevers. As if that were not enough, twenty years earlier, in 1759, when Lord Oxford's Norfolk Regiment was sent there on its first call-out, it found the place infected with smallpox, the flux and putrid fever.[3]

Was there any cure for the ague? The 1811 dictionary refers to ague drops which were composed of arseniate of potash in a water solution and the use of Peruvian bark (quinine), which was considered to be very efficacious. Nelson himself makes no reference to taking any medicine and in fact attributes his feeling better to a change in wind direction.

The dictionary points out that a peculiarity of the fever is its susceptibility to renewal from very slight causes such as the prevalence of an easterly wind. Certainly, weather conditions in Portsmouth can be debilitating, as anyone who has been caught out on Southsea Common in the midst of a bitingly cold north-easterly wind and a hot sun can testify.

As for the noyeau, according to *Law's Grocer's Manual*, it was the stone of a fruit which was macerated in distilled spirit to make a sweet liqueur or cordial, which is presumably why duty was payable on it.

To Philip Stephens, Esq., Admiralty.

Boreas, *Portsmouth, August 17th, 1787.*

Sir,

I am this moment honoured with your letter of yesterday, wherein you acquaint me of their Lordships' surprise at finding William Clarke discharged from the Rattler *by my order, and desiring to know my reasons for giving the order. In return, I beg leave to acquaint you, that it was at the request of the poor man, backed by the desire of the deceased Captain Collingwood. I certainly thought it was proper, as I exactly followed the steps of the late Commander-in-Chief on the Leeward Island Station, in the case of William Ray, Seaman, deserter from the Unicorn.*

I had also always understood, that when a man was condemned to suffer death, he was from that moment dead in Law; and if he was pardoned, he became as a new man; and, there being no impress, he had the choice of entering or not his Majesty's Service. There was no want of a good man to supply his place.

If I have erred in discharging him, I am sorry; but I had at that time no doubts, as I conformed to the manner of the late Commander-in-Chief's treatment of a man in a similar situation; and I beg you will assure their Lordships, that I only wish to know the exact Rules of the Service in this respect, to have conformed most strictly to them.

I have the honour, &c.,
Horatio Nelson.

A New Church for Portsea

Left: While Captain Nelson was in Portsmouth on the *Boreas*, the foundation stone was being laid for the fourth Anglican church to be built on Portsea Island. This was the Church of St John the Evangelist and it was situated in Prince George Street, Portsea. Henry Slight notes that it was projected and erected by two eminent architects, John Munday and John Sheen but the design were prepared by Nicholas Vass junr, presumably. The church was consecrated by the Bishop of Winchester in 1789. (COURTESY OF PORTSMOUTH CITY MUSEUMS AND RECORDS SERVICE)

St John's stood for over 150 years but was eventually destroyed in the bombing of the Second World War. One of the many building in Portsmouth that Nelson might have seen but which we will never see – we have to rely on Henry Slight to describe it for us:

Externally it presents a fine elevation, the front embellished with a large Venetian window and fan-light over the entrance. The two stories on each side have each two elegant windows and wings containing the staircases; and there is a large clock and bell in a lofty and noble cupola above the grand entrance.

The interior is in the most florid and exquisite style of Venetian architecture. In four of the six compartments dividing the side-walls are four large sash-windows, both above and below; a spacious gallery, supported by small columns and enlightened by a large window, extends round three sides; the communion-table, which is of marble, is in a semicircular recess, separated by a screen of fluted Corinthian columns from the body of the church, and on each side are doors leading to the vestry and organ-gallery above, in which is a noble and costly instrument.

The recess is highly decorated in imitation of marble, and on the panels are appropriate scriptural texts &c. The cornices and panels are of stucco, and the arched ceiling is supported by four highly decorated Corinthian columns, with their acanthus, &c.: the highly finished cornices are exceedingly decorative and appropriate; while the splendid chandeliers, elegant pulpit and reading-desk, and the pews adorned with mahogany, render this fabric most impressive to every person of real taste. Attached is a commodious residence for the minister, in the same style of magnificent architecture.

INTERIOR. ST-JOHN'S CHURCH PORTSEA

Left: This photograph shows the interior in about the 1880s with the original box pews and a fine stained-glass window. In the destruction of St John's, Portsmouth obviously lost a fine Georgian church. The Vass family, father and son, have made a important, yet neglected, contribution to Portsmouth. At least one of their two churches, St George's, and the model dockyard stand as a memorial to their work. (COURTESY PORTSMOUTH MUSEUMS AND RECORDS SERVICE)

St Ann's – The Dockyard Church

On the other side of the wall in the dockyard another new church was being constructed. In 1785 it was decided to build a new residence for the commissioner of the yard in order that royalty could be appropriately entertained when they visited the dockyard. The site chosen for this was that of the chapel built in 1703. This building was demolished and the new Church of St Ann's completed in 1786. The architect was Mr Marquand, the admiralty surveyor of works, who was in charge of all the building within the dockyard.

It still stands today but during the Second World War it was badly damaged by bombing and when restored was 16 feet shorter than the original. St Ann's is the Parish Church of HM Naval Base and is staffed by chaplains. As John Winton says in his book on the naval heritage of Portsmouth, 'St Ann's is the perfect spiritual and architectural symbol of the Royal Navy's close links with the City of Portsmouth.'

In addition, a book of remembrance is maintained which lists the names of all those whose ashes have been committed to the deep in burials at sea in a consecrated area off Spithead since 1972.

Right: This photograph shows the west entrance with its portico. The architecture echoes the utilitarian elegance of the dockyard buildings, long and narrow with its stairs to the gallery enclosed inside instead of out. (COURTESY THE VERGER OF ST ANN'S CHURCH); AUTHOR'S PHOTOGRAPH, 2004)

Left: The interior. The east end has a large Venetian style window which makes the church light and airy. By the late 1780s, Baroque-style memento mori have been replaced by ornamental swags picked out in blue and gold and Greek oil lamps. The original box pews remain in the gallery but downstairs they have been replaced with a more modern design. (Courtesy the Verger of St Ann's Church); author's photograph, 2004)

Above right: St Ann's has many wall memorial tablets and this one provides another example of exquisite calligraphy in a Portsmouth church, this time by the famous twentieth century artist Eric Gill (1882–1940). Gill was a wood engraver, sculptor, letter designer and carver who created this plain-looking memorial tablet in 1937. As sculptor, he would have been a popular choice, as in the 1930s Gill was very fashionable and his spare, unfussy style merged in well with the eighteenth century tablets. It is the only inscription of his in Portsmouth.

The tablet, made of Portland stone, is dedicated to the memory of Sir John Donald Kelly, admiral of the fleet, who ended his career as commander in chief, Portsmouth on HMS *Victory*. At first glance, the tablet seems very unassuming but there is a lot more going on than meets the eye: four lines of capital letters in red at the top are followed by 17 lines of grey in raised lower case listing all his appointments.

Then an indentation, the pace changes; a change of colour to red and six lines of italics justified to the left. A further indentation to the right – a masterly pause – and then, '...where they would be'. (Courtesy the Verger of St Ann's Church); author's photograph, 2004)

Nelson is now to spend five years on half pay in England during the period of peace and the next letter from Portsmouth will not be for another five and a half years.

References
[1] *Mrs Jordan's Profession*, p.111.
[2] *A Military Heritage*, p.36.
[3] *The English Militia in the Eighteenth Century*, pp.383–384. I am indebted to Dr Val Fontana for this reference.

Chapter V

1793:
'THERE IS NO CERTAINTY IN WINDS AND WAVES'

The war with Revolutionary France has commenced and Nelson was given the command of the *Agamemnon* in January 1793 where he was to remain for three and a half years.

To Mrs. Nelson.

Spithead, April 29th, 1793.

We arrived at Spithead last night, and this morning have got my orders to go to Sea until the 4th of May, when I shall be at Portsmouth. Lord Hood will then be there, and it is now certain that I am going with him. We are all well: indeed, nobody can be ill with my Ship's company, they are so fine a set. Don't mind what newspapers say about us. God bless you.

Horatio Nelson.

❈❈❈

Spithead, April 30th, 1793.

We should have gone to Sea yesterday, but it blew so strong we could not get up our anchors, and to-day, unless the wind changes in the afternoon, we shall not get out to Sea, which is a great mortification to me; for something might be done, it we were at Sea, and I fear orders may come to stop us. I must be here on Sunday at the farthest, as Lord Hood sails, if the wind is fair, on Thursday, May 9th.

I am, &c.,
Horatio Nelson.

❈❈❈

To Mrs. Nelson.

Spithead, May 6th, 1793.

I arrived here last night, and rather expected to have seen you here; but Mr. Matcham told you right, there is no certainty in winds and waves. We had some blowing weather, but nothing for Agamemnon *to mind. We fell in with two French frigates, and two armed Vessels, who got into La Hogue harbour, where we could not follow for want of a pilot. I was again ordered to Sea this morning, but am now stopped, as my ship wants many things before she sails for the Mediterranean. Lord Hood is expected to-night. Maurice came to me, and it blew so hard I could not land him: he consequently went to Sea with us.*

Believe me, most affectionately yours,
Horatio Nelson.

❈❈❈

Fanny did eventually get to say goodbye to Nelson just before he left for the Mediterranean – this was one occasion at least when a member of Nelson's family was in Portsmouth. They said farewell to each other on 10 May 1793 and the *Agamemnon* sailed on 11 May: they would not meet again for four years. It was a more fateful parting than they knew, as by that time Nelson had met the love of his life, Lady Emma Hamilton (1765–1815), in Naples.

Chart of Spithead: By Heather and Williams Published on 1 December 1797

For Nelson, out of all the staging posts between London and the English Channel, the last two at sea were probably the most important. They were the anchorages at Spithead and St Helen's. There are more letters in this book addressed from these two anchorages than from Portsmouth itself, so what was their significance?

Firstly, Spithead. This was a stretch of water not only linked to Portsmouth Harbour by the deep water channel, but was also very extensive, measuring over three miles by eight. This allowed fleets and large numbers of transports and storeships to assemble without danger of collision. In addition, the Isle of Wight sheltered the area from south-westerly winds.

During the French Wars (1793–1815), when Portsmouth was the Royal Navy's principal naval base, Spithead functioned as the main anchorage for the Channel fleet. From here, as we can see from Nelson's letters, ships and convoys were despatched all over the world.

This sea chart produced in 1797 provides an opportunity to look at the anchorages in detail. It had been produced by William Heather (fl. 1740–1812) who had set up as a publisher and dealer in charts and nautical instruments at 157 Leadenhall Street, London, under the sign of the 'Little Midshipman' in 1765. During the next forty years he produced a series of important sea charts and pilot-guides.

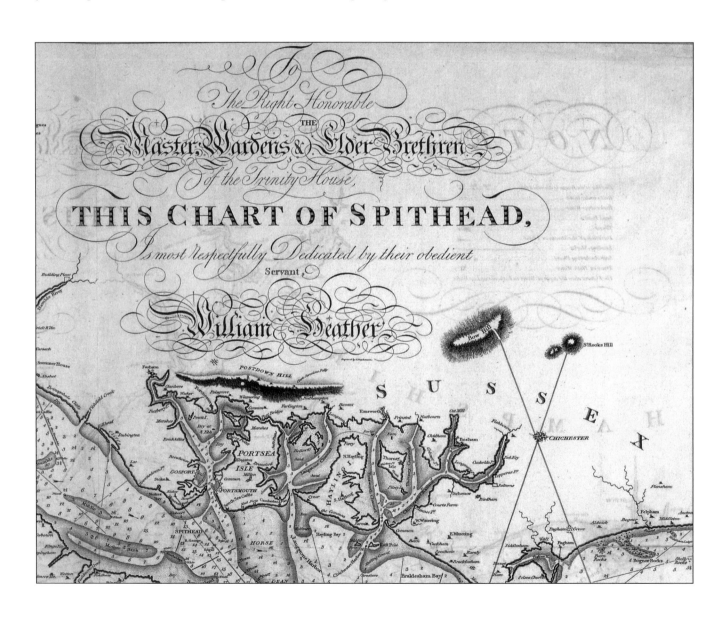

In spite of the work of Murdoch Mackenzie, a state hydrographic service was not set up until 1795 so, during the eighteenth century, ships of the Royal Navy were forced to rely on privately published charts both British and foreign. Nelson himself used French charts on board HMS *Victory* but despite the fact that the sea chart was an indispensable tool of his trade, there is no separate collection of charts that can be attributed to his use.

In contrast to the plain admiralty charts, Heather's privately published chart included an elaborate decorated title and a dedication to the master wardens and elder brethren of the Trinity House. Trinity House was the royally approved pilotage authority and professional body which had been set up by charter in 1514. (COURTESY ROYAL NAVAL MUSEUM)

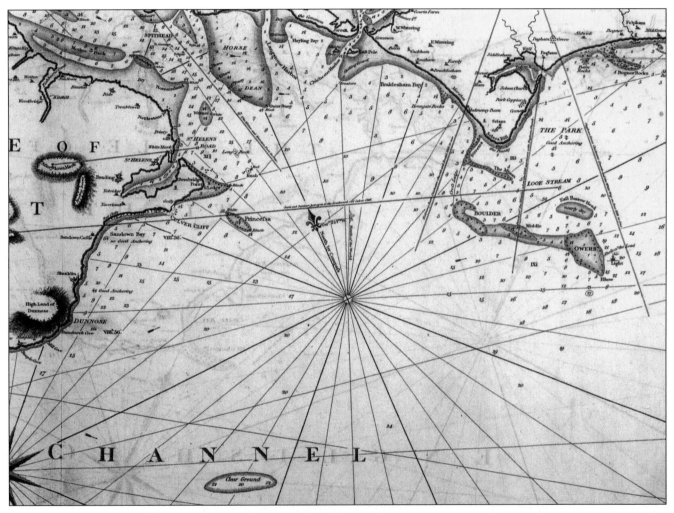

This segment of the chart shows Spithead, the Mother Bank, St Helen's Road and part of the Isle of Wight – all parts of the Solent that Nelson would have been very familiar with, perhaps more so than the surrounding land. The chart is very informative, for example, Sandown Bay has the legend, 'No good anchoring', while Shanklin has 'Good anchoring'. As in the 1766 chart the depths are shown in fathoms. (COURTESY ROYAL NAVAL MUSEUM)

The Ashey Down Seamark

The rhumb-lines link up two well known Isle of Wight landmarks that Nelson would have known and are still used as navigational sea marks today. Firstly, the Ashey Down Sea Mark, which is situated on the highest point of Ashey Down just off the road to Yarbridge near Brading. This is a truncated pyramid of hewn stone about twenty feet high with the apex obliquely cut off. The lower part is painted black and the upper part white to make it more visible against the countryside. It was constructed in 1735 at public expense. (AUTHOR'S PHOTOGRAPH, 2004)

The pyramid has a carving inset into one side with the inscription GR II and date, 1735. (AUTHOR'S PHOTOGRAPH, 2004)

This picturesque vista is by George Brannon (1784–1860), the well-known artist, engraver and author who lived on the Isle of Wight and produced many such scenes of it between 1820 and 1860. He also published a series of local guide books. Although this engraving is dated May 1, 1840, over forty years after the sea chart, we can catch a glimpse of the view as it was in the eighteenth century and in fact, is hardly altered today. (AUTHOR'S COLLECTION)

The Semaphore Station

However, Ashey Down sea mark was not just a scenic attraction. A vital part of Nelson's Portsmouth was communications and for this, Portsmouth has to be considered in conjunction with the Isle of Wight. During the wars with France, Ashey had a very important role to play, as the Navy built four semaphore stations at key high points on the Isle of Wight. Their job was to relay to the admiral at Portsmouth via the station on the Square Tower, the details of all the shipping seen off the island with the final messages all passing through Ashey.

Another lovely rural vista from George Brannon dated May 20, 1839, shows the sea mark from Newchurch. This time he adds in the signal station itself, which was a small, two-roomed building with an adjoining shed in which the signalling tackle was kept. Near the signal house was set a topmast and a topgallant mast of a man-of-war, with a yard crossing them and set on an east-west axis.

The signals were made by raising a certain number of balls at the ends of the yard and sometimes by hoisting a flag at the end of the topgallant mast. The station was considered to be a naval station and was always manned by a lieutenant, a midshipman and two seaman.

The signal masts were carefully set on the Portsmouth side of the seamark to leave clear visibility, giving the commander at Portsmouth a full picture of all the shipping movements within sight of the island. Messages could get through to Portsmouth in less than thirty minutes even from the cliffs overlooking the Needles, the most distant station.

Eventually though, the signal station became redundant when semaphore was replaced by telegraphy and then radio. The sea mark stolidly stands there still, rather like a stone milestone on a busy modern motorway, reminding us of a slower and more ancient way of life.[1] (AUTHOR'S COLLECTION)

The White Mark at St Helen's

The second navigational aid that Nelson would have known is the White Mark at St Helen's. This is shown in another fine view from George Brannon. The White Mark is actually one side of the ruins of the old church tower on the shore which is painted white to act as a sea mark. This engraving is dated 16 June 1839.

Brannon's depiction of the woodland reaching right down to the shore though, is not just an artistic device to make a pretty picture. St Helen's was the second anchorage to be used by the Royal Navy and was renowned for its safety and shelter which was provided by the trees.

After assembling at Spithead, ships would move down to St Helen's to wait for suitable winds and tides before setting off on their main departure route which was southwest around the point of St Helen's. It was here, for example, that HMS *Victory* waited for Nelson to embark from Portsmouth in 1805 before leaving to join Vice-Admiral Collingwood's fleet at Cadiz.

St Helen's itself developed as a victualling depot, supplying beef, mutton, poultry, eggs, beer and in particular, sweet drinking water. The spring water of St Helen's was valued for its property to stay fresh on long voyages while other water went stagnant. One disadvantage of the presence of the Navy was visits from the pressgang, but the resourceful locals would fire a cannon from the old Watch House as a warning to fishermen and farmers of its presence.[2] (AUTHOR'S COLLECTION)

The scene is very similar today but with only one ship on the horizon: people still walk along the shore line and further on is a pleasant, secluded beach. The Victorian St Helen's Fort can be seen in the distance. (AUTHOR'S PHOTOGRAPH, 2000)

References
[1] *Isle of Wight Curiosities*, p.94.
[2] *Diamond Coast*, pp.102-103.

Chapter VI

1798:
'THE TIMES ARE BIG WITH EVENTS'

Since his last letter from Portsmouth in 1793 Nelson had been promoted to commodore in 1796 and rear admiral in 1797. The Battle of Cape St Vincent on 14 February 1797 had made him a hero for which he received the Knight of the Bath with the right to style himself Sir Horatio Nelson. On 24 July 1797 however, he suffered a defeat at Tenerife in the Canary Islands and the loss of his right arm. Nelson was sent home on half pay to recover.

The arm took longer to heal than expected, but eventually Nelson was able to join the *Vanguard* in March 1798 as rear admiral. He prepared to go to the Mediterranean with orders to destroy a French expeditionary force under the command of Napoleon Bonaparte.

***

To Evan Napean. Esq., Secretary to the Admiralty.

Vanguard, *Spithead, 29th March, 1798. Wind N.N.E.*

Sir,

There being twenty-five men at the Hospital, who cannot return to the Ship before she proceeds to sea, nor can they be 'DSQ', (Discharged to Sick Quarters), they not having been twenty-eight days at the Hospital, and also five or six men absent without leave, who cannot be 'Run' on the Ship's Books, not having been absent three musters; therefore I beg leave to observe that after the Ship has been a few days at sea she will be considerably short of complement. I have therefore to request that their Lordships will be pleased to order the same number of men as will be left on shore, in order that she may sail with her numbers complete.

I am, Sir, &c.,

Horatio Nelson.

***

To the Reverend Mr. Nelson, Hilborough.

Portsmouth, March 31st, 1798.

My dear Brother,

You will not, I hope, attribute my not answering your two letters to any other cause than that of really being hurried by my approaching departure. I participate in your sorrow at G. Thurlow's deficiency of rent, and his determination to give up the farm, but all landlords are at times plagued with their tenants. In short, the times are big with events, and before the year gets round we shall either have a good Peace, or what I dread to think on. But God's will be done. The wind is fair: in two hours I shall be on board, and with the lark I shall be off to-morrow morning; therefore I have only time to say God bless you and yours, and ever believe me,

Yours most affectionately,

Horatio Nelson.

***

To Lady Collier,

Vanguard. *St Helen's, April 8th, 1798.*

Dear Madam,

I am only this moment favoured with your letter of the 2nd, the weather having prevented our communicating with the shore. You may rely that your son shall spend as little as possible, for he will be a very lucky fellow if he gets on shore twice in a year. With every sentiment of respect, believe me,

Your Ladyship's most obedient servant.
Horatio Nelson.

I beg my best respects to Mrs. Mills: desire her to remember my advice; it may do good, and cannot be hurtful. The more I see, the more necessary to follow my advice.

❋❋❋

To John Locker, Esq.,

St Helen's, 8th April, 1798

My dear Sir,
It as only last night that I was favoured with your letter of the 4th, it having blown so strong as to prevent all intercourse with the shore.

Captain Faddy is embarked in the Ship, and assure your good father of my attention to whoever he recommends. Captain F. appears a very good kind of man. Captain Berry has taken his son on board.

I am sorry to hear that your father's head yet troubles him, but I hope that he and you will very soon recover. I am fast tied with the wind at S.W., and likely to continue. I beg my kindest remembrances to your good father, sister, and brothers, and believe me ever yours most affectionately,

Horatio Nelson.

❋❋❋

To William Suckling, Esq.,

St Helen's, April 9, 1798.

My dear Sir,
I cannot quit England without thanking you and Mrs. Suckling for the great kindness you both have shewn to my dear wife and myself; and, [from] my heart, I wish you health and every other blessing; and I hope soon to meet you in Peace. With my kindest respects to Mrs. Suckling and all your family, believe me,

Yours most obliged and affectionate Nephew,
Horatio Nelson.

The Battle of the Nile came four months later on 1 August. Nelson and his fleet destroyed the French force in Aboukir Bay in a decisive victory which gave him instant popular fame and ensured that he was known as the Hero of the Nile from then on. He was wounded in this battle too and lost the sight of his right eye. Rather than return to England to recover, this time he went to Naples and stayed with Sir William (1731–1803) and Emma Hamilton until they were all recalled home in 1800.

Some months later, Captain William Locker died on 26 December 1800: with him went the end of the eighteenth century. Nelson had lost an important mentor of twenty-three years standing whom he had last seen in July 1797. He had hoped to see him again before his death but that was never possible. The next day, Nelson sent his son a letter of condolence, the absolute model of what such a letter should be:

27 December 1800.

My dear John,
From my heart do I condole with you on the great and irreparable loss we have all sustained in the death of your dear worthy father – a man whom to know was to love, and those who had only heard of him, honoured. The greatest 'earthly' consolation to us his friends that remain, is that he has left a character for honour and honesty which none can surpass, and very, very few attain. That the posterity of the righteous will prosper, we are taught to believe, and on no occasion can it be more truly verified than from my dear much lamented friend, and that it may be realized in you, your sisters and brothers, is the fervent prayer of
My dear John, your afflicted friend,
Nelson.

Nelson also attended his funeral in Greenwich. One of Nelson's attributes was the ability to attract and retain father figures to him. First of all his uncle, Maurice Suckling, then Captain Locker and last of all Sir William Hamilton, who regarded him as a son.

Strangely enough, Nelson's own father was actually alive during all this time and did not die until 1802, just three years before Nelson. Having lost his mother at the age of nine and one of a large family, perhaps in reality these mentors were mother figures who could provide Nelson with unconditional love and support.

A year later in a conflict with the Baltic States, Nelson won another victory at the Battle of Copenhagen on 2 April 1801. Returning home in the July, he was appointed commander in chief of a fleet of over one hundred vessels in the Channel with the mission of defending the south coast from attack.

By October 1801 the threat from France had receded and he was able to join the Hamiltons at the house in Merton, south-west London, that Emma Hamilton had found for him. There are no more letters now from Portsmouth until 1803.

The Floating Prison

Returning to the question of the French prisoners of war who had to be accommodated during the Napoleonic Wars, one answer had been to put them in fortified shore establishments such as Portchester Castle. Another solution was the use of prison hulks which were moored in the harbour to prevent the prisoners from escaping. They were old vessels of two or three decks and to ensure that they could not be sailed anywhere, the masts were taken out and anchors used to keep them in place.

These hulks were a prominent feature of Portsmouth Harbour between 1797 and 1817 and would have been very familiar to Nelson. They are sparsely documented though, probably because as soon as the Napoleonic wars ended the vessels were broken up and the prisoners sent home.

This view of them was painted by Ambroise-Louis Garneray, known as Louis Garneray (1783–1857), a prisoner who wrote an account of his nine years' captivity from 1806 to 1815. Garneray was also a marine artist who painted a number of views of the hulks, but unfortunately, did not sign or date his early work.

To us, they appear as a rather pleasant seascape, but this impression belies their reality to someone who was to be a prisoner in them. Garneray was to be imprisoned on the *Prothee*, a French ship captured in 1780, which was used a prison between 1795 and 1815. He describes his first reaction to it:

Seen from afar, anchored in a line with eight other floating prisons at the mouth of the Portchester River, her shapeless black hulk resembled an immense sarcophagus.

Once on board:

I sustained a fearful shock when I was led between files of soldiers on the deck and found myself brutally tossed into the midst of the Prothee's *miserable and hideous inhabitants. No description however forceful, no pen however powerful, could describe the spectacle that suddenly met my gaze.*

Imagine a generation of the dead coming forth from their graves, their eyes sunken, their faces haggard and wan, their backs bent, their beards wild, their bodies terrifyingly thin and scarcely covered by tattered yellow rags, and still you have no more than a feeble and incomplete idea of how my companions in misfortune appeared.[1]

At one point Garneray and a companion tried to escape, thinking it would be a simple matter to dive overboard, swim to the shore and make their escape. However, they were reckoning without the mud in Portsmouth Harbour which formed a most effective prison wall. Their efforts to swim or wade ashore through the mud exhausted them so in the end they climbed aboard a Danish ship.

The captain considers England to be his country's ally and returns Garneray to the prison hulk. His companion is not so lucky and is found lying dead in the mud the next day. The mud of Portsmouth Harbour still claims its victims today when people having waded out at low water, misjudge the speed of the incoming tide and find themselves stranded.[2]

Life in the prison hulks did not exist independently of life in Portsmouth and Gosport. Far from concerning themselves about the conditions on the hulks, local traders regarded the prisoners as a lucrative source of income. Conversely, local people were an important source of income for the prisoners too, as they had no other means of support. Garneray, for example, got quite a nice little business going by selling his paintings to dealers from Portsmouth.

Entertainments were also held on the hulks, for example there was a boxing match between prisoners which was considered a great draw. It was attended by fashionable local people who came over in boatloads, including, according to Garneray, 'Several English ladies rigged out with the startling splendour and vile taste that are so essentially British'. (© National Maritime Museum, London, Ref. No.: BHC 1923)

A closer view of a prison ship by E. W. Cooke, showing the convicts being taken aboard. The prisoners' washing hung out to dry is a poignant domestic detail. (© National Maritime Museum, London, Ref. No.: PW 3148)

St Helen's Road, Spithead, Portsmouth and Langstone Harbours

This segment is part of a sea chart which was surveyed in 1783 by Lieutenant Murdoch Mackenzie junr (1743–1829), who had succeeded his uncle Mackenzie senr as admiralty surveyor in 1771. It shows Portchester and the castle very clearly facing the channel of deeper water known as Portchester Lake. At the lower edge of the map is Portsmouth Dockyard and on the left, Gosport and Elson.

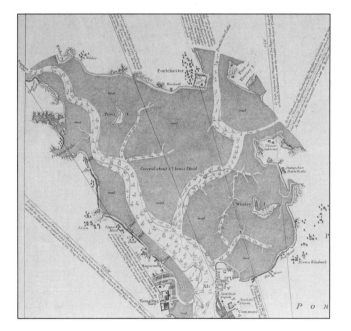

The prison hulks were probably moored in Portchester Lake and Mackenzie has labelled very clearly the mud which surrounded them on all sides. If by chance any prisoner did get through, they would then have to contend with the armed guards at the castle.

The *Universal Magazine* attributed the development of Portsmouth itself to the fact that the northern reaches of the harbour had begun to silt up:

There was anciently a small castle and a town called Port-Peris or Portchester... but the sea retiring from it the inhabitants followed and built the town of Portsmouth which is said to be the only regular fortification in Britain and the key of England.

(© National Maritime Museum, London, Ref. No.: FOO90)

References
[1] *The Floating Prison*, p.5.
[2] A report in *The News* on 25 May 2004 describes the rescue of a man stranded waist-deep in mud about 400 metres off Priddy's Hard, near Elson, Gosport, who had been trying to reach a moored dinghy. The Solent Coastguard was alerted and the man winched to safety by helicopter from a rising tide.

Chapter VII

1803: 'THAT HORRID PLACE PORTSMOUTH'

Nelson had been promoted to vice-admiral in 1801 but it was not until war with France broke out again in May 1803 that he was given his most important appointment, the command of the Mediterranean fleet. A month earlier, on 6 April 1803, Nelson had experienced another personal loss when Sir William Hamilton died in London with him and Lady Hamilton at his side. However, his death did release them to live more freely as a couple.

Nelson left Merton to take up his command, taking the post-chaise to Portsmouth to join the fleet at four o'clock in the morning of 18 May 1803. In a note to Lady Hamilton he commented that, 'Either my ideas are altered or Portsmouth. It is a place, the picture of desolation and misery but perhaps it is the contrast to what I have been used to'.

To Sir Evan Nepean, Bart., Admiralty.

Portsmouth, 18th May, 1803.

Sir,

You will be pleased to acquaint the Lords Commissioners of the Admiralty, that I arrived here about one o'clock this afternoon, and have hoisted my Flag on board his Majesty's Ship Victory. *Captain Sutton informs me that she will be in every respect ready for sea on Friday morning. I am, &c.,*

Nelson and Bronte.

❋❋❋

To Admiral The Earl of St Vincent, K.B.,

May 18th, 3 P. M. (1803)

My dear Lord,

As the Victory *will be ready, Captain Sutton tells me, to sail on Friday morning at daylight, (and I am trying to make that to-morrow night,) I have, on many accounts, thought it best to hoist my Flag in her. If Admiral Cornwallis wants her – which is very improbable according to what I have heard – but if he does, I shall remove nothing from the Frigate but my cot: and, therefore, be gone in five minutes. You may rely, my dear Lord, that nothing shall be left undone by me, by a vigorous and active exertion of the force under my command, to bring about a happy Peace. I am ever my dear Lord, your most obliged and faithful,*

Nelson and Bronte.

❋❋❋

To Admiral The Earl of St Vincent, K.B.,

May 19th, 1803.

My dear Lord,

This will be presented to you by my nephew, Sir William Bolton, and now he stands in so near a situation to me, it must be my anxious wish to get him employed, and with me, and promoted. If the Devil stands at the door, the Victory *shall sail to-morrow forenoon. Keep your health, my dear Lord, and ever believe me your most obliged and affectionate,*

Nelson and Bronte.

❋❋❋

To the Right Honourable Admiral Lord Gardner Commander-in-Chief at Portsmouth.

May 20th, 1803, 3 P. M.

My dear Lord,

However I felt on reading the order you showed me this morning, yet I am not of a disposi-

tion to complain; for if I got safe to the Mediterranean, my mind was made up to dismantle some Ship of War, for I believe the honour of the Country ought not to be risked by having the Victory *half manned. But the more I felt, the more truly am I sensible of your Lordship's goodness; and thanking you sincerely, and wishing you, my dear Lord, health and happiness, believe me your much obliged and obedient servant,*

Nelson and Bronte.

❈ ❈ ❈

To Admiral the Earl of St Vincent, K.B.,

May 20th, 1803.

My dear Lord,
You may rely that I shall be off Brest as expeditiously as possible, and there wait for Admiral Cornwallis. I am mad at losing a moment of this wind, but I cannot help myself. She is to be paid at eight o-clock, and I shall be on board at nine. Ever, my dear Lord, yours most faithfully.

Nelson and Bronte.

Many thanks for your kind letter by the Post. May every blessing attend you, and may we soon met in Peace.

❈ ❈ ❈

To Sir Evan Nepean, Bart., Admiralty.

Victory, at Spithead, 20th May 1803.

Sir,
I was honoured with your letter, sent by a Messenger at half-past four yesterday, at half-past one this morning; and I beg leave to assure you that I hold it impossible for any Officer, under such orders as their Lordships' to me, to designedly miss Admiral Cornwallis off Brest. Their Lordships may rely on my strict obedience to their orders, and I rely with confidence on their liberal constructions of my actions. The Victory *shall sail the moment she is paid. I have the honour to be, &c.,*

Nelson and Bronte.

❈ ❈ ❈

In quite a different vein to his formal correspondence, on 20 May 1803, Nelson also wrote a letter from HMS *Victory* to Lady Hamilton, a copy of part of which is displayed in The Lady Hamilton, a pub on the Hard. He writes:

My Dearest Emma, you will believe that although I am glad to leave that horrid place Portsmouth yet being afloat makes me now feel that we do not tread the same element. I felt from my soul but God is good and in his due wisdom will unite us...

Merton Place

Nelson has referred indirectly to his house in Merton but where exactly was it? Martyn Downer in his book on Nelson's purse describes it as being situated in, 'The golden triangle of gentlemen's villas west of London': the three points of the triangle being formed by Merton, Wimbledon and Morden in south west London.

So what was golden about them? Located about seven miles away from central London, Merton in the seventeenth century was not just another collection of streets in the conurbation of outer London that it is today. To the wealthy London merchants and officials it was an ideal place for their country retreats and residences as it was near enough to reach London quickly but far enough away to seem like the country.

More country houses were built in the eighteenth century, in particular, Spring House which was built in 1726 and was occupied by James Lackington, a well-to-do London bookseller in 1791. Its location was known as upper Merton, 'The most rural village in Surrey.' It was very fashionable at the time to refer to these estates as 'Paradise', a surprising description for anyone familiar with this part of south-west London today. For example, the Dukes of Devonshire used Chiswick as a place for peace and relaxation and for Duchess Georgiana it was 'earthly paradise'.

In 1801, Nelson purchased what was to be his paradise, Merton Place and its surrounding estate, which is thought to have been built in the beginning of the eighteenth century and which cost him £9000. The surveyor summed the house up, 'In short, it is altogether the worst place under all its circumstances that I ever saw pretending to suit a Gentleman's family.'

Nelson bought it anyway, on the grounds that he could not afford anything larger. It may also be that the fact that it has a similar name to Merton Hall, near Norwich in Norfolk, not far from his birthplace and the seat of the de Grey family for 650 years, appealed to his desire for social standing.[1] In addition, it was a fashionable place to live and there were members of the aristocracy in the vicinity.

However, Sir William Hamilton, who of course lived in the house with Nelson and Lady Hamilton until his death in 1803, liked the house. He wrote to Nelson on 16 October 1801:

The proximity to the capital and the perfect retirement of this place, are for your Lordship, two points beyond estimation; but the house is so comfortable, the furniture clean and good, and I never saw so many conveniences united in so small a compass. You have nothing but to come and enjoy immediately.[2]

In addition, Nelson liked to entertain on a large scale and have members of his family to stay. The nearness of London meant that the more luxurious items required by the household which could not be obtained in the small village of Merton could be brought by the servants from stores in the capital, as was the practice in the large houses nearby.[3]

Nelson was to own the house for four years from 1801 until his death and his estate was eventually to cover over 160 acres in the parishes of Merton, Wimbledon and Mitcham. Merton itself though, was not to last much longer as a rural paradise. Nelson knew it in the last years of its heyday and must have thought that it would be there for ever.

However, its very success was to lead to its downfall. After Lady Hamilton had sold the house and estate in 1809, fashions changed and the Georgian rural paradise gave way to suburban development. Developers eventually took the opportunity to break up the estate to build housing and the house itself was finally demolished by

1823. A development grew up called Nelson's Fields consisting of narrow roads, cramped houses and small businesses. The coming of the railway in the 1860s finally completed its transformation into a London suburb.

Several pictures were produced of the house between 1804 and 1806. This one shows the north façade with its classical details. It is from an engraving by W. Angus which was published on 1 March 1804 after a painting by Edward Hawke Locker (1777–1849), a commissioner of Greenwich Hospital. As the youngest son of Captain William Locker RN, he was not only to write about his father's relationship with Nelson but was also to paint his house.

Locker's picture includes all the elements one would expect in a picturesque eighteenth century rural vista, an elegant house in a woodland setting; a narrow river with the ornamental, Italianate bridge across it emphasising its width; a fisherman under the trees; an attractive group in the foreground, two children and their pet dog, the gardener with his besom and the strong temptation for the viewer to identify the woman as Lady Hamilton.

In reality, the surveyor of the estate described the river as, 'a dirty black looking canal or rather a broad ditch, which keeps the whole place damp'. Nelson wanted to fill it in but Lady Hamilton considered it to be a feature of the garden and called it 'The Nile' after Nelson's victory in Aboukir Bay. (COURTESY OF MERTON LIBRARIES AND HERITAGE SERVICES)

Merton's Other Admiral – Rear Admiral Isaac Smith (1753–1831)

Nelson was not the only seafaring man to make his home in Merton. Dawn Muirhead, a member of the Merton Historical Society points out that Smith was a close neighbour of Nelson's: five years older, he survived him for many years. He spent his summers in Abbey Gate House, a building which is also now demolished, with his brother Charles.

Smith had joined the Navy in 1766 aged 13 and had sailed with Captain Cook on his first and second voyages between 1768 and 1775, having previously demonstrated his mapping ability. Later he fought in the West Indies and served in the East India station. He retired on health grounds in 1807 and died in 1831.

Admiral Smith's tomb stands outside St Mary's Parish Church in Merton Park and inside a marble monument commemorates the Smith brothers, their nephew Isaac Cragg Smith and his wife Caroline (née Wyatt). At the time of writing, it is not known how much contact, if any, the admiral would have had with the Nelson household during his life. In death, however, his funeral hatchment hangs inside the church alongside those of Nelson and Sir William Hamilton.[4]

References

[1] *The Character of Horatio Nelson; A Note*, p.50.
[2] *A History of Lord Nelson's Merton Place*, p.8.
[3] *The Marquess of Rockingham's House in Wimbledon*, p.259.
[4] *Merton Historical Society, Bulletin No.153*, March 2005, p.5.

Chapter VIII

August 1805:
'THIS IS THE FIRST TIME I HAVE BEEN IN QUARANTINE'

Just over two years later we are now on the count-down to Trafalgar. Napoleon by this stage, was hoping to launch an invasion of Britain by joining forces with the Spanish fleet. Meanwhile, Nelson had been blockading the French fleet in harbour but eventually, it evaded him and tried to escape to the West Indies.

That plan was foiled however, and Nelson drove them back to European waters. Sensing a respite in the conflict he returned to England to recuperate. Nicolas included a chronological analysis of Nelson's life which allows us to follow the events of the next two months as they unfold:

August 1st: Vice-Admiral of the White, with his Flag in the Victory, *on his passage to Ushant from Gibraltar, after returning from the pursuit of the French Fleet to the West Indies.*
August 15th: Off Ushant, joined the Channel Fleet under Admiral Cornwallis, and proceeded to Spithead accompanied by the Superb.
August 17th: Anchored at Dunose [off the Isle of Wight.]
August 18th: Anchored at Spithead.

❄❄❄

To William Marsden, Esq., Admiralty.

Victory, *at Spithead, 18th August, 1805.*
Sir,
You will be pleased to acquaint the Lords Commissioners of the Admiralty, that on the evening of the 15th inst. I joined the Honourable Admiral Cornwallis off Ushant, with His Majesty's Ships named in the margin (Victory, Canopus, Superb, Spencer, Belleisle, Spartiate, Conqueror, Tigre, Leviathan, Donegal, Swiftsure); *that on doing so I received an order from him to proceed immediately with the* Victory *and* Superb *to Spithead, where I arrived this morning.*

I enclose for their Lordships' information, a duplicate list of the state of the Ships therein mentioned, the original of which I transmitted to Admiral Cornwallis, not having the honour of paying my respects to him, as he was good enough (being the close of the day when we joined) to end me his order by one of the Cutters, with a request that I would not think of coming out of the Victory *at that time of night, but proceed as before mentioned. The Companies of the* Victory *of* Superb *are in most perfect health, and only require some vegetables and other refreshments to remove the scurvy.*

I am, Sir, &c.,
Nelson and Bronte.

❄❄❄

To William Marsden, Esq., Admiralty.

Victory, *at Spithead, 18th August, 1805.*
Sir,
You will herewith receive an account of specie on board His Majesty's Ships named in the margin, found in the Military chests belonging to the Regiment of Castile, and on board the several detained Spanish Merchant Vessels mentioned in the said list, which you will be pleased to lay before the Lords Commissioners of the Admiralty, that such directions may be given about its disposal on the arrival of the Ships in Port, which it is on board of, as their

Lordships shall think proper. At the same time you will be pleased to acquaint their Lordships that the uncertainty of any of the Squadron (late under my command) returning to England, prevented me from ordering the specie to be put on board the Superb, which otherwise was my intention.

I am, Sir, &c.,
Nelson and Bronte.

P.S. – The 6808 dollars taken out of a Spanish Vessel by the Spencer, were supplied to the respective Captains, being in distress for money, and for which my Secretary, Mr. Scott, has their bills and receipts, and will deliver them when directed.

❄❄❄

To William Marsden, Esq., Admiralty.

Victory, at Spithead, 18th August 1805.

Sir,

I must beg you will be good enough to recommend James Marguette [Pilot], the bearer hereof, mentioned in my letter in original and duplicate dated the 10th ult., to their Lordships' kind attention. He is a most valuable and useful man as a Pilot for the Leeward Islands, and very handsomely volunteered his services to me, as mentioned in my said letters; and as he is a prefect stranger in London, and consequently will be apt to be imposed upon, I must beg that he may be taken particular care of, and put in a way for a speedy passage to Barbadoes. I have paid him, as per Certificate from the Captain of the Victory, at the rate of 5s. per day, from the 14th of June to the date hereof, as he has no money to defray his expenses during his stay in England; and beg, if their Lordships consider him entitled to more, that they will be so good as order him to be paid; and also furnish him with such a further sum as they may think proper, to defray his expenses, and be some compensation for the inconvenience and loss he may sustain in the absence from his home. I must also beg, when their Lordships order him a passage in any of His Majesty's Ships, that they will be pleased to direct him to be borne as a Pilot, that he may receive the allowance as such till he arrives at Barbadoes.

I am, Sir, &c.,
Nelson and Bronte.

❄❄❄

To the Collector of the Customs, or those it may concern.

The Victory, with the Fleet under my command, left Gibraltar twenty-seven days ago, at which time there was not a fever in the Garrison, nor, as Doctor Fellows told me, any apprehension of one.

The Fleet late under my command I left on August 15th with Admiral Cornwallis, at which time they were in the most perfect health. Neither the Victory, or the Superb, have on board even an object for the Hospital, to the truth of which I pledge my word of honour.

Nelson and Bronte.

❄❄❄

To William Marsden, Esq., Admiralty,

Victory, at Spithead, 18th August, 1805.

Sir,

I herewith transmit you, for the information of the Lords Commissioners of the Admiralty, a letter from Captain Hardy of the Victory, with the one therein alluded to from the Surgeon of the said Ship, representing the very bad state of Captain Hardy's health, and the necessity of his being permitted to go on shore for a shore time, for the recovery thereof. I also enclose you a letter from the Physician of the Mediterranean Fleet on the above subject; and as my personal knowledge of these facts, as well as the reluctance with which Captain Hardy is under in making this application, I have to beg you will be pleased to move the Lords Commissioners of the Admiralty to grant that valuable Officer such indulgence of absence as they shall think proper, for the recovery of his health.

I am, sir, &c.,
Nelson and Bronte.

To Alexander Davison, Esq.,
My dear Davison,
You will have heard before I write this line, that the Victory *is at Spithead. I hope we are not to be put in Quarantine; for we have neither sick, or have had in the Fleet. Neither this Ship, or* Superb, *which is come with me, have one man to send to the Hospital. You will have felt, I am sure, for all my ill-luck, or rather d-n General Brereton. As I shall see you very soon, I will only say that I am as ever, my dear Davison. Your most obliged and faithful friend,*

Nelson and Bronte.

August 19th: Nelson moved to the Motherbank.

To William Marsden, Esq., Admiralty.

Victory, *Motherbank, August 19th, 1805.*

My dear Sir,
I am much obliged by your kind letter of yesterday, and the inclosure; this is the first time in my life that I have been in Quarantine. We are now out twenty-eight days; and the most rigorous in the Mediterranean for a Ship of War, is only twenty days from our last communication with an unhealthy place, if the Ship is healthy. I shall see you as soon as I can, and thank you for your mind attentions. Ever, my dear Sir, your obliged

Nelson and Bronte.

❈ ❈ ❈

To Captain Keats, H.M. Ship Superb.

Victory, *August 19th, 1805.*

My dear Keats,
I would not ask you to dine here yesterday, as we were to move just at dinner time. I have made the signal for the Cutter's boat under whose orders we are, to know if we may communicate: if he says 'Yes,' I will hoist the Assent *and* Superb's *Pendants; if 'No,' the Negative. If we can communicate, I shall expect of course to see you, and to stay dinner. I do not expect* Pratique *before to-morrow. Ever yours faithfully,*

Nelson and Bronte.

Nelson struck his flag and went to Merton; he lived principally at Merton, but occasionally in London.

He was to have just 25 days in England from 20 August to 14 September 1805.

Chapter IX

September 1805:
'BUT MY FATE IS FIXED AND I AM GONE'

The period of respite was short lived. A fleet was to be assembled to attack the combined fleets of the French and Spanish which was sheltering in Cadiz and Nelson was ordered to take command of it. His priority now was to travel to Portsmouth, embark on the *Victory*, sail to Cadiz to join the main fleet and prepare for battle.

Nicholas continues his chronology:

September 2nd: Informed at Merton by the Hon. Captain Blackwood, that the Combined Fleet had put into Cadiz. Ordered to resume the command of the Mediterranean Fleet.

September 13th: Left Merton.

At some point on the journey Nelson wrote in his diary:

Friday night at half-past ten drove from dear, dear Merton, where I left all which I hold dear in this world, to go to serve my King and country. May the Great God Whom I adore enable me to fulfil the expectations of my Country and if it is His good pleasure that I should return, my thanks will never cease being offered up to the throne of His Mercy. If it is His good providence to cut short my days upon Earth, I bow with the greatest submission relying that He will protect those so dear to me that I may leave behind.
His Will be done.
Amen. Amen. Amen.

The Last Journey

Nelson obviously regarded this journey from Merton to Portsmouth as momentous as it turned out to be, so is it possible to recreate it and visualise where he went at each stage? Firstly, his departure from Merton. One of the criticisms made by the surveyor of his estate was that the land was entirely detached by the Turnpike Road and was surrounded by public roads possessing not the least privacy.

For Nelson, who had no time to spare, this proximity to the main road was the great advantage of the estate and the turnpike was exactly opposite the drive. Judith Goodman of Merton Historical Society who has studied Nelson's journey from Merton Place, believes that the entrance gate to the house was where a pub call the Nelson Arms now stands.

So how would he travel down to Portsmouth? There were many stage coach services down to the coast of course, but they were slow and carried a number of other passengers. The stage coach arrived at inns at inconvenient hours and allowed insufficient time for eating and sleeping.

By contrast, the post-chaise was faster, there might only be one other passenger and the travellers had more control over their journey. They could select their own inns and be sure of spending the nights in bed as opposed to on the road. The post-chaise was also considered to be more gentlemanly. No doubt speed would have been the most important consideration for Nelson at this time but comfort would have been a factor too, especially for anyone travelling through the night as Nelson did. The road surfaces in 1805, of course, bore no resemblance to the tarmac that we are used to today.

Where would Nelson have hired the post-chaise from? Just along the road was the

King's Head, the local coaching inn which was busy and well-known and could always be relied upon to provide a post-chaise for the admiral for hire to Portsmouth. Presumably, it would have driven through the main gate up to the house but the exact route of this is unknown.

The Portsmouth Road – the Sailor's Highway

As for the road that Nelson would have taken, there is only one possibility. The Portsmouth Road, now the A3, is not so different today 200 years later: it is still the umbilical cord between London and Portsmouth. The Victorians considered the roads of Old England to have romantic associations, in a way which we do not today. In 1895, Charles Harper wrote a book called *The Portsmouth Road*, which set out the stories, legends and travellers' anecdotes relating to 'The Sailors' Highway'.

More usefully perhaps, he also included mileages between the start of the Portsmouth Road which was deemed to begin at Stone's End, Borough, (now the junction of Newington Causeway and Borough High Street, just along from the Elephant and Castle in south east London) to various points along the way. The journey between Stone's End and the Landport gate in Portsmouth was 71½ miles.

This mythologizing of a road chimed in tune with the nostalgia for 'Ye good old days' and 'Merrie England', which was very prevalent in the inter-war years (1920–1939). So much so, that the book was reprinted in an illustrated version in 1923.

In 1935, a book for children published just before another war, notes that in the nineteenth century, when there were many sailors who had lost all their money making their way from Portsmouth to London, every parish along the road had to give a penny to every poor sailor in need of it.

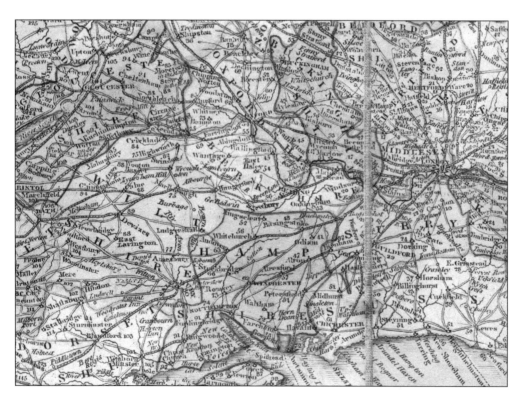

Returning to 1805, Merton Place was on the Epsom Road, a good turnpiked 'Direct' road which survives as the present A24: this map published in 1812 takes us all the way down to Portsmouth. 'Direct Roads' are shown as double lines, 'Mail Roads' as double lines with dots, and 'Cross Roads' as single lines.

Judith Goodman suggests that Nelson would have taken this road as far as Leatherhead, which can be identified on the map as the point between Epson and Dorking where the road crosses the River Mole. Here, he would have taken the 'Direct Road' to Guildford, now identifiable as the modern A246 and joined the Portsmouth Road, a good turnpiked mail road.

She points out that it would have been a shorter distance for Nelson to take the road from Merton to Kingston and pick up the Portsmouth Road there, but this was only a parish road, with a very poor surface and probably slower in the end. (PRIVATE COLLECTION)

The Royal Anchor, Liphook

Nelson's journey from Merton to Portsmouth took a total of seven and a half hours to cover 46¾ miles. The same team of horses could not be expected to run this distance without stopping so where would they have been changed? E. Hallam Moorhouse in his book on Nelson in England wrote:

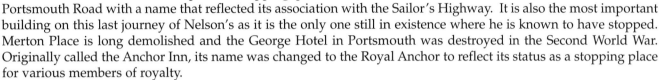

> All through the night he drove, through Guildford and over Hindhead on his way to Portsmouth. At Liphook, at the Anchor Inn, he snatched a hasty breakfast, and in his hurry left a sextant behind him.

The horses were probably changed while Nelson was eating.[1]

The Anchor Inn was an important stopping place on the Portsmouth Road with a name that reflected its association with the Sailor's Highway. It is also the most important building on this last journey of Nelson's as it is the only one still in existence where he is known to have stopped. Merton Place is long demolished and the George Hotel in Portsmouth was destroyed in the Second World War. Originally called the Anchor Inn, its name was changed to the Royal Anchor to reflect its status as a stopping place for various members of royalty.

Today, as in 1805, the Royal Anchor is situated at the junction of five major roads, an obvious setting for a former coaching inn and one of a number in the vicinity. It is now a popular pub with quite a history, convicts awaiting transportation were kept chained in the cellar and their fetters can still be seen.

The pub also has its own ghost, a highwayman who was murdered there. Samuel Pepys recorded in his diary that his party lost their way in the forest around Cobham while travelling to Portsmouth to inspect naval vessels. They eventually emerged at the inn at Liphook where he found there, 'good honest people'.

A local guidebook published in 1908 described it as follows:

> The Anchor at Liphook was a famous posting house in days of yore, and many an honoured guest has stopped by its great chestnut tree. Blucher and other memorable visitors came here on their way to the great Portsmouth gathering, [1814] and among other Royal travellers, there are memories of the Duchess of Kent and her little daughter who was to be Britain's best-loved Queen. In the good old times as many as 26 public conveyances pass in the day.

(AUTHOR'S PHOTOGRAPH)

Left: Inside there is a plaque commemorating Nelson's visit. It reads, 'Lord Nelson supp'd at the Royal Anchor on 14th September 1805, the night before he set sail to gain victory at Trafalgar some 5 weeks' later.'

Nelson however, would not be expected to eat his egg and chips perched at the bar on a stool. Throughout the seventeenth and eighteenth centuries inns did not have common dining-rooms. Each party, particularly those travelling by their own post-chaises such as Nelson, dined in a private room.

Is there a room specially associated with Nelson? The layout of the pub is now open-plan and according to the landlord, there is no tradition which associates any room with Nelson. There is however, a brass lock and key displayed on the wall which was taken from Queen Victoria's bedroom following her stay there in 1859.

As for the sextant which he allegedly left behind him, there is no trace of that either. Had there been, the landlord said that he would have displayed on the wall as a prime exhibit!

There is also a note painted on the wall inside to say that Nelson stayed there with Lady Hamilton. While at first glance this seems unlikely as she was never in Portsmouth with him, the pub was, at that time, the main stopping-off place from London to Bristol, so it is possible that they could have been on their way to the West Country. (COURTESY ANCHOR INN; AUTHOR'S PHOTOGRAPH, 2004)

Right: The main entrance to the Royal Anchor – did Nelson go through this door? (AUTHOR'S PHOTOGRAPH, 2004)

The Milestone

One unobtrusive re-minder of earlier days are the milestones set either side of the modern A3. This one is at the side of the northbound carriageway to London and is inscribed 'Hyde Park Corner 40, Godalming 8 Miles, Liphook 4 miles'. The Ordnance Survey arrow indicates that the stone is government property. (AUTHOR'S PHOTOGRAPH, 2004)

Portsea Island

The post-chaise would have been on its way again about 4.30a.m. on the third stage of the journey. The view of Portsea Island from the crest of Portsdown Hill is familiar to any traveller to Portsmouth. In 1801, Thomas Pennant who was travelling from London to the Isle of Wight wrote his impression of it:

The Isle of Wight rose sublime in the distant view; the Channel, intervening between the main land and the isle, stretched far to the east and closed beyond Southampton, bounded on each side by low shores. Beneath us lay the flat dreary Isle of Portsea, with Portsmouth at its end.

Its noble harbour filled with ships of war, at this peaceful time laid up, yet divested as they were of their terrific apparatus, could not fail of striking us with admiration. The idea of our naval strength, and the vast power we could, when called to arms, so immediately exert, raised in us the most pleasing reflection. Here only the sublimity of the scene appeared to us; but everything else which could please the eye, or affect the imagination, vanished; and we were truly disappointed by the strong and partial painting of the fond admirers of this boasted hill.

Let us turn towards the west; the prospect is most horribly disgusting: a great extent of shallow estuary stretches from Portsea Isle quite to the county of Sussex, at low water presenting an extensive tract of mud, divided by a few channels, or at high water covered with a thick embrowned tide....

We descended into the Isle of Portsea, and in a short time reached the Lines; passed by Portsbridge-battery, and crossed, on a drawbridge, the narrow water which insulates the island; then by Hilsea barracks, and through a series of villages of recent growth, which will soon unite and form a large town; after which we crossed two other draw-bridges, and, passing through a gate, entered the town of Portsmouth.[2]

The Landport Gate: 'Getting up to Meet Nelson'

Right: The gate referred to here is of course the Landport Gate, Nelson has arrived in Portsmouth. This photograph shows its front façade and closed inner doors which now faces the recreation-ground but in 1805 was the entrance to Portsmouth. There was no point in arriving at the gate before 4a.m. because it was closed for the night. Anyone who did so had to wait outside until morning. (COURTESY HMS *TEMERAIRE*; AUTHOR'S PHOTOGRAPH, 2004)

It is impossible today of course, to recreate Nelson's approach exactly because of the realignment of the road leading up to the gate and the removal of the two drawbridges. However, this is the nearest to it. Anyone who feels like getting up to meet Nelson at the Landport Gate, so to speak, has to remember that sunrise on 14 September is 6.37a.m. However, this is British Summer Time which did not exist in 1805 as it was introduced in 1916 during the First World War.

Below: Sunrise at the Landport Gate on 14 September 1805 was an hour earlier at 5.37a.m, now Greenwich Mean Time. Nelson said he arrived in Portsmouth at 6a.m. which would be 7a.m. today. Assuming that the weather was as good in 1805, this is how the Landport Gate might have looked just after sunrise on a September morning as Nelson approached in his post-chaise. (AUTHOR'S PHOTOGRAPH, 2004)

Nicolas comments:

September 14th: Arrived at Portsmouth, and re-hoisted his Flag on board the Victory.

Nelson's diary entry reads:

Saturday, September 14th, 1805: At six o' clock arrived at Portsmouth, and having arranged all my business, embarked at the Bathing Machines with Mr. Rose and Mr. Canning at two; got on board the Victory at St Helen's, who dined with me; preparing for sea.

The George Hotel – Nelson's Arrival

14 September 1805 is Nelson's last day in England. This succinct diary entry gives no hint of the timetable of all his activities during the eight hours he was in Portsmouth. On arrival he went to the George Hotel. This hotel is probably the only hotel in the country that is more famous for its back entrance than its front. Why that should be we will find out shortly, but meanwhile, it is worth pausing a moment on Nelson's journey to look at its background.

It was situated in the centre of the High Street and dated back to 1612. From 1693–1716 it was known as the Wagon and Lamb and by the eighteenth century, it was a well known coaching inn. The 'Royal Mail' and the 'Regulator' left outside daily for London.

Originally, it had had a thatched roof and a water trough outside but as the town grew and prospered this rusticity disappeared. It was redesigned as an elegant Georgian hotel and was very popular with senior naval officers. Its nearness to the Sally Port at the end of the High Street gave easy access to Point, the harbour and dockyard and for fashionable society it was within easy travelling distance of London.

It was always a good hotel but once Nelson died, however, it acquired the additional status of a shrine as the last place in England in which he stayed. This was recognised by two plaques, one on the front and one on the rear entrance. This postcard shows the hotel as it was at the end of the nineteenth century: the plaque on the façade reads, 'Sept. 14 1805 It was here Lord Nelson Spent his last hours in England'.

The photograph was taken by a French photographer by the name of Louis Levy, generally known as L.L., who travelled around the continent and Britain taking pictures of well-known places and then making them into postcards. L.L.'s cards are always worth looking at as he usually managed to include some interesting social details in his pictures. Here, we can see two handcarts which have not yet been replaced by the motor car.

The buildings on either side of the hotel were, of course, destroyed as well and in fact, the next building in this photograph still in existence is the one just beyond the nearer handcart of the two at No.24. The two lampposts indicate where the stage coach would pull up, the passengers alight and enter the hotel. (AUTHOR'S COLLECTION)

Luckily, the hotel management remembered which room Nelson had stayed in and this had become a local tourist attraction. For instance, the guide-books to Southsea and Portsmouth published by the Portsmouth Corporation in 1908 and 1910 include a section on the George Hotel.

They say that it was capable of accommodating 40 guests. Both books agree that Nelson had breakfast there in room No.15.

As to the reason why the back entrance is so famous, Nelson left the hotel this way to avoid the crowds which had gathered in the High Street to see him leave. This photograph is taken from *Nelson in England*, which was published in 1913. The picture itself is undated but must date from before the First World War. This is the nearest representation that we ever are likely to get of what it looked like in 1805.

So much for the romantic Victorian depictions of Nelson's farewell to Portsmouth. In reality, he had to pass the old dog sitting patiently by the door, push his way through hotel laundry hanging on a washing line and walk over the cobbles past yet another handcart out in to what is now Penny Street. (COURTESY PORTSMOUTH CITY COUNCIL)

Above: As for the plaque at the rear, this was located on the wall next to the garage entrance. By the time that this photograph was taken, probably in the 1930s, the age of the stage coach was long past and the back entrance had been altered to accommodate the motor car. (COURTESY ANTHONY TRIGGS)

Above: After the end of the Second World War the site of the George Hotel was developed as a block of flats which was officially opened in 1954 as The George Court. These flats now have three commemorative plaques. The first one is the tablet from the rear entrance which has now been moved round to the front as the original back exit no longer exists. It has been placed on the façade with an explanatory plaque underneath – this is plaque number two. (COURTESY ANTHONY TRIGGS)

Above: More or less the same view taken from 'Smitten City' and dated 1940 after the *Luftwaffe* have had a crack at it. (COURTESY THE NEWS)

Left: The plaque came in for it too. Here it is on a piece of wall still standing. It was retrieved safely though and can now be seen in Portsmouth City Museum. (COURTESY THE NEWS)

Left: A close-up of the two plaques. The lower one reads:

The above plaque was formerly over the Penny Street entrance of the George Hotel which stood on this site until destroyed by enemy action in 1941. This plaque [probably a replacement] was repositioned here in 1954.

(AUTHOR'S PHOTOGRAPH, 2004)

Right: The two lampposts are post-war replacements. (AUTHOR'S PHOTOGRAPH, 2004)

Below: Plaque number three is inset into the pavement between the two lampposts. (AUTHOR'S PHOTOGRAPH, 2004)

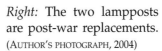

Visitors at the George and a Letter to Emma

On arrival at the hotel Nelson found people waiting for him. First of all, was the Revd Thomas Lancaster, the rector of Merton. He had come to Portsmouth with his 14-year-old son Henry who was to join the *Victory* as a first class volunteer.

Henry Lancaster (1791–1862) joined the *Victory* that very day but left the hotel before Nelson. The coincidence of his joining the *Victory* on such a fateful occasion is very striking. The obvious thought too is, did he survive the Battle of Trafalgar? Unlike his admiral, he did survive and subsequently had a very successful career in the Navy being promoted to commander in 1851. On his return from Trafalgar though, Merton can never have been the same for him.[3]

Once he had seen his son off, Revd Lancaster was to return to Merton, but just before he left, Nelson wrote a quick note to Lady Hamilton for him to take back to her:

> *My dearest and most beloved of women, Nelson's Emma, - I arrived here this moment and Mr. Lancaster takes it. His coach is at the door and only waits for my line.* Victory *is at St Helen's, and if possible, shall be at sea this day. God protect you and my dear Horatia prays ever your most faithful Nelson and Bronte.*

Also waiting, having arrived from London, was George Rose (1744–1818) who was vice-president of the Board of Trade from 1804–1806. He was attended by George Canning (1770–1827) who was the newly-appointed treasurer of the Navy and would go on to become prime minister in 1827 but sadly died very shortly afterwards. Both men were to wait for Nelson to conclude his business and then accompany him to the *Victory* to dine on board.

The Last Visit to Portsmouth Dockyard

To resume Nelson's schedule. In his diary he had mentioned arranging all his business, but what business was this and where did he go? The *Hampshire Telegraph* on 14 September reports that he did have breakfast at the George, perhaps the second one that day, and then went to the dockyard on a visit to Sir Charles Saxton.

However, it is not known at what time he went, how long he stayed there or even how he got there. The obvious constriction on his time would be the state of the tides. On Saturday 14 September 1805, low water at Portsmouth Harbour was at 7.27a.m. (Standard Local Time) and high water, seven hours later at 14.19p.m.

The quickest way for him to travel would have been by boat which he could have picked up at the Sally Port, indeed, the admiral's barge from the *Victory* could have been despatched to collect him. However, unless he went soon after his arrival the tide would now be coming in and against him. This might explain why Henry Lancaster had already left for the *Victory* by the time that Nelson arrived at the George in order to catch the outgoing tide.

Once at the dockyard, Nelson probably alighted at the King's Stairs, shown here in a photograph taken by W. J. Lawrence in 1937. HMS *Victory* can be seen in the background. (COURTESY J.C. LAWRENCE)

Above: So what did he do when he got there? He probably would have paid a courtesy call at some point on his old friend Captain Sir Charles Saxton (1732-1808). Sir Charles had been appointed commissioner of the Navy at Portsmouth in 1789 and held the post until 1806. He died in November 1808 and this print by J. Northcote was published after his death on 31 December 1808. (© NATIONAL MARITIME MUSEUM, LONDON, REF. NO.: PU 3125)

This postcard shows the building that was the commissioner's residence and is now the admiral's residence. It is undated but this is probably how it looked just before the First World War. It is hard though, to know how it would have appeared in 1805 because considerable alterations were made to it. (AUTHOR'S COLLECTION)

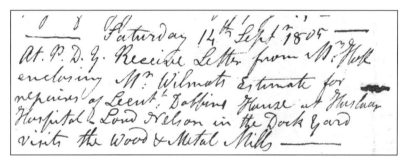

This is an entry from the journal of Simon Goodrich (1773–1847), the Deputy Inspector General of Naval Works from August 1805 who would have escorted Nelson around. This occasion was not only a fateful encounter for him on Nelson's last day, but showed how Nelson was so keen to see the latest developments that he made a detour from his tight schedule.[5] (COURTESY SCIENCE MUSEUM LIBRARY)

Nelson's main aim was most likely to assess the state of readiness of a number of vessels still at Spithead which were due to follow the *Victory* out to Cadiz. For example, the *Agamemnon*, the *Defiance* and the *Royal Sovereign* were not ready and were instructed to follow as quickly as they could.

While he was in the dockyard, Nelson also took the opportunity to visit the Block Mills, built in 1802 and encompassing both wood and metal mills. Here the range of pulley blocks for the Royal Navy was manufactured. These blocks were an example of the latest technology as applied to the sailing ship and the mills were often shown to important visitors to the dockyard.[4]

This seems to be the conclusion of Nelson's business. Now the tide was coming in and would have been against him assuming that he returned by boat to the Sally Port. One question is why did he go back to the Sally Port at all and not straight out to the *Victory* at St Helen's? The incoming tide would not have been much of a hindrance for St Helen's. Had he done this of course, history would have been quite different as there would have been no last walk down to Southsea beach.

As it was, two naval men accompanied him back to the George: Captain John Conn, who was Nelson's cousin by marriage and a protégé, and Admiral Sir Isaac Coffin (1759–1839), the port admiral's second in command. The party is assembling to accompany Nelson on what was to be his last walk on English soil.

Nelson's Last Walk

Left: This time, Nelson decided that in order to avoid the crowns who were gathering, he would not embark at the Sally Port but would leave the George from the back entrance and make his way down to Southsea beach. This is what the rear of The George Court flats look like today, the whole area, was of course, rebuilt after the Second World War. (AUTHOR'S PHOTOGRAPH, 2004)

Right: Looking out down into Penny Street. In 1805, it was known as Great Penny Street and extended right the way along to Grand Parade. Pembroke Road was known as Fighting Cock Lane. (AUTHOR'S PHOTOGRAPH, 2004)

How did Nelson's party get to Southsea beach? This postcard is one of the many representations of him on this walk – in this version he is accompanied by another senior naval officer, with Mr Canning and Mr Rose nowhere in sight. (AUTHOR'S COLLECTION)

In spite of all the pictures of this famous walk, the exact route that Nelson took is not known. This is a segment from a panorama of Portsmouth as seen from the top of the Semaphore Tower which was situated on the top of the Square Tower between 1822 and 1848. It was drawn and illustrated by Admiral Spencer Smyth while he was charge of the Semaphore Tower Station and is dated 1825.

So just twenty years after Nelson, this is what the area looked like. Portsmouth cathedral surrounded by houses is on the far left; the old Town Hall is still in the middle of the High Street; the Royal Garrison Church has yet to be redesigned and the Governor's House will not be demolished until 1826.

The quickest point of access on to the beach where the admiral's barge can collect Nelson and his two companions is the Spur Redoubt. This is the triangular-shaped fortification protruding into the sea on the right-hand side just below the horizon. To reach it the quickest route would seem to be along Great Penny Street and through the Governor's House complex. (PRIVATE COLLECTION)

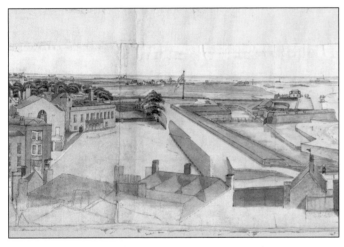

Here is a close-up of the fortifications from the panorama. It is surprising that Nelson's exact route is unknown considering the number of people in the vicinity. One reason could be that the military allowed his party access through the Governor's Garden and they were just lost sight of. Then, they had to gain access to a tunnel through the fortifications which brought them out on to the wooden bridge leading to the Spur Redoubt. (PRIVATE COLLECTION)

Right: This is what a view of the High Street taken just slightly lower down from the top of the Square Tower looks like today. Trees and greenery now surround the cathedral and the old Town Hall has gone, but other than that, it looks very much the same. (COURTESY PORTSMOUTH CITY MUSEUM AND RECORDS SERVICE; AUTHOR'S PHOTOGRAPH, 2004)

Above left: This is the scene today. (Courtesy Portsmouth City Museums and Record Service; author's photograph, 2004)

Above right: This is the tunnel entrance through the fortifications – presumably Nelson and the others passed through it. (Author's photograph, 2004)

The Spur Redoubt

The Spur Redoubt was built in 1680 by Sir Bernard de Gomme and extended during the 1730s to 1750s. It was a small fort which was detached from the main fortifications and designed to strengthen the seaward line in front of an exposed corner of the King's Bastion.

Nowadays, the tip of the iceberg where fortifications are concerned, its construction has been studied in detail by Russell Fox, monuments officer of Portsmouth City Council from 1968–1998. He found overall that:

> *...in effect the whole plan of the town's fortifications (particularly with regard to post-seventeenth century works) exists in a recoverable form below modern ground level.*[6]

This very lively painting of the Spur Redoubt in 1818, just thirteen years after Nelson passed through it, shows many details of its construction. He would have gone along the wooden bridge to enter the fort and then through the little Sally Port next to the outhouse with the roof and chimney seen here on the left.

(Courtesy Portsmouth Museums and Record Service Ref. no. 52/1952)

This photograph shows the fortifications as they are today, the Spur Redoubt, the stretch of moat, the long curtain wall and the King's Bastion. Unfortunately, the Spur Redoubt has not lasted as well as the curtain wall and bastion.

It fell derelict, then in 1934, the upper levels of at least two metres high were removed, the lower levels covered and the public promenade created. In 1988, a restoration programme revealed standing masonry which was restored. However, any positive effect this work might have had was completely erased by the erection of the timber footbridge. The Spur Redoubt remains the signature work of Bernard de Gomme and epitome of Portsmouth's seventeenth and eighteenth century fortifications which still exists but awaits complete restoration.

The canon on the far right has a plaque which reads:

24 pounder gun from the armament of the frigate HMS Foudroyant *presented to the City of Portsmouth by the* Foudroyant *Trust 10th July 1974 to mark the association between the City and the training ship HMS* Foudroyant *(ex Trincomolee) at the time still active in the service of youth.*

The gun carriage and cannon were subsequently refurbished by marine engineering artificers of HMS Sultan *during 1994/95.*

(AUTHOR'S PHOTOGRAPH, 2004)

On to the Beach

We now come to the last section of Nelson's walk. The party would have emerged through the tunnel in the long curtain wall and crossed the wooden footbridge shown here. This bridge was constructed in 1976 but had deteriorated badly by the 1990s. It has now been replaced but the photograph does give a good idea of the width of the moat. (AUTHOR'S PHOTOGRAPH, 2004)

Above: Next, they entered the passage shown here through the stone walls of the Spur Redoubt to the Sally Port which gave access to the beach. (AUTHOR'S PHOTOGRAPH, 2004)

Above: This is the end of the line for us today. (AUTHOR'S PHOTOGRAPH, 2004)

Right: This is the beach at low tide. Of course, it is very different from 1805, the shore line has been built up and is much steeper. The bathing machines that Nelson is to mention in his letters have been replaced by Clarence Pier.

However, we can imagine the admiral's barge, thirty-two feet long with its twelve oarsmen, six on each side, waiting to take him and two of his companions to HMS *Victory*. The admiral and captain remain on the beach. (AUTHOR'S PHOTOGRAPH, 2004)

Nelson found time to write a letter which presumably he gave to Captain Conn to send off for him.

To Rear-Admiral Murray,
My dear Admiral,
Many thanks for your kind note and haunch of venison. I am this moment getting in the Boat at the Bathing Machines, - May every success attend you, and health, that greatest of blessings. I beg my best respects to Mrs. Murray; and ever, my dear Murray, believe me your most faithful friend,

Nelson and Bronte.

Nicolas adds here, 'This is supposed to be the last letter Lord Nelson ever wrote in England.'

There are to be no more letters from Portsmouth itself so we have to revert to the local paper to find out what happened, the complete report reads:

Lord Nelson arrived at the George this morning at six o'clock. After breakfast, he went to the Dockyard on a visit to Sir Charles Saxton; and at one o'clock, his Lordship embarked from the Southsea beach and went on board the Victory *which had dropped down to St Helen's.*

Sir I. Coffin and Capt. Conn attended his Lordship to the boat; G. Rose Esq., and George Canning Esq., accompanied his Lordship and dined on board the Victory, *after which those gentlemen went to Southampton in the Commissioner's yacht. A number of people followed his Lordship and cheered when he embarked. The* Victory *with the* Euraylus *frigate will sail tomorrow.*

Citizen Hero – Secular Saint

Perhaps this report is a bit too mundane for us today, the reporter did not have to grope his way through the fog of legend and hindsight and was able to take things as they came. Robert Southey (1774–1843) was to write a much more romantic account in his biography of Nelson entitled, *The Life of Nelson*, which was first published in 1813:

> Early on the following morning he reached Portsmouth; and, having despatched his business on shore, endeavoured to elude the populace by taking a by-way to the beach; but a crowd collected in his train, pressing forward to obtain a sight of his face – many were in tears, and knelt down before him, and blessed him as he passed.
>
> England has had many heroes, but never one who so entirely possessed the love of his fellow-countrymen as Nelson. All men knew that his heart was as humane as it was fearless; that there was not in his nature the slightest alloy of selfishness or cupidity; but that, with perfect and entire devotion, he served his country with all his heart, and with all his soul, and with all his strength; and, therefore, they loved him as truly and as fervently as he loved England.
>
> They pressed upon the parapet to gaze after him when his barge pushed off, and he was returning their cheers by waving his hat. The sentinels, who endeavoured to prevent them trespassing upon this ground, were wedged among the crowd; and an officer who, not very prudently upon such an occasion, ordered them to drive the people down with their bayonets, was compelled speedily to retreat, for the people would not be debarred from gazing, till the last moment, upon the hero, the darling hero of England.[7]

Southey is a little known writer now, but in his time he was one of England's literary giants, a poet and historian and for thirty-two years, poet laureate. What significance does his interpretation have and is there any relevance to Portsmouth? His description of the crowd genuflecting before Nelson gives us a glimpse of a much older, pre-Reformation England and its long-neglected religious observances.

This approach would not have been acceptable to the Hanoverian Protestantism of the eighteenth century, but times had changed and Regency society had embraced the cult of patriotic heroism and self-sacrifice. In his interpretation of these events, Southey encapsulates in three paragraphs the mixture of religion and patriotism which Nelson embodied.

The episode is, of course, set in a mythical Portsmouth, the reporter from the *Hampshire Chronicle* did not record anyone kneeling down on the fortifications. Nelson's last walk has this resonance precisely because it is his last walk – there was to be no coming home.

As to its relevance to us today, Nelson's last walk is timeless. It symbolises an experience which is specific to Portsmouth and other sea-port towns which see so many people leaving not knowing whether they will ever return and of course, so many never do.

Following the end of the Napoleonic Wars in 1815, in the popular mind, both Nelson and Wellington had become secular saints who symbolised national virtues. Nelson, though, unlike the aristocratic Duke of Wellington, had acquired the romantic status of a citizen hero as well.

Large scale monuments symbolising these virtues were set up as they were seen as universal symbols of national pride. The forms they took were based on the monuments of classical antiquity, the culmination of this being Nelson's column in Trafalgar Square which was commenced in 1838 and finally completed in 1867.

As time went on, while monuments on a grand scale declined in popularity, unusually, there was no reaction against Nelson himself. The combination of his slight form, the empty sleeve and much decorated admiral's uniform, epitomised patriotic self-sacrifice to the late-Victorians just as it does to us today.

At Sea

Once on board HMS *Victory*, at some point Nelson wrote the following prayer:

May the great God whom I adore enable me to fulfil the expectations of my country. And if it is his good pleasure that I should return my thanks will never cease being offered to the throne of His mercy. If it is His good providence to cut short my days upon the earth I bow with the greatest submission; relying that He will protect those so dear to me that I may leave behind. His will be done. Amen, amen, amen.[8]

The letters resume from St Helen's:

To William Marsden, Esq., Admiralty.

Victory, at St Helen's, 14th September, 1805.

Sir,
You will please to acquaint the Lords Commissioners of the Admiralty that I arrived at Portsmouth this morning at six o'clock, and hoisted my Flag on board the Victory *at this anchorage about noon. The* Royal Sovereign, Defiance, *and* Agamemnon, *are not yet ready for sea, so that I must leave them to follow, the moment they are complete. The Ships named in the margin (*Victory, Euryalus *– Captain the Honourable Henry Blackwood), only accompany me. I am, Sir, &c.,*

Nelson and Bronte.

❋ ❋ ❋

To William Marsden, Esq.,

Victory, at St Helen's, 14th September, 1805.

Sir,
Not knowing where His Majesty's Ships named in the margin [Chiffone, Unite, Nautilus, Beagle, Pylades, Moselle, Scout, Merlin, Entreprenante, Pickle] are at present, I beg to transmit orders for their respective Captains, and request you will be so good as forward them as early as possible. Inclosed is a copy of the said Orders and Rendezvous for their Lordships' information, and also a copy of the Order given to the Captains of His Majesty's ships Renommée *and* Melpomené, *directing them to proceed to Malta with money, agreeably to their Lordships' instructions, communicated to me in your letter of the 12th instant. The Orders for the* Ajax *and* Thunderer *are gone to Plymouth; and those for the* Amazon *to dock and refit, not knowing when she may arrive, are herewith transmitted. L'Aimable will proceed with the Lisbon Convoy, agreeably to their Lordships' orders of the 11th and 12th instant, and join me on my Rendezvous the moment the service is performed. I am, Sir, &.,*

Nelson and Bronte.

❋ ❋ ❋

To Captain Robert Dudley Oliver, H.M. Ship Melpomené.
Victory, at St Helen's, 14th September 1805.
You are hereby required and directed to complete His Majesty's Ship under your command with the utmost dispatch for Foreign Service; and the moment that is done, and the Melpomené *in all respects ready for sea, you are to receive the amount of two hundred and fifty thousand pounds sterling in dollars on board the said Ship, and instantly proceed and join me on the enclosed Rendezvous in your way to Malta; but should you learn that the Fleet under my command has gone into the Mediterranean, and that it would be taking you out of your way to join me, it is my directions that you proceed direct to Malta; and after having delivered the said money to Sir Alexander Ball, you will return and join me wherever you may learn the Fleet under my command may be.*

Nelson and Bronte.

N.B. – An order of the same tenor and date given to the Captain of the Renommée.

To Captain....... of H.M. Ship.........

Victory, St Helen's, 14th September, 1805.

As I am about to proceed from hence down Channel, you are hereby required and directed to join me in His Majesty's Ship under your command on the enclosed Rendezvous; and I am to desire that every possible exertion is used to put the said Ship in a state for immediate service, with stores and provisions complete to six months, and that you will join me as above directed.

Nelson and Bronte.

❊❊❊

Nicolas continues with his chronology:

September 15th: Sailed in company with the Euryalus.

To Captain William Lechmere, H.M. Ship Thunderer.

Victory, *at Sea, 15th September, 1805.*

Secret Rendezvous.
Off Cape St Vincent, where a Frigate will be stationed to give information where I am to be found. In the event of not meeting the said Frigate, after cruising twenty-four hours, the Ship in search of me must call Cape St Mary's and Cadiz, approaching them with the utmost caution.

Nelson and Bronte.

❊❊❊

September 16th: Off Portland.
To Alexander Davison, Esq.,

Victory, *September 16th, 1805,*
Off Portland, Wind W.S.W.

My dear Davison,
I regret most exceedingly, for many reasons, my not having had the pleasure of seeing you; but my fate is fixed, and I am gone, and beating down the Channel with a foul wind. I am, my dear friend, so truly sensible of all your goodness to me, that I can only say, thanks, thanks; therefore I will to business. I wish I could have been rich enough, with ease to myself, to have settled my Account with you; but as that is not done, I wish for my sake that you would have it closed, and receipts pass between us; and then I will give you a bond for the balance, as for money lent. Those bonds relative to Tucker, being all settled, should be returned to me. Be so good as to give them to Haslewood. If you and I live, no harm can happen; but should either of us drop, much confusion may arise to those we may leave behind. I have said enough. Haslewood will settle the Account with all legal exactness.
I have requested you to pay Chawner's account for work to be done in his line; and what is ordered, viz. the kitchen, ante-room, and for altering the dining-room, which you would have been provoked to see spoiled. The alteration will cost three times as much as if it had been done at first. However, Chawner now knows all my plans and wishes. Poor blind Mrs Nelson I have given 150l. (£) to pay her debts, and I intend to pay her house-rent in future, in addition to the 200l. a year, which I take will be about 40l. a year. I wished also to have seen you respecting my Proxy, for as it passed through your hands without an immediate communication with Lord Moira, so it should have returned that way. I ever was against giving my Proxy to any man, and now I have it again, it will probably never be given again. Lord Moira made me break my intention; and as very few can equal our friend for honour and independence, it is not very likely that I shall give it, without strong reasons, again. With every good wish, believe me ever, my dear Davison, your most obliged and faithful friend,

Nelson and Bronte.

I have settled Chawner's account for all which has been hitherto done at Merton.

❊❊❊

The *Victory* is on course for Cadiz, the letters from St Helen's come to an end and Nelson's voice from Portsmouth falls silent.

Nicolas continues:
September 17th: Off Plymouth.
September 18th:Off the Lizard.
September 23rd:Off Cape Finisterre.
September 25th: Off Lisbon.
September 26/27th: Off Cape St Vincent,
September 28th: Joined the Fleet off Cadiz, under Vice-Admiral Collingwood. In command of the Fleet off Cadiz.
October 19th: The Enemy's Fleet put to sea.
October 21st: Battle of Trafalgar. At 1.30 P.M. Mortally wounded, and at 4.30. dies.

The News Breaks in Portsmouth

The news of the victory at Trafalgar and the death of Nelson did not reach Britain until 5 November. The first edition of the *Hampshire Telegraph* to report it is that of Monday 11 November 1805. This carries reports from the previous week and in one dated Saturday 9 November, the leader proposes that, ' ...a statue or bust or some trophy erected here record the love and veneration of the inhabitants for the departed hero'.

On Thursday 7 November there was general rejoicing:

...at 7 o'clock the guns were fired on the platform and were followed by a feu de joye from a line extending along the walls and Southsea Beach consisting of the Royal Artillery and Artificers, the North Hants., North and East Devon Militia and the Portsmouth and Portsea Battalion of Volunteers. After firing the troops cheered.

At 8 o' clock, three vollies were fired on board of each ship at Spithead which was succeeded by cheers from the manned yards and shrouds.

This print by Heath shows the Saluting Platform in 1817 which was situated next to the Square Tower: the guns would have been fired from here. Also in the picture is the semaphore station which was placed here from 1816–1822. In 1822, it was transferred to the top of the Square Tower. Back in 1805 however, the semaphore station did not exist and communications were passed via the shutter telegraph station near the King's Bastion. (© NATIONAL MARITIME MUSEUM, LONDON, REF. NO.: PU 1068)

Nelson Immortal

In the town itself, the Crown Inn, the Mitre and Mr Hoad's house in Portsea displayed 'very elegant' transparencies. These were hung festooned with crepe and depicted such topics as Britannia with the French and Spanish colours lying at her feet; views of the *Victory*, phrases such as 'Nelson Immortal' and an urn representing Nelson's death. The bells rang the whole evening.

The following Tuesday:

… a most sumptuous dinner was given, at the Crown Inn by the Russian Admiral Senevin, to the principal Officers of the Navy and Army at this place. The table was set out in a style of uncommon elegance. The Marine Band played during the whole entertainment. Many loyal toasts were given; and the Russian Officers expressed their unfeigned admiration and joy at the late memorable victory.

Not less than fifty persons of distinction were present among, whom were Admirals Montagu and Sir I. Coffin, all the Naval Captains in this port; and General Hope with other Officers of rank. The company expressed the highest satisfaction with the whole of the entertainment.

'And England's Trident Rule the Wat'ry World!'

Admiral Senevin's dinner was the first of many celebratory dinners in Portsmouth. The mayor and corporation dined out at the George, there was an assembly at the Crown Inn and a public dinner at the Beneficial Society's Hall attended by the mayor for which tickets cost 15 shillings each. Those attending of course, were also expected to dig into their wallets and contribute to Lloyd's Patriotic Fund which had been set up to provide relief for people who had become destitute through war or injury.

Music was a very important part of life in Portsmouth and the first concert of the subscription season was held on 5 November at the Beneficial Hall. The series of six concerts included appropriate music such as excerpts from Handel's oratorios and a piece composed specially for the occasion. This was an ode entitled, 'O the Victory of Trafalgar' written by the Revd H. Donne of Portsea. A Mr Norris composed an elegy for four voices, 'O'er Nelson's Tomb'.

Frank Warren and Irwen Cockman in their monograph on music in Portsmouth, comment that there was also a patriotic concert organised by Stephen Sibly. Sibly had been appointed as the organist of St John's Chapel in Portsea in 1789 and for the next fifty years organised concerts and musical events. They point out however, that although £30 was raised, no mention was made of this in the local press.[9]

The Return of the *Victory*

The mood changed in Portsmouth when the damaged *Victory* with Nelson's body aboard anchored at St Helen's on December 4. On December 7, the *Hampshire Telegraph* commented:

…it is a circumstance of no small consolation to England, that the honoured remains of the late Lord Nelson are arrived in safety; and we state with much reluctance, that it is expected here that they will be conveyed to Town by water...

...we therefore still hope, that an order will arrive to convey the beloved remains to Town by land.

The order never arrived and on 11 December the *Victory* sailed on to Chatham for repairs. Local people had to accept that Nelson's body would not be landing at Portsmouth and in fact, the Admiralty ordered the removal of his body to Greenwich on 21 December. Meanwhile:

...Admirals Montagu's and Sir Isaac Coffin's Flags and the pendants and colours of all the ships at this port, are lowered to half-mast high, and the Captains and Officers of the Ships wear crepe round their arms.

The *Hampshire Telegraph* reported on 7 December:
...a Day of Thanksgiving for the late victories was observed here with a formality becoming the great occasion. Every place of worship, of all descriptions was fully attended, and praise and thanksgiving were sent forth, we cannot doubt, from the altar of every heart.

A collection was made for Lloyd's Fund. We were happy to see that every man felt it his share of the general duty to express his gratitude to the brave men, and their widows and children, who on the great day of Trafalgar, did their duty to the everlasting honour of their country.

The sums raised were Portsmouth church £100; the Garrison Church £65; St John's Chapel £60 and St George's Chapel £30.

By the 21 December, a subscription had been opened for a, 'plain marble pillar and bust' in memory of Nelson by means of an advertisement placed in the *Hampshire Telegraph*, 'at the express desire of several respectable inhabitants in this Town'.

Then on 23 December:

A Bust and Pillar to the memory of Lord Nelson. Several gentlemen of this Town and neighbourhood having intimated a wish that some Public Token of Respect to the memory of Lord Nelson should be made, the inhabitants and others are informed that Mr. Mottley will receive the names of such Persons as may be willing to subscribe towards erecting in this Town a PLAIN MARBLE PILLAR AND BUST commemorative of the Glorious Achievements of the fallen Hero.

On 23 December Nelson's body landed at Greenwich.

On 6 January 1806, the *Hampshire Telegraph* commented:
We are happy to notice the progress that is making in the subscription for a Pillar or other monument to the memory of Lord Nelson. This place, from its importance as a port and naval arsenal, ought to stand forth distinguished in such an expression of gratitude to that great character.

It was beside, the last place in which Lord Nelson planted his foot on land, and surely it would be much mortification to every friend of the place, if it were the last or least, in concurring with others to honour his beloved name.

The Funeral

Nicolas continued:
January 8th 1806: Conveyed to the Admiralty.
January 9th: Deposited in St Paul's Cathedral.

Sir Isaac Coffin attended Nelson's funeral and then on 25 January 1806 returned to his post of second-in-command at Portsmouth. That day just over four months ago when he stood on Southsea beach watching Nelson getting into the admiral's barge must have seemed a long time ago.

References
[1] *Nelson in England*, p.252.
[2] *A Journey from London to the Isle of Wight*, pp.123–124.
[3] *The Men Who Fought With Nelson in HMS Victory at Trafalgar*, p.70.
[4] *Dockyards*, vol.10, Issue 1, February 2005, p.1.
[5] *Goodrich papers B: Vol 10, pages 66-67. I am greatly indebted to Jonathan Coad for this reference. His latest book*, The Portsmouth Block Mills, *English Heritage, 2005, describes the pioneering work of the Block Mills and highlights the work of Simon Goodrich.*
[6] *Portsmouth's Ramparts Revisited*, pp.29–30.
[7] *Southey on Nelson*, pp.264–265.
[8] *The letter from St Thomas's Cathedral, Edition34, Spring 2005.*
[9] *Music in Portsmouth 1789–1842*, p.6.

Chapter X

2005:
THE IMMORTAL MEMORY

The Monuments

The *Hampshire Telegraph* was quick off the mark in proposing a monument to Lord Nelson on 9 November. However, the Navy was even quicker. On the 2 November Admiral Collingwood had sent a memorandum to the captains of the ships off Trafalgar:

> *Vice-Admiral Collingwood, in attending to the wishes and feeling in common with all lately serving under the orders of Vice-Admiral Nelson, those sentiments of attachment and affection due to so exalted a character, submits to the Admiral, Captains, Officers, Seamen, and Marines, his compliance with the request made him of assenting to the erecting, at the general expense of the Squadron, on Ports Down Hill, a lasting Monument to their late Chief's memory and great name; he does, in consequence, request the Captains of the respective Ships will make the same known to their crews, that if approved it may be adopted; and in order to procure a fund for so laudable a purpose, that the sum of £2,000 shall be deducted and paid by the Agents for that object, out of the prize-money arising from the Action off Cape Trafalgar, the 21st ultimo, subject to the disposal of the Commissioners to be named by the Commander-in-chief.*
>
> *The Commander-in-Chief invites Rear-Admiral Louis, with those of the Squadron under his orders at that time, to unite with him in the way he thinks most advisable, for the accomplishment of this National object.*
>
> *Should this meet your concurrence, as well as those on board the Ship you command, you will be pleased to note it in your Log Book, and report to me in writing, signed by yourself, First Lieutenant, and signing Officers,*
>
> *Cutht. Collingwood.*

The Nelson Monument

The admiral was wise in organising a secure source of funding first and then deciding on the monument afterwards. While it was easy to put forward suggestions for memorials, as today, raising the money to construct them proved to be much more difficult. For example, the pillar and bust proposed for Portsmouth never materialised. Even a proposal reported in the local press in February 1806 for a monument in St George's Square, Portsea never came to anything, in spite of the fact that a local merchant had donated a large piece of granite for the pedestal.

The Nelson monument was constructed on Portsdown Hill between 1807, when the foundation stone was laid on 4 July, and 1808 when the final visit was made to check that everything was in order. It still stands today, situated in Monument Lane on farmland just over the border from Portsmouth and within the area covered by Fareham Borough Council.

It takes the form of a Portland stone column, 120 feet high set on a granite base. The shaft is tapered and recessed in the centre of each side. The curved niche at the top contains a bust of Nelson on the north side.

Now, the monument is maintained by the Navy at HMS Collingwood. Regarding its listing status, the monument was dual listed: in 1967 it was given Grade II* listed status and in 1970, scheduled as an ancient monument. However, in 2001 it was descheduled as Grade II* was deemed sufficient for its care.

This print was published in a magazine called, *The Penny Illustrated* in 1865, although there are earlier versions in existence and entitled, *Portsmouth Harbour, the Meeting Place of the French and English fleets.* Fort Nelson is under construction on the right-hand side and on the left, fashionably dressed visitors are making their way up the hill to look at the monument. In the manner of an eighteenth century prospect, the view has been adjusted to improve the composition of the picture. Today, it is mostly obscured by trees.

Nevertheless, it is still a very dramatic setting. This small picture sums up the monument's attributes, its design as a Greek revival column with the acroteria (the curves at the corners of the pedestal) designed to resemble a ship's prow and its vantage point overlooking Portsmouth Harbour enabling it to be used as a sea mark. (Courtesy Portsmouth City Museums and Record Service Ref. no: 129/1962)

To look more closely at the detail, this photograph shows the bust of Nelson and underneath in Gothic-style script is the word, 'Trafalgar'. The architect of the column itself was John Thomas Groves (c.1761–1811) but the name of the sculptor of the bust is not known for sure. Richard Walker in his book on the portraits of Nelson describes it as a Coade stone bust and attributes it to John Bacon, presumably the junr (1777–1859).

During the early nineteenth century, the elevation of a bust in this way was considered to raise the status of the person from earthly and mortal to that of deified hero. The onlooker looks up to the hero who, 'looks down' from a position of permanence. The contemplation of such antique monuments was considered to stimulate the imagination and the height created a sense of sublimity.

Generally at this time, heroes were depicted as idealised nudes or Greco-Roman warriors. To depict Nelson as a nude was found to be problematical because of his lost arm. There was also no need to use Roman dress to convey the idea that he was a hero because his idiosyncratic admiral's uniform always did that. Thus Nelson was almost always shown as a ordinary man in naval dress. By the 1830s in any case, it had become the fashion to depict the hero in modern costume. (Courtesy Allan Smith, 2004)

The pedestal has two inscriptions set in recesses, this one, in a plainer script is on the north face:

Consecrated to the memory of Lord Viscount Nelson by the zealous attachment of all those who fought at Trafalgar to perpetuate his triumph and their regret MVCCCV.

(COURTESY ALLAN SMITH, 2004)

The second, on the south face is in an elegant eighteenth century hand:

The British Fleet consisted of Twenty seven Ships of the Line: of France and Spain Thirty three, Nineteen of which were taken or destroyed.

(COURTESY ALLAN SMITH, 2004)

The Nelson monument is a most subtle and poignant memorial, sombre but not depressing. This is particularly so when compared with the much later column in Trafalgar Square, which may be very grandiose and imposing but it is weighty and bland and most importantly, landlocked.

Nelson described himself as a 'sea-person' and might spend seven to eight hours each day on deck. In contrast, seventy miles away from central London, his bust in the eye of the delicate wand of the compass needle, so to speak, measures the passage of the sun across the heavens from sunrise to sunset. At night, the stars above Portsmouth Harbour wheel around him.

Lastly, its setting. The monument stands in the midst of the ancient farmland of Portsdown Hill yet its design is un-English. This combination of rural English landscape and the monument's quality of foreignness, reminds us that Nelson was from solid Norfolk stock yet fought all his famous battles well away from English shores. It combines an impression of outward oriental fatalism with an profound inner strength which is in sympathy with the modestly-worded inscriptions. (COURTESY ALLAN SMITH, 2004)

A Governor's Gift – the Lost Statues

There were two monuments set up near the King;s Rooms to commemorate Nelson in mid-Victorian times, both by Lord Frederick Fitzclarence (1799–1854). He was one of the ten illegitimate children of William IV and the actress Dorothy Jordan and had made his career in the military. From 1847 to 1851 he was the lieutenant governor of Portsmouth and did much to promote the town.

In 1850 at his own expense, he presented two statues to the mayor and corporation of the town. They depicted Nelson and the Duke of Wellington on a grand scale, the statues were seven feet high and their pedestals eleven feet. They were sculpted in stone by W. Milligan of Old Cavendish Street, London (fl. 1845–1850). This is an engraving from the *Illustrated London News* dated 18 May 1850 and is probably the only detailed picture of them.
(COURTESY *ILLUSTRATED LONDON NEWS*)

However, the statues were never popular and their surfaces soon deteriorated in the corrosive sea air. By 1865 too, the King's Rooms had become derelict and the whole area was to be re-developed. In the process, the two statues disappeared never to be seen again. William Gates reports that they were defaced and thrown in the sea by a party of sailors. A more mundane explanation is that they were just demolished and removed to make way for the terminus for the new horse drawn trams which opened in 1865.

A Governor's Legacy – The *Victory* Anchor

The second monument to Nelson set up by Lord Frederick Fitzclarence lasted a lot longer and still stands today albeit in a different form. It consists of an anchor from HMS *Victory* set on a pedestal but its exact date is not known. Originally, it was set up on Southsea beach near the present day Clarence Pier with an inscription on the pedestal that read:

Close to this spot embarked the Hero of the Nile, alas for the Last time, to take command of the British Fleet, That fought and conquered at Trafalgar, where our Nelson fell. This tribute of respect is placed here in humble admiration of the departed Hero by Lord Frederick Fitzclarence Lieutenant Governor of Portsmouth, 1852.

This engraving from the *Illustrated London News* shows the anchor in 1854.
(COURTESY *ILLUSTRATED LONDON NEWS*)

At some point, it is believed to have been resited on the King's Bastion and then moved from there in the 1880s to its present location on Clarence Parade where it is one of a number of Victorian memorials. It was remounted on a granite plinth with two granite stepped bases.

There are tablets with inscriptions inset into each face of the plinth. The north face has:

The Battle of Trafalgar. The British fleet consisted of 27 sail of the line; that of the allies of France and Spain 33. Of these, 19 were taken or destroyed by Lord Nelson.

The south has:

Near this memorial on the 14th. September, 1805, Admiral Lord Nelson embarked for the last time, being killed on the following 21st. October at the victorious Battle of Trafalgar.

The west face has, 'Ready Aye Ready', and the east, 'England expects every man to do his duty'. On the anchor itself are the words, 'Victory's Anchor Oct. 21st 1805.' The *Victory* anchor was Grade II listed in 1972 and on 10 May 1973, this photograph was taken by the City Council's Department of Architecture and Civic Design. (COURTESY PORTSMOUTH CITY MUSEUM AND RECORDS SERVICE)

1905: An Edwardian Centenary – Send a Card

One hundred years on the immortal memory proved to be just that and Nelson was still the fallen hero. So much so, that Arnold White and E. Hallam Moorhouse wrote a book entitled *Nelson and the Twentieth Century*, to celebrate the centenary of the Battle of Trafalgar. In it the Victorian ideals of self-sacrifice and heroism were shown to be still valid in the twentieth century, a concept which was not to be challenged until the First World War.

Nationally, large exhibitions were organised and as in 1805, pieces of music composed specially, the most famous of which is probably, 'Fantasia on British Sea Songs' by Sir Henry Wood which was first performed at a special Promenade Concert on 21 October 1905.

So how was the centenary celebrated in Portsmouth? One way was to send a picture postcard. By 1905, although the craze for the new picture postcards was in full swing, they were still a novelty. The 1905 centenary was the first large-scale commemorative national event to occur since their mass production started in about 1900. Local publishers were quick to take advantage of this and published postcards which commemorated Nelson's victory and included local views.

This one gives good value for money as it combines a picture of Nelson with a copy of his prayer, four views of the *Victory*, one of Nelson's Column, one of the *Victory* anchor and a general one of, 'the wooden walls'. It was postally used on 22 October 1905. The card was printed in Saxony as many postcards were before the First World War but this stopped abruptly in 1914. (AUTHOR'S COLLECTION)

Left: This card is aimed at the local market and the views are only of Portsmouth: the house where Charles Dickens was born, the Town Hall, the harbour and floating bridge and Southsea front. Presumably, to update an existing design to include 1905 was a simple matter. (AUTHOR'S COLLECTION)

Right: The cigarette card was also very popular and in 1905 a set of 50 was issued by Wills's Cigarettes to commemorate the centenary. This is No.34 in the Nelson Series and the text on the reverse reads:

The Victory's Anchor. This famous anchor, now serving as a monument on Southsea Common, near the spot where Nelson embarked on his last fateful voyage, is a fit emblem of the tenacity and endurance which made Lord Nelson England's greatest naval hero. It fittingly serves to commemorate his naval greatness and his last message: England expects that every man will do his duty.

(AUTHOR'S COLLECTION)

Left: The localised picture postcard commemorating Nelson continued after 1905. This is a picture of the 'toast rack car' which was bought in 1919 and was the only such tram operated by Portsmouth Corporation. It was built to resemble a boat and here, it is shown decorated to commemorate Trafalgar during a Navy Week, the year is not known. The message on the back reads, 'Dear Mum and Dad, just a card to let you know I've got back OK. Hope you are feeling better. Bill'. (AUTHOR'S COLLECTION)

Post-War Reconstruction – The Nelson Statue

Right: During the bombing of the Second World War, Nelson's Portsmouth was not the only part of the city to be swept away. The postwar period saw a massive programme of reconstruction and in the process, a Dr Aldous decided to take a leaf out of Lord Fitzclarence's book and donate a statue of Nelson to the city. Even before the war ended he had set aside money to pay for it and in 1945, set about realising his ambition.

Eventually the statue was completed. It was made in bronze, the sculptor was F. Brook Hitch and it was placed on a high plinth of rough grey granite with bronze plaques inset on the north, west and east sides and on the south, the date of 21 October 1805 incised in the granite.

Dr Aldous had hoped that the statue would be set up on Cathedral Green which was still in the process of redevelopment, but in the event, a site in Pembroke Gardens was selected. It was unveiled on 11 July 1951 by Admiral Sir Arthur Power and this is where it stands today. The statue and its plinth were Grade II listed in 1951. (AUTHOR'S PHOTOGRAPH, 2004)

Left: This close up shows the detail of Nelson's uniform. Dr Aldous was most particular in stipulating that Nelson was to be shown in the undress uniform in which he left Portsmouth and was mortally wounded at Trafalgar. He also wanted an informal pose to contrast with the stiff, unbending poses of the 1830s and 40s and the stance to be easy and natural.

In his letter to the City Council dated 1946, Dr Aldous wrote:

I hope that when the statue is erected, it will be hailed as the best and most correct representation of Lord Nelson, and that it will help to remind, not only visitors, but also the residents in this City in years to come, of Nelson's close association with Portsmouth.

(COURTESY ALLAN SMITH, 2004)

Right: We feel the weightlessness of that empty right sleeve in the back view of the statue. The sculptor has indeed caught Nelson in an informal pose, the left leg bearing his weight with the right bent in front of him subtly indicates how his body compensated for the uneven balance of the missing arm. (AUTHOR'S PHOTOGRAPH, 2004)

Regarding the plaques, the one on the north side reads, 'Presented by Herbert J. Aldous, LRCS., LSA., from whose designs the sculptor worked F. Brook Hitch, FRBS.'

Right: The west side carries Nelson's Prayer.
(AUTHOR'S PHOTOGRAPH, 2004)

Far right: This plaque is on the east side.
(AUTHOR'S PHOTOGRAPH, 2004)

Left: While fashions had changed a lot from the 1830s they had not changed entirely. Dr Aldous also wanted a 'heroic' plinth which was to be the same height as the statue, eight foot nine inches. In this view, Nelson looks down on us from a great height in the manner of the nineteenth century hero and we look back up to him, the hero. On the steps are the words, 'Here served Horatio Nelson You who tread his footsteps Remember his glory'. (AUTHOR'S PHOTOGRAPH, 2004)

Right: However, Dr Aldous wanted to emphasise that Nelson was an ordinary man too. About 30 yards away from the statue is a short, free-standing plinth also in granite though a slightly darker colour, with a bronze tablet inset into the top which reads:

'The Statue'. Lord Nelson is in the undress uniform he wore when leaving Portsmouth for Trafalgar. The coat which he was wearing when mortally wounded has been carefully copied. He passed over this spot where the statue stands 14 September 1805. It faces the place on the beach were he embarked for HMS Victory. He was short and thin but this cannot be shown in a single statue for it made thus, he appears tall.

The uniform is correct to the smallest detail. The sword is a copy of the one he always wore. Portsmouth was the last English town he ever saw.

Viewed from behind this plaque, Nelson ceases to be the elevated hero and becomes life-size. The use of perspective in this way is a most unusual and subtle aspect to the statue and is probably the only monument in the country to Nelson in two parts.

Every year to commemorate Lord Nelson, wreaths are laid at the statue on Trafalgar Sunday prior to a procession to St Thomas's Cathedral for the annual service of prayer for seafarers and a committal of a wreath to the sea from the Hot Walls. (AUTHOR'S PHOTOGRAPH, 2004)

The Field of Hope

Near Nelson's statue on 29 March 2004, the Lord Mayor of Portsmouth and the Dean of Portsmouth cathedral plus 250 people attended a ceremony to bless a circular field of 6,500 daffodils planted in memory of loved ones who had died from cancer. More than £10,000 was raised to support the Marie Curie Cancer Care Charity in Hampshire and a plaque was placed at the edge of the field.

This photograph shows the Lord Mayor Councillor Tom Blair talking to local people after the ceremony. He wears the Lord Mayor's gold chain which was bought in 1858 and is set with decorated medallions. The names of former mayors and Lord Mayors and their dates are inscribed on plain rectangular links. (COURTESY CLLR TOM BLAIR; AUTHOR'S PHOTOGRAPH, 2004)

Portsmouth Dockyard Today

As the 200th anniversary of Trafalgar approaches, the memory of Nelson and his Navy lives on in a variety of different ways. Portsmouth Dockyard has been reborn as the tourist attraction Portsmouth Historic Dockyard and the work of the shipwright is celebrated in the Dockyard Apprentice Exhibition in Boathouse No.7. Over the road, this 'Productivity meter' is a solitary legacy from earlier days. (COURTESY SECURITY OFFICER, HM NAVAL BASE; AUTHOR'S PHOTOGRAPH, 2004)

This shot shows the colonnades of the storehouse and the timber floor and ceiling. (COURTESY SECURITY OFFICER, HM NAVAL BASE; AUTHOR'S PHOTOGRAPH, 2004)

HMS *Victory*

Nelson's flagship, HMS *Victory* is the most accessible living memorial to Nelson and has been in dry dock in the dockyard since 1922. She is the oldest commissioned warship in the world but is more than just a museum of eighteenth century naval life. HMS *Victory* is the flagship of the Second Sea Lord, Commander in Chief of the Naval Home Command, and is saluted by all naval vessels entering Portsmouth Dockyard.

The ship has a most impressive figurehead as shown in this 1930's postcard. This is a copy of the original which was replaced before Trafalgar between 1801 and 1803. In heraldic terms it forms the Second Achievement of George III and was carved by George Williams at a cost of £50.

As in other royal coats of arms, two cupids act as the supporters of the shield and each wears a coloured sash, blue for starboard (right) and red for larboard (left). The shield is surrounded by the Latin inscription of the Order of the Garter, *Honi Soit Qui May Y Pense* (shame to him who evil thinks).[1]

The card was postally used on 16 August 1938 and on the reverse, the archetypal message from Portsmouth, 'Dear Flossie, Went to Portsmouth yesterday to go round the Victory. Everything here OK. Weather very good. Cheers, D.' (AUTHOR'S COLLECTION)

This atmospheric view of the quarterdeck is also from the 1930s. One of the ship's anchors can be seen in the background and in the centre, the plaque denoting the spot where Nelson fell. On the right-hand side, the clock tower is just visible through the rigging. This is of course, the original clock tower that Nelson would have known. (AUTHOR'S COLLECTION)

Lastly, a close-up of the plaque itself with its Victorian script as it used to be set proud of the deck before the days of Health and Safety. Now, it has now been reset flush with the deck. (AUTHOR'S COLLECTION)

Peter the Great – the Russians are Back

The Russian Tsar Peter the Great and his connection with Portsmouth is not forgotten today. On 16 September 2004, the plaque which commemorates his visit to the dockyard in 1698 was rededicated and blessed with Holy Water.

The service was conducted by the naval chaplain, the Revd Chris Luckraft and a Russian Orthodox priest, Father Maxim from the Russian Orthodox Patriarchal Cathedral of the Dormition and All Saints, Knightsbridge, London.

Here they are shown standing next to the plaque. In the centre, against the background of HMS *Victory*, the Russian Ambassador Grigori Karasin addresses the congregation. (Courtesy Security Officer, HM Naval Base; author's photograph, 2004)

Alan Eades, the churchwarden of the Russian Orthodox Community of St Peter and St Paul, Portsmouth, holds the censer. Also present was the naval base commander, Commander Amjad Hussain, the Lord Lieutenant of Hampshire Mrs Mary Fagan, and the Lord Mayor of the city of Portsmouth, Councillor Jason Fazackerley. The music was provided by the Royal Marines School of Music based in the naval base. (Courtesy Security Officer HM Naval Base; author's photograph, 2004)

Monitor M33

Dockyard scenes are still popular subjects for artists. Lorraine Abraham, a member of the Royal Society of Marine Artists, in a study of light and shadow, depicts the *Monitor M33* in dry dock against a backdrop of HMS *Victory* and dockyard buildings.

The vessel is a gunboat dating from 1915 and is the only British warship still in existence in Great Britain from that period. She is owned by Hampshire County Council and is undergoing an extensive programme of renovation.
(Courtesy Lorraine Abraham)

The Dockyard From the Air – A Twenty-First Century Prospect

Portsmouth Dockyard as it is today shown from the top of the Spinnaker Tower on 27 November 2004. The last 200 years have seen some changes but just as we knew where we were in the 1774 dockyard model, so Nelson would still be able to find his way around were he to alight at the King's Stairs today.

He could still see the admiral's residence, the Naval Academy, the officers' houses, the ropehouse, the store houses and St Ann's Church plus a few more things besides. The Vass father and son would be pleased to see some familiar places still left too and just down the road out of sight, is St George's Church. (Courtesy *The News*)

Naval cutlass drill and the Royal Navy Amateur Fencing Association (RNAFA)

A sailor in the eighteenth century Navy was not only expected to sail a ship but had to fight as well – with a sword. As Mark Barton says in his book on naval cutlass exercise:

It is difficult to visualise a more evocative image of hand-to-hand fighting at sea than the boarder armed with a cutlass. This is true whether the subject is a disciplined sailor of the Royal Navy or a pirate attacking an innocent merchantman.[2]

Cutlass drill was an important part of a seaman's training and in fact, the cutlass was not withdrawn from service until 1936. This engraving from the *Illustrated London News* dated 23 March 1878 shows Victorian sailors at cutlass drill. (COURTESY MARK BARTON; *ILLUSTRATED LONDON NEWS*)

The Royal Navy attached much importance to swordsmanship in general and formalised provision for training was established as far back as 1733. While no longer needed in everyday life and not usually seen by the public, the skill is considered to be an essential part of naval and Royal Marine history and tradition. The Royal Navy Amateur Fencing Association was founded just after the First World War and is very active in keeping the sport alive today.

Mark Barton is the honorary secretary of the RNAFA and together with his colleague John McGrath has written a series of books on the history of cutlass drill, officers' swords and Royal Naval fencing from 1733–1948.

They are keen to ensure that as much information as possible on all the aspects of swordsmanship is collected and preserved before it disappears for good. This photograph shows Royal Naval fencers in action at the royal tournament in 1979. (COURTESY MARK BARTON)

Right: Another action shot from the royal tournament 1979. (Courtesy Mark Barton)

Left: Ladies get involved too these days. This photograph is entitled, 'Sue Bullock charging down the piste' and is dated late 1980s–early 1990s. (Courtesy Mark Barton)

The Garrison Town Today – The Defence Diving School and Horsea Island

The headquarters of the garrison commander of Portsmouth closed on 31 March 1961. The fortifications of course, had gone long before having demolished by the Victorians in the 1870s and 1880s as redundant.

Now, the legacy of Portsmouth as a garrison town rests with the Defence Diving School on Horsea Island whose commanding officer is the senior army officer, Portsmouth. Since 2002 this has been Lt-Col. A. P. Taylor RE. This is the coat of arms in the entrance to the school. (Courtesy Defence Diving School; author's photograph, 2004)

The Defence Diving School was set up in 1995 with the primary purpose of training divers for service both in the fleet and the field army. Command of the School alternates between a royal naval commander and a lieutenant-colonel from the Royal Engineers.

Horsea Island was originally two small islands. When first taken over by the Admiralty in 1885 they were combined and converted from agricultural land into a research establishment concerned with the testing of torpedoes.

In 1970, the island was connected to the mainland as part of the Portsmouth Harbour Reclamation Scheme. Today, no longer an island, there are special facilities for diver training including a 1000m lake with several jetties and a dive tank plus over one hundred members of staff.

Horsea Island can usually be seen on old maps and on the 1766 sea chart on page 44 just a single habitation appears. Basil Ripley wrote a monograph on the history of Horsea Island in 1982 and said that originally, there was a Georgian farmhouse on the Island but by then, that had gone.

The only permanent inhabitants were a couple in a 1930s bungalow near the site of the farmhouse. The bungalow was very isolated with only the birds for company and electricity had to be obtained from a generator. Now, over twenty years later, it is abandoned and derelict. (COURTESY DEFENCE DIVING SCHOOL; AUTHOR'S PHOTOGRAPH, 2004)

Keep out! (COURTESY DEFENCE DIVING SCHOOL; AUTHOR'S PHOTOGRAPH, 2004)

The island has always been known for its wildlife, its wide variety of birds and in particular, its orchids. Two rare types can be found there, the deep pink and purple coloured pyramidal orchid and the lesser-spotted orchid. The plants were introduced on to the site in the 1880s when the two islands were merged into one and soil was imported from Portsdown Hill.

The soil is rich in limestone which suits the orchids very well, they attract butterflies which then help pollinate the plants. The Royal Navy runs many projects to protect wildlife and many of its sites, including Horsea Island are sites of special scientific interest. Here is one of the purple orchids taken in full bloom by Royal Navy photographers. (COURTESY FLEET REGIONAL PHOTOGRAPHIC UNIT, 2004)

The Garrison Commanders

Portsmouth's military history has been neglected in favour of its naval history yet it is just as important. This is probably because it is much more fragmented as the garrison was home to many different regiments for short periods of time only.

There is no association in the public mind between Portsmouth and any one regiment and no building associated with the garrison such as a military museum. However, this aspect of the past is an essential part of the character of Nelson's Portsmouth.

The Defence Diving School does its best to preserve what history there is and unseen by the public, the school maintains boards which list the names of the lieutenant generals commanding Southern District from 1878, the garrison commanders from 1920 and the senior army officers from 1961. Field Marshall Lord Montgomery was the garrison commander in 1937 when a brigadier. (COURTESY DEFENCE DIVING SCHOOL; AUTHOR'S PHOTOGRAPH, 2004)

The Keys to the Fortress of Portsmouth

The keys shown in the photograph are, in symbolic form, the keys to the fortress of Portsmouth and are the responsibility of the senior army officer. However, they never leave the Guildhall and are kept with the City plate. Here, they are shown here resting on their specially designed decorative velvet cushion with gold tassels. It also has a velvet band across it with the letters E.R.II at one end and the Achievement of Portsmouth embroidered on the other end. In the centre is a regimental bow with a gold fringe.

The keys appear in public on three occasions only, firstly, when the sovereign visits Portsmouth; secondly, at the election of the Lord Mayor of the city of Portsmouth at the annual meeting of the City Council which is held at the Guildhall and thirdly, when the freedom of the city is awarded.

The present set of keys are thought to have been made by John Owen, the uncle of Thomas Ellis Owen, the architect of Southsea, in 1814 for the visit of the Prince Regent and Tsar Alexander of Russia. It consists of the key to the Landport Gate, shown here on the right which bears a crown and the key to the town or St George's Gate on the left, which bears a crescent and star.

Each key is about nine inches long, weighs well over a pound and is made of brass. On each key is carved the names of the most important people present for the visit although this is not obvious from the photograph. Originally, they used to be kept in the custody of the governor and to lie on the table in front of him at dinner. (COURTESY PORTSMOUTH CITY COUNCIL; AUTHOR'S PHOTOGRAPH, 2004)

The Ceremony of the Keys

Right: The public has the opportunity to see the keys at least once a year in a dramatic and colourful ceremony when they are presented at the election of the Lord Mayor. The senior army officer has the responsibility to provide an escort for this ceremony which is known as the Ceremony of the Keys and consists of himself, a warrant officer and two NCOs.

This photograph was taken at the rehearsal for the ceremony in 2004 and shows Lt-Col. Taylor with the sword; WOI T. Gauci R.E., carrying the keys; Sgt. T. Garvey RE, on the left and on the right, Cpl. A. Marshall RLC. The escort wears Number 2 Dress. The escort enters the Guildhall, approaches the Lord Mayor, formally presents the keys to him and then returns the way it came. (COURTESY LT-COL TAYLOR; AUTHOR'S PHOTOGRAPH, 2004)

Below: The general salute – present arms. (COURTESY LT-COL. TAYLOR; AUTHOR'S PHOTOGRAPH, 2004)

Above: The salute to the Lord Mayor. The officer lowers his sword. (COURTESY LT-COL. TAYLOR; AUTHOR'S PHOTOGRAPH, 2004)

Left: The officer addresses the Lord Mayor:

My Lord Mayor, the Keys of the City of Portsmouth have been returned to me by your predecessor and I thus now return them to the City for safekeeping. This is on the understanding that should our Sovereign visit Portsmouth the Keys will be returned to me or my successors for presentation to Her Majesty, or on other occasions as is required by tradition.

The Lord Mayor replies, I am very happy to receive the Keys into the safe custody of the City and undertake to make them available to you and your successors for presentation to the Sovereign, should she visit Portsmouth and on other occasions as required by tradition.

(COURTESY LT-COL. TAYLOR; AUTHOR'S PHOTOGRAPH, 2004)

Trafalgar 199 – A Commemorative Dinner, a Family Connection and a Last Look

Left: The commemorative dinners first held in 1805 have continued ever since. Held on 21 October, Trafalgar Day, they are an annual feature of naval establishments and many other places throughout the world. The Royal Naval Club in Old Portsmouth is no exception to the rule and on the 199th anniversary of the Battle of Trafalgar, the guest of honour was Anna Tribe, Nelson's great-great-great-granddaughter descended from his daughter Horatia.

Traditionally, the dinner includes Grace, the traditional Parade of Beef, the Parade of Sail (frigates made of chocolate illuminated with sparklers) and Nelson's Prayer. A toast is proposed to the Queen and the guest of honour proposes a toast to the immortal memory of Admiral Lord Nelson. The evening rounds off with the vigorous singing of sea shanties.

Here, Mrs Tribe arrives at the Royal Naval Club and is greeted by the chairman, John Galley. (COURTESY ANNA TRIBE; THE ROYAL NAVAL CLUB; AUTHOR'S PHOTOGRAPH, 2004)

Right: The Royal Naval Club possesses a number of Nelsonian relics. Mrs Tribe holds up the most intimate which is a card displaying the shirt studs that Nelson wore at the Battle of Trafalgar. The wording underneath reads:

These studs were taken from a shirt worn by Vice Admiral Viscount Lord Nelson shortly after the mortal wound received by him 21 October 1805 on board HMS Victory *by Boatswain Bufrey by whose Grandchild they were given to Mr James Mills February 1847.*

(COURTESY ANNA TRIBE; THE ROYAL NAVAL CLUB; AUTHOR'S PHOTOGRAPH 2004)

'Nelson and His Emma'

This picturesque corner of Lombard Street and St Thomas's Street has been reproduced many times in books and on postcards. On this occasion, the ambience of the group of late-eighteenth century houses is heightened by the presence of 'Lord Nelson' and 'Lady Hamilton' who were also in Old Portsmouth on the day of the 199th Anniversary. Here, they pause to chat to a local resident, a poignant last view of the famous couple, the only time they were ever seen in Portsmouth together. (AUTHOR'S PHOTOGRAPH, 2004)

The Letter Home – Keeping Portsea Island Afloat

Looking back over the letters that Nelson wrote from Portsmouth, three topics spring to mind as having particular relevance for the city today. The main one is the provision of a public drainage system and the health problems caused by lack of proper sanitation. This was already an issue in the eighteenth century but as time went on and the population increased, epidemics of cholera occurred and became more frequent. By late-Victorian times, it was accepted that something radical had to be done.

By 1868, a main drainage system had been installed consisting of 11 miles of main sewer and 56 miles of branches. The untreated sewage was pumped out to sea on the ebb tide at the entrance of Langstone Harbour.

However, due to the low-lying nature of Portsea Island, the force of gravity was insufficient to help the sewage on its way and it accumulated in the sewers. More effective pumps had to be installed and by 1887, Eastney pumphouse with its powerful beam engine powered by steam had been constructed.

The Beam Engine House is a fine example of Victorian industrial architecture using polychrome brickwork. It is now a scheduled ancient monument and maintained by Portsmouth City Council. Nowadays, the beam engine is disconnected from the main sewage system but it still functions and is now open to the public.
(AUTHOR'S PHOTOGRAPH)

Everything is on a gigantic scale. In this shot, Tim Gower, the site manager, stands next to the beam engine holding a ring spanner which is used for adjusting nuts. (COURTESY PORTSMOUTH CITY COUNCIL; AUTHOR'S PHOTOGRAPH, 2004)

The modern pumping station, situated next door, is run by Southern Water and of course is now powered electronically. Portsea Island is dependant on the pumps to keep it afloat. On 15 September 2000, the pumps could not cope with the amount of water collecting in the system and central Southsea was flooded.

Today, the pumps work throughout the 24 hours and a diesel engine is used as back-up should the power fail. They not only deal with sewage but any excess water. The sewage is of course treated before it is discharged, being routed through a station at Budd's Farm for this process.

Here, Ron Shipp, the Process Operator points out the channels for excess water to the author during her visit to Eastney Pumping Station in November 2004. The channels seem very large for such low water levels but they need to be able to accommodate many thousands of gallons of water if necessary. The tide mark on the sides shows how high water levels can be. (COURTESY SOUTHERN WATER)

Portsmouth Harbour – The Pilot and the Camber

Many aspects of life in Portsmouth Harbour are the same now as they were in Nelson's time. In one of his letters he mentions the pilot, with an expletive deleted in front of it, because the pilot had run his ship aground although this was not in Portsmouth. Nelson was furious and this shows the importance of pilot's work which is still the case today.

The pilot's little orange boat is a familiar sight to local residents as it goes about its business in the Camber and in the harbour. Yet how many people actually know what the pilot does? The service is independent of the Royal Navy and the City Council employs three Pilots who have their main base at the Continental Ferry Port. There are two boats, one moored in the Camber, the other on stand-by.

Historically, the role of the Pilot developed because of the lack of sea charts. Ships needed to be guided into harbours and pilots would tout for trade from in-coming ships and then guide them in. All ports have their own pilots and their use is compulsory. Portsmouth is one of the three Queen's Harbour Master ports in the U.K, the other two are Plymouth and Faslane.

In this photograph Paul Fryer, senior pilot and assistant harbour master stands in front of his boat moored at the Camber. (AUTHOR'S PHOTOGRAPH, 2004)

The commercial port of Portsmouth functions alongside the naval port and the Camber, the most ancient port of Portsmouth, is still very much in use. It is both an attractive tourist location with berths for pleasure craft and a working port with dedicated pontoon systems for the exclusive use of the fishing industry.

Fresh fish bought at the Camber is a popular local delicacy but this plaque commemorating the loss of the fishing boat *Wilhelmina J* and six crew members, reminds us of the dangers that fisherman face at sea every day. (AUTHOR'S PHOTOGRAPH, 2004)

The Old Merton and the New Southsea

'Paradise Merton' was of course, close to Nelson's heart and although his house no longer survives in south west London, a reference to it lives on in Southsea. Mention has been made of the architect and developer Thomas Ellis Owen (1805–1862).

He was the son of Jacob Owen (1778–1870) who in July 1805, had been appointed Assistant Clerk of Works for the R.E. Department of the Board of Ordnance and moved to Portsmouth with his family where he spent much of his early career. In 1832, Jacob Owen was appointed the Architect and Engineer to the Dublin Board of Works and went over to Ireland when he was to develop into the major figure of nineteenth century Irish public works architecture.

His son Thomas Ellis Owen was born on 11 March 1805 – just in time to be present in Portsmouth at the time of Nelson's last walk – and although generally associated with Southsea, actually lived in the High Street, Old Portsmouth for 15 years, from 1833 until 1848 when he moved to his new house, Dovercourt, in Kent Road, Southsea.

The house was No.16, High Street in Old Portsmouth and No.18 next door was used as a workshop. This photograph shows No.16 which still exists as a substantial, elegant Georgian house. Number 18 was destroyed in the bombing but its front door and door-case can be seen in the City Museum. It is an imposing classical portico dating from 1780. (AUTHOR'S PHOTOGRAPH, 2004)

✳ ✳ ✳

Thomas Ellis began his career by assisting his father, but when Jacob Owen moved to Dublin Thomas remained in Southsea and set up in practice on his own account. He worked hard to develop the new suburb of Southsea as a watering-place and designed many terraces and villas. He was to name one of his roads in central Southsea Nelson Road and a road next to it, Merton Road.

While there are many roads and buildings in Portsmouth, in particular public houses, named after Nelson, this is especially appropriate because Owen developed Southsea along the lines of the park villages near Regent's Park in London which were designed by John Nash (1752-1835) in the 1820s.

There are other roads in Southsea with romantic names with sylvan associations such as The Retreat, Woodpath, The Thicket, The Vale and The Circle (almost The Clearing!) but no other roads entwine themselves into a figure of eight in the way that Nelson and Merton Roads do. This interlacement of roads was one of a number of clever devices adopted by Owen to make a small development look larger by concealing its boundaries. The roads form the core of his Southsea, now an important conservation area.

Owen could of course, have named the roads Nelson and Trafalgar but always with an eye to the main chance, he neatly sidestepped the cliché and called one Merton. Its rural associations and connection with the hero of Trafalgar would appeal to the middle classes who bought or rented his villas.

However, the middle classes, particularly the ladies, would not want to be linked with any suggestion of the scandal that had enveloped Nelson and Lady Hamilton. A

Hamilton Villa had been built in a discreet setting tucked away off Osborne Road in 1850. Unfortunately, this no longer exists.

Ray Riley in his work on the development of Southsea has highlighted the disproportional numbers of single women who chose to live there, especially the unmarried daughters of admirals and military men. Peter Borsay in an article on the landed elite in provincial towns goes further:

...There was also a growing pool of polite individuals and families – daughters, younger sons and widows of country gentlemen – who retained close social (and perhaps financial) links with the rural elite, but chose to reside permanently in fashionable towns.

Such places provided an ideal environment for those with comfortable but limited incomes seeking to lead a leisured and gentle life. In particular, well-off spinsters and widows found urban living, especially in locations where they congregated together in large numbers, an opportunity to construct an independent but respectable lifestyle, free from the potentially severe constraints of marriage.

The high ratio of women to men found in the spas and seaside resorts, was in part a reflection of this, and some fashionable towns, such as Preston, were well known for their large cohorts of genteel single women.[3]

Maybe the life of a spinster in Owen's Southsea did have its good points. Merton Road though, was developed late and not built up until the early 1860s, just before Owen's own death in 1862. By this time, Nelson, his wife and Emma Hamilton had been dead for many years and presumably, the name had become more closely associated with an idyllic country retreat than with a long-forgotten scandal. This photograph shows the vista from Grove Road South. (AUTHOR'S PHOTOGRAPH, 2004)

The Letter From Home

Lastly, the number of people who received letters from Nelson and presumably, sent ones in reply, have played a minor role in this book. To redress the balance a little and to pay tribute to all those who waited anxiously at home for letters from those on active service, here are two photographs of a statue unveiled on 4 June 1997, by the Duke of Kent.

Set outside the D-Day Museum in Southsea, it was sculpted by Vivian Mallock and entitled 'A Soldier of World War II', although it could have just as easily been called, 'The Letter From Home'. Let the inscription have the last word:

Decades of easy peace may go their way and tide,
and time, may drift us far apart,
but you who shared our savage yesterday
will hold the highest places in our heart.

(AUTHOR'S PHOTOGRAPHS 2004)

A SOLDIER OF
WORLD WAR TWO

DECADES OF EASY PEACE MAY GO THEIR WAY
AND TIDE, AND TIME, MAY DRIFT US FAR APART,
BUT YOU WHO SHARED OUR SAVAGE YESTERDAY
WILL HOLD THE HIGHEST PLACES IN OUR HEART

References
[1] *Nelson's Victory*, p.56.
[2] *Naval Cutlass Exercise*, p.3.
[3] *The Landed Elite and Provincial Towns in Britain 1660–1800*, p.290.

BIBLIOGRAPHY

Primary Sources

A Survey and Description of the Principal Harbours with their Accomodations [sic] and Conveniences for Erecting and Moaring, Secureing and Refitting the Navy Royall of England viz: the Rivers of Thames and Medway containing Chatham and Sheerness Dockyards on the latter, Woolwich and Deptford and on the former. Also the Port of Portsmouth and Southampton Water with the Dockyard on the former. Plymouth Sound with the coast of Devonshire to Torbay, with the late erected New Dock Yard at Hamouze and the Navy Office near Tower Hill, London, illustrated By generall Plans and proper views or Prospects of Each Place To which the particular Buildings thereof are confined. Together With An Account of the Emprovements which have been made at Each Yard since the Revolution of 1688 giving a Numericall Account of severall Kinds of Buildings with their Quantity and value which by an estimate Rate they maybe accounted worth to the nation. Also An Account of the Nature and Usefullness of the late Erected New Docks at Portsmouth and the Yard at Plymouth. Concluding with some remarks of the Beginning and Encrease of the Navy Yards from the Time of Henry the 8th, also a short specimen of the manner and Dependances of the Surbordinate Offices thereof in Relation to the Practise and execution of the General Business, British Library ref. no.: Kings MS. 43, 1698.

Goodrich, Simon, Goodrich Papers B, Journals and Memoranda, Volume 10, 1805 Aug. 1 – Nov. 23, Science Museum Library.

Pennant, Thomas. *A Journey from London to the Isle of Wight*, vol.II, Oriental Press, Wilson & Co., 1801.

Secondary Sources

Addis MBE, RN, Lt Cdr, C.P. *The Men Who Fought With Nelson in HMS Victory at Trafalgar*, The Nelson Society, 1988.

Balfour, Alan. *Portsmouth*, Studio Vista, 1970.

Barton, Mark. *Naval Cutlass Exercise*, Royal Navy Amateur Fencing Association, 2002.

Barton, Mark. *Fencing in the Royal Navy and Royal Marines, 1733–1948*, Royal Navy Amateur Fencing Association, 2004.

Benford, Mervyn. *Milestones*, Shire Publications Ltd, 2002.

Birbeck, Eric (ed.). *A Visit to Haslar, 1916, by Major-General John B. Richardson, Colonel Commandant, Royal Artillery*, Royal Hospital Haslar, 2004.

Birbeck, Eric and Holcroft, Alain. *Historical Guide to the Royal Hospital Haslar*, Royal Hospital Haslar, 2003.

Blake, John. *The Sea Chart: the Illustrated History of Nautical Maps and Navigational Charts*, Conway Maritime Press, 2004.

Borsay, Peter. *The Landed Elite and Provincial Towns in Britain 1660–1800*, The Georgian Group Journal, vol.XIII, 2003, pp.281–294.

Bramshott Parish Council. *Liphook and Bramshott*, Hampshire, Official Guide, 1971.

Brewer, E. Cobham. *Brewer's Dictionary of Phrase and Fable*, revised by Ivor H. Evans, Cassell & Co. Ltd, 1977.

Bryant, Roger. *Monty: The Pompey Connection*, Ragged Right, 1993.

Burke, Thomas. *Britain in Pictures, the British People in Pictures: English Inns*, William Collins of London, 1944.

Burton, Lesley and Musselwhite, Brian. *The Book of Gosport: Celebrating a Distinctive Coastal Town*, Halsgrove, 2004.

Buxton Ian. *His Majesty's Monitor M33, 1915–2001*, Hampshire County Council, 2001.

City Planning Officer, P. S. Newbold, Conservation Area No.4: *Old Portsmouth Guidelines for Conservation*, Portsmouth City Council, 2004.

Clifton, Gloria and Rigby, Nigel (eds.). *Treasures of the National Maritime Museum*, National Maritime Museum, 2004.

Course, Edwin. *Drainage on Portsea Island: Eastney Pumping Station*, Portsmouth City Museums, 1975.

Curl, James Stevens. *Egyptomania, the Egyptian Revival: a Recurring Theme in the History of Taste*, Manchester University Press, 1994.

Dixon Hunt, John. *The Picturesque Garden in Europe*, Thames and Hudson Ltd, 2002.

Downer, Martyn. *Nelson's Purse: An Extraordinary Historical Detective Story Shedding New Light on the Life of Britain's Greatest Naval Hero*, Bantam Press, 2004.

Du Garde Peach, L. *The Story of Nelson: An Adventure From History*, A Ladybird Book, Wills & Hepworth Ltd, Loughborough, first edition, 1957.

Esmond, Richard. *The Charm of Old Portsmouth*, Gale and Polden Ltd Portsmouth, 1959.

Fox, Russell. *Portsmouth's Ramparts Revisited, Fortress: The Castles and Fortifications Quarterly*, No.11, November 1991, pp.29–38.

Fox, R. and Barton, K. J. 'Excavations at Oyster Street, Portsmouth, Hampshire, 1968–1971', reprinted from *Post-Medieval Archaeology*, No.20, 1986, pp.31–255.

Fox, R.T., and Hall, R.B. *The Clay Tobacco Pipes of the Portsmouth Harbout Region*, Portsmouth, 1979.

Friar, Stephen. *The Sutton Companion to Heraldry*, Sutton Publishing, new edition, 2004.

Gardiner, Robert (ed.). *Fleet, Battle and Blockade: the French Revolutionary War 1793–1797*, Chatham Publishing, London, in association with the National Maritime Museum, 1996.

Garneray, Louis. *The Floating Prison: The Remarkable Account of Nine Years' Captivity on the British Prison Hulks During the Napoleonic Wars, 1806–1814*, translated from the French with a foreward and notes by Richard Rose, Conway Maritime Press, 2003.

Gates, William G. *Portsmouth in the Past* (with a new introduction by Margaret Guy, ALA), first published Portsmouth 1926, republished S.R. Publishers Ltd, 1972; *Portsmouth Through the Centuries: Historical and Topographical Notes*, no publisher, 1931; *History of Portsmouth: A Naval Chronology*, the Evening News and *Hampshire Telegraph*, Charpentier Ltd, 1931.

Gatt, Laurence. *The Portsmouth Beneficial School 1755–1939*, Portsmouth Paper, Number 46, Portsmouth City Council,1986.

Geddes, Alistair. *Portsmouth During the Great French Wars 1770–1800*, Portsmouth Paper No.9, 1980.

Goodman, Judith. *Merton and Morden: A Pictorial History*, Phillimore & Co. Ltd, 1995.

Goodrich, Simon. *Goodrich Papers B, Journals and Memoranda*, vol.10, Aug. 1–Nov. 23 1805, Science Museum Library.

Goodwin, Peter. *Nelson's Victory: 101 Questions and Answers About HMS Victory, Nelson's Flagship at Trafalgar 1805*, Conway Maritime Press, 2004.

Graves, John. *George III's Miniature Dockyards, The Maritime Year Book: Annual Journal of the Friends and Corporate Members of the National Maritime Museum*, No.2, 1994–1995, pp.15–17; *The Dockyard Models of George III*, unpublished notes of a lecture to the Naval Dockyards Society, 1999.

Guillery, Peter. *The Small House in Eighteenth Century London: A Social and Architectural History*, Yale University Press in Association with English Heritage, 2004.

Halpern, Linda Cabe. 'Wrest Park 1686–1730s: Exploring Dutch Influence' in *Garden History, Journal of the Garden History Society*, vol.30, No.2, Winter 2002, pp.131–152.

Harper, Charles G. *The Portsmouth Road: The Sailor's Highway*, Cecil Palmer, first edition 1895, second and revised edition 1923.

Hasler, Charles. *The Royal Arms – Its Graphic and Decorative Development: An Essay on the Development of Britain's Royal Arms in Terms of Graphic and Decorative Design Together with References and Notes on the Cross-Links with Versions in Three Dimensions and in Turn Their Transformation into Flat Graphic Form*, Jupiter Books, 1986.

Holmes, Richards (introduction), David Crane, Stephen Hebron and Robert Woof (catalogue entries). *Romantics and Revolutionaries: Regency Portraits from the National Portrait Gallery*, London, National Portrait Gallery, 2002.

Holmes, Richard (ed.). *Southey on Nelson, the Life of Nelson by Robert Southey*, Harper Perennial, 2004.

Holmes, T. W. *The Semaphore: The Story of the Admiralty-to-Portsmouth Shutter Telegraph and Semaphore Lines 1796–1847*, Arthur H. Stockwell Ltd, Devon, 1983.

Hooper MD, R. *Quincy's Lexicon-Medicum: A New Medical Dictionary; Containing an Explanation of the Terms in Anatomy, Physiology, Practice of Physic, Materia Medica, Chemistry, Pharmacy, Surgery, Midwifery and the Various Branches of Natural Philosophy Connected with Medicine, Selected, Arranged and Complied from the Best Authors*, London, 1811.

Hopkins, Peter. *A History of Lord Nelson's Merton Place*, Merton Historical Society, 1998.

Howse, D. and Sanderson, M. *The Sea Chart: An Historical Survey Based on the Collections in the National Maritime Museum*, David and Charles, Newton Abbott, 1973.

Hudson, Gilbert. *Nelson's Last Diary September 13 – October 21 1805*, Elkin Mathews, Cork Street, London, 1917.

Jones, Jack. *Isle of Wight Curiosities: A Guide to Follies, Curious Tales, Unusual People and Architectural Eccentricities*, The Dovecote Pres Ltd, 1989.

Kelly's *Directory of Portsmouth, Portsea, Landport, Southsea and Gosport and Suburbs*, Kelly & Co., 1886.

Latham, Robert and Matthews, William (eds.). *The Diary of Samuel Pepys*, vol.II 1661, vol.III, 1662, G. Bell & Sons Ltd, 1970.

Lavery, Brian. *Jack Aubrey Commands: An Historical Companion to the Naval World of Patrick O'Brian*, Conway Maritime Press, 2003.

Law, James, T. (compiler and arranger). *Law's Grocer's Manual: A Practical Guide for Tea and Provision Dealers, Italian Warehousemen, Chandlers, Shipstore Dealers, Bakers, Confectioners, Fruiterers, and General Shopkeepers.* J.T. Law, Liverpool, c.1895.

Leslie, Fiona. *Inside Outside: Changing Attitudes Towards Architectural Models in the Museums at South Kensington, Architectural History: Journal of the Society of Architectural Historians of Great Britain*, vol.47, 2004, pp.159–200.

Lloyd, David. *Buildings of Portsmouth and its Environs: A Survey of the Dockyard, Defences, Homes, Churches, Commercial, Civic and Public Buildings*, City of Portsmouth, 1974; *Historic Towns of Hampshire and Surrey*, Victor Gollancz Ltd, 1992.

Locker FRS, FSA, Edward Hawke. *Memoirs of Celebrated Naval Commanders, Illustrated by Engravings from Original Pictures in the Naval Gallery of Greenwich Hospital by one of the Commissioners of the Institution*, Harding and Lepard, 1832.

Longstaffe-Gowan, Todd. *The London Town Garden 1740–1840*, Yale University Press, 2001.

Madariaga, de, Isabel. *Catherine the Great: A Short History*, Yale University Press, 1990.

Marcus, G. J. *Heart of Oak: A Survey of British Sea Power in the Georgian Era*, Oxford University Press, 1975.

Marriott, Leo. *What's Left of Nelson*, Dial House, 1995.

Matthew, H. C. G. and Harrison, Brian (eds.). *Oxford Dictionary of National Biography*, Oxford University Press, 2004.

McCreery, Cindy. *Ports of the World: Prints from the National Maritime Museum*, Greenwich c.1700–1870, Philip Wilson Publishers/the National Maritime Museum, 1999.

McGrath, John. *Swords for Officers of the Royal Navy*, Royal Navy Amateur Fencing Association, 2004.

McInnes, Robin. *The Isle of Wight Illustrated*, Crossprint, Newport, Isle of Wight, 1989.

Moorhouse, E. Hallam. *Nelson in England: A Domestic Chronicle*, Chapman and Hall Ltd, 1913.

Mountfield, David. *The Coaching Age*, Robert Hale & Co., 1976.

Moutray Read, D. H. *Highways and Byways in Hampshire*, Macmillan and Co. Ltd, London, first edition 1908, reprint 1928.

Myers, Robin and Harris, Michael (eds.). *Spreading the Word: the Distribution Networks of Print 1550–1850*, St Paul's Bibliographies Winchester, 1990.

Naish, John. *Seamarks: Their History and Development*, Stanford Maritime Ltd, 1985.

National Union of Teachers Conference Souvenir 1937: Portsmouth, University of London Press Ltd, 1937.

Nicolas GCMG, Nicholas Harris. *The Dispatches and Letters of Vice Admiral Lord Viscount Nelson with Notes by Sir Nicholas Harris Nicolas*, vols.1–7, Chatham Publishing, 1997.

Nicols FSA, R. H. and Wray, F. A. *The History of the Foundling Hospital*, Oxford University Press, 1935.

O'Dwyer, Frederick. 'Building Empires: Architecture, Politics and the Board of Works 1760–1860' in *Irish Architectural and Decorative Studies: the Journal of the Irish Georgian Society*, vol.V, 2002, pp.108–175.

Offord, John. *Churches, Chapels and Places of Worship on Portsea Island*, John Harman, 1989.

Oman, Carola. *Nelson*, Hodder and Stoughton Ltd, reprint 1948.

Otter, R.A. (ed.). *Civil Engineering Heritage: Southern England*, Thomas Telford Ltd, 1994.

Pack, Captain A. J. *Nelson and the Portsmouth Scene*, unpublished notes of the Nelson Birthday Lecture, Portsmouth Central Library, 1984.

Patterson, B. H. *A Military Heritage: A History of Portsmouth and Portsea Town Fortifications*, Fort Cumberland and Portsmouth Militaria Society, 1984.

Peace, David. *Eric Gill: The Inscriptions: A Descriptive Catalogue*, David R. Godine, Publisher Boston, first U.S. edition, 1995.

Peers, Sir Charles. *Portchester Castle, Hampshire, Ministry of Works, Ancient Monuments and Historic Buildings*, Her Majesty's Stationery Office, London, 1953, reprinted 1957.

Pevsner, Nikolaus and Lloyd, David. *The Buildings of England: Hampshire and the Isle of Wight*, Penguin Books, 1990.

Phillips, Edward J. *The Founding of Russia's Navy: Peter the Great and the Azov Feet 1688–1714*, Greenwood Press, 1995.

Portsmouth Cathedral: A Pitkin Cathedral Guide, Pitkin Pictorials, Andover, Hampshire, 1994.

Portsmouth Corporation, *Southsea and Portsmouth at a Glance: A Guide to that Charming and High Class Summer and Winter Resort*, July 1908; *A Guide to Southsea and Portsmouth: the Fashionable South Coast Watering Place of Renown Facing the Silvery Solent*, June 1910.

Portsmouth Historic Dockyard, *The Clock Tower at Storehouse No.10: History and Reconstruction*, Information Panel, Portsmouth Historic Dockyard, 28 July 1992.

Portsmouth Reference & Information Centre, *Public Monuments in Portsmouth*, the Central Library, Guildhall Square, Portsmouth, PO1 2DX, no date.

Portsmouth & South East Hants CAMRA, Winterfest XIII, *The Penguin's Revenge*, Thorngate Halls, Gosport, 18 & 19 February 2005.

Quail, Sarah. *Southsea Past*, Phillimore & Co. Ltd, 2000.

Quarm, Roger. 'An Album of Drawings by Gabriel Bray R.N., HMS *Pallas*, 1774–75' in *The Mariner's Mirror: The Journal of the Society for Nautical Research*, vol.81, No.1, February 1995, pp.32-44.

Richardson, Harriet (ed.). *English Hospitals 1660–1948: A Survey of Their Architecture and Design*, Royal Commission on the Historical Monuments of England, 1998.

Riley, R. C. *Portsmouth Royal Dockyard: A Short Photographic History*, Portsmouth Royal Dockyard Historical Society, Publication No.4, 1984; *Windows to the Past*, Portsmouth Royal Dockyard Historical Society, Publication No.6, 1991.

Riley, Ray. *The Houses and Inhabitants of Thomas Ellis Owen's Southsea*, Portsmouth Paper No.32, Portsmouth City Council, 1980.

Portsmouth: Ships, Dockyard and Town, Tempus Publishing Ltd, 2002.

Ripley, Basil. *Horsea Island and the Royal Navy*, Portsmouth Paper No.36, Portsmouth City Council, 1982.

Roberts, Jane. *The King's Head: Charles I: King and Martyr*, with a note on portrait busts by Jonathan Marsden, Exhibition Catalogue, The Royal Collection, 1999.

Rodger, N. A. M. *The Wooden World*, Collins, 1986; *The Insatiable Earl: A Life of John Montagu, Fourth Earl of Sandwich 1718–1792*, Harper Collins, 1993.

Ryder, Richard, D. 'The Character of Horatio Nelson: a Note' in *Trafalgar Chronicle: Year Book of the 1805 Club*, No.14, 2004, pp.47–52.

Saunders, Andrew. *Fortress Builder: Bernard de Gomme, Charles II's Military Engineer*, University of Exeter Press, 2004.

Sherwood, Cynthia. *Monuments of Portsmouth*, unpublished catalogue, no date about 1991.

Slight, Henry. *A Metrical History of Portsmouth with Delineations, Topographical, Historical and Descriptive of the Port and Arsenal*,

Hollingsworth and Price, White-Horse-Street, 1820; *A Chronicle History of Portsmouth*, third edition, 1838, no publisher.

Slight, Julian, *Chronicles of Portsmouth*, Lupton Relfe, 1828.

Smith, Jane (ed.). *Blimey! What a War…: Sgt. Stark, H. L.,10531706, Royal Army Ordnance Corps, Writes to Bessie Constance Fisher, 1941–1946*, unpublished collection of letters, Portsmouth, 1998; *Dear Mum and Dad, I Haven't Seen Any Battleaxes Yet…: Musician Stark P. J., W/425499,Women's Royal Army Corps Staff Band, Writes to Harry and Bessie Stark, 1965–1969*, unpublished collection of letters, Portsmouth, 1999.

Smith, Wendy. *St Ann's Church: A Brief History*, HM Naval Base, Portsmouth, First Edition, 2001.

St George's Parochial Church Council. *A Brief History of St George's Portsea by the Congregation and Others*, no date.

Stedman, John. *Images of Portsmouth*, The Breedon Books Publishing Company, Derby, 1993.

Steen, Marguerite. *A Pride of Terrys: Family Saga*, Longmans, Green & Co. Ltd, 2nd impression, 1962.

Stevenson, Christine. *Medicine and Magnificence: British Hospital and Asylum Architecture 1660–1815*, Yale University Press, 2000.

Sugden, John. *Nelson: A Dream of Glory*, Jonathan Cape, 2004.

The Evening News. *Portsmouth, Smitten City: the Story of Portsmouth in the Air Raids 1940–1944*, first edition, c.1946.

Tomalin, Claire. *Mrs Jordan's Profession: The Story of a Great Actress and a Future King*, Viking, 1994.

Triggs, Anthony. *Portsmouth: History in Hiding*, Ensign Publications, 1989; *Portsmouth First*, Halsgrove, 1999; *Portsmouth: The Good Old Days*, Halsgrove, 2002; *Portsmouth: A Shattered City*, Halsgrove, 2003.

Veale, Elspeth. *The Marquess of Rockingham's House in Wimbledon, the Georgian Group Journal*, vol.XIV, 2004, pp.243–260.

Walker, Richard. *The Nelson Portraits: An Iconography of Horatio, Viscount Nelson, K.B., Vice Admiral of the White*, Royal Naval Museum Publications, 1998.

Walter, Edna L. *Life in Many Lands IV: In Britain Today*, James Nisbet & Co. Ltd, 1935.

Warren, Frank and Cockman, Irwen. *Music in Portsmouth 1789–1842*, The Portsmouth Papers No.69, Portsmouth City Council, 1998.

Watkin, David. *The Architect King: George III and the Culture of the Enlightenment*, Royal Collection Publications, 2004.

Watts, Eric. *Fares Please: The History of Passenger Transport in Portsmouth*, Milestone Publications, 1987.

Webb, J., Quail, S., Haskell, P. and Riley, R. *The Spirit of Portsmouth: A History*, Phillimore & Co. Ltd, 2001.

Western, J. R. *The English Militia in the Eighteenth Century: The Story of a Political Issue 1660–1802*, Routledge & Kegan Paul, 1965.

Weston, Agnes. *My Life Among the Blue-Jackets*, James Nisbet & Co. Ltd, fourth edition, 1910.

White, Arnold and Moorhouse, E. Hallam. *Nelson and the Twentieth Century*, Cassell & Co. Ltd, 1905.

White, Colin. *Nelson's Last Walk*, The Nelson Society 1996, reprint from *The Nelson Dispatch*, vol.5, Part 11, July 1996; *The Nelson Companion*, Bramley Books, 1997 edition; *The Nelson Encyclopaedia*, Chatham Publishing in Association with the Royal Naval Museum, 2002; *Nelson: The Pitkin Biographical Guide*, Jarrold Publishing, Norwich, 2003.

Whitehead, John L. M. D. *The Undercliff of the Isle of Wight: Past and Present*, Simpkin, Marshall and Co., Stationers, Hall Court, 1911.

Williams, G. H. *The Keys of the Fortress*, The Gosport Historic Records and Museum Society, Gosport Records, Issue Number 13, May 1977.

Williams, Ian. *Diamond Coast: The Story of the Isle of Wight's Coast*, The Dovecote Press Ltd, 2004.

Winton, John. *The Naval Heritage of Portsmouth*, Ensign Publications, 1989.

Yarrington, Alison. 'Nelson the Citizen Hero: State and Public Patronage of Monumental Sculpture 1805–1818' in *Art History*, vol.6, No.3, September 1983, pp.315–329; *The Commemoration of the Hero 1800–1864: Monuments to the British Victors of the Napoleonic Wars*, Garland Publishing Inc. 1988.

Newspapers, Journals and Periodicals

Dockyards: Newsletter of the Naval Dockyards Society
Friends of Portsmouth Cathedral Yearbook
Hampshire Chronicle
Hampshire Telegraph, and Sussex Chronicle: Or, Portsmouth and Chichester Advertiser
Illustrated London News
Merton Historical Society Bulletin
The Builder
The Kedge Anchor: Newsletter of the 1805 Club.
The Mariner's Mirror: The Journal of the Society for Nautical Research.
The Nelson Dispatch: Journal of the Nelson Society.
The News: Portsmouth
The Universal Magazine of Knowledge and Pleasure
The Times
Trafalgar Chronicle: Year Book of the 1805 Club